Dr Hugh Schonfield, eminent historian and ⟨...⟩ and educated at St. Paul's School and Glasg⟨...⟩ ⟨...⟩ in Near Eastern Affairs, and was for many years historian of the Suez Canal and contributor on the subject to the Encyclopaedia Brittanica Year Books. During the Second World War, Dr Schonfield worked for a time with the Near East Department of the Ministry of Information and wrote the section on Libya for the government-sponsored volume *Islam Today*. His major interest was in archaeology, especially in the field of Christian origins, and he was one of the scholars who worked on the newly-discovered Dead Sea Scrolls. He was the first Jew to translate the New Testament, a work which received the highest praise for its accuracy and realism from distinguished churchmen and scholars. His best-known work was his portrayal of Jesus in *The Passover Plot*, a book which has widespread appeal (it even influenced John Lennnon of The Beatles) and sold more than three million copies. He wrote over thirty books, including *An Old Hebrew Text of St. Matthew's Gospel; The Lost 'Book of the Nativity of John' – A Study in Messianic Folklore and Christians Origins; The History of Jewish Christianity – From the First to the Twentieth Century; According to the Hebrews – A New Translation of the Toldoth Jeshu; Jesus – A Biography; The Jew of Tarsus; Saints Against Caesar; Secrets of the Dead Sea Scrolls; The Original New Testament* (translator)*; The Politics of God; For Christ's Sake; After the Cross; The Pentecost Revolution; Those Incredible Christians* and *The Essene Odyssey*.

He was President of the Commonwealth of World Citizens and of the International Arbitration League, and was nominated for the Nobel Peace Prize in 1959 for his services towards international harmony.

Proclaiming the Messiah The Life and Letters of Paul of Tarsus shows conclusively that Paul was not, as Christians claim, the founder of a new religion, but a Jewish mystic who believed in the coming of the Messiah, whom he saw in Jesus. After many years of careful study Schonfield reached the conclusion that much of what is said about St Paul's writings stems from misunderstanding and partly deliberate misrepresentation. Schonfield's new translation, with notes and references, fully recognizes the Jewish religious ideas which lie behind the letters. He completed *Proclaiming the Messiah* shortly before his death in 1988, and it is now published posthumously.

Paul of Tarsus holding a scroll – Courtesy of Catacombe di S. Domitilla, Rome

Proclaiming the Messiah

THE LIFE AND LETTERS OF
Paul of Tarsus
Envoy to the Nations

Hugh J. Schonfield

OPEN GATE PRESS
LONDON

First published in 1997 by Open Gate Press
51 Achilles Road, London NW6 1DZ

British Library Cataloguing-in-Publication Programme
A catalogue record for this book is available from the British Library.

ISBN 1 871871 32 8

Printed in Great Britain by
Redwood Books, Trowbridge, Wiltshire

Contents

PART ONE

THE LIFE

PART TWO
THE LETTERS

Cover portrait of Paul – Courtesy of Catacombe di S. Domitilla, Rome
Oxyrhynchus 2157. 4th. century fragment of Paul's letter to the Galatians –
    Photograph p.112 courtesy of the Egypt Exploration Society.
Map by J F Horrabin

*To the High Master of St. Paul's School
in token of my gratitude as an Old Pauline
for the Classical education I received.*

Part One

THE LIFE

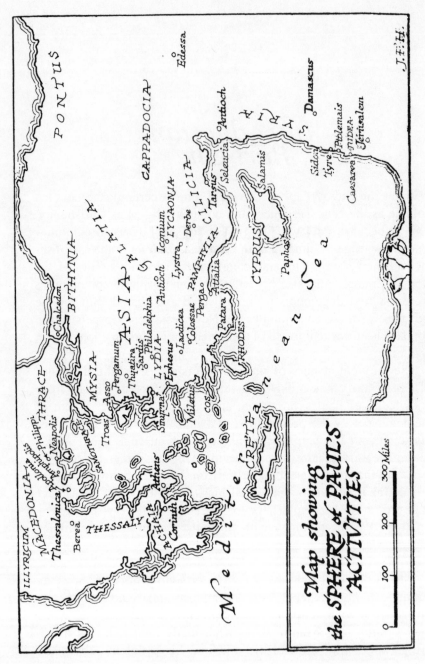

Map showing the SPHERE of PAUL'S ACTIVITIES

Map by J F Horrabin

Introduction

Without the Envoy Paul there would almost certainly be no such volume as the New Testament and no such religion as Christianity. This is because Paul was the first follower of Jesus to communicate knowledge of him to pagan Gentiles, resulting in the establishment of non-Jewish Christian communities in various cities of the Roman Empire. And also his letters to some of these communities were the first documents to be collected and shared. But for the existence of these communities the New Testament Gospels would not have been written; for all of them were for the information of such communities.

The momentousness of these circumstances for the doctrines of Christianity has most unfortunately detracted greatly from knowledge of Paul as a person, and reduced him to a system of theology. Yet by the preservation of Paul's letters we can learn of his ideas and his feelings and experiences at first hand, which cannot be said of any other individual in the Bible. Indeed, we must say that Paul's teaching arose from his personality, his background, and the events that befell him; and if they had been other than they were he would have expressed himself very differently. To study Pauline theology without Paul the man – a very strange and most misunderstood man – is another case of Hamlet without the Prince of Denmark.

It has to be said right away that no orthodox Christian, however erudite, can comprehend Paul, and almost equally no rabbinically informed Jewish scholar. Both concentrate on doctrine, when they should have been seeking what made Paul tick, his imaginings about himself and his mission, his problems about the unattractiveness of his appearance, his mysticism partly arising from physical disabilities, possibly epilepsy. And above all his inner loneliness.

A good deal about Paul's biography is traced by the author of the *Acts of the Apostles*. Much of it may be quite reliable; but the aim of the work is to reconcile the positions of Paul and the other envoys, who had known Jesus personally. The harshness of the conflict between them is considerably toned down, as we can see by comparing Paul's own statements in his letters.

One of the factors we dare not neglect is the problem confronting Paul in trying to communicate to Gentiles, not only the nature and function of the Messianic, something totally alien to Gentile thought, but the mysteries of Jewish occultism which so powerfully influenced Paul's own convictions. He wrote about this problem to the community at Corinth: 'It was impossible, brothers, for me to speak to you as spiritually-equipped people, only as physically-equipped people, as infants in Christ. I had to feed you with milk rather than solid food, for you were not equal to it. Neither are you equal to it yet, for you are still at the physical stage.' (*I.Cor*.iii.1-3).* We have to recognise also that Paul was powerfully affected by his own psychic experiences.

Another factor we have to apprehend at the outset in dealing with Paul's doctrines is that very often the only way he could get through to his only recently pagan hearers and readers was to seek to find in the heathen expressions, concepts, and customs, with which they were familiar, some kind of equivalents to what he wished to convey. Much in Paul's teaching was the outcome of this difficulty of communication. It was not that his Jewish beliefs had changed; but that he was forced to improvise, creating in effect a Christian jargon, to get some of his ideas across, some of them being very complex and impossible to convey with complete success.

Unfortunately, this problem of communication, especially of mystical matters, has not sufficiently registered either with Christian or Jewish exegetes.

The need to accomodate to the comprehension of persons with a different background is a familiar problem of communication. In the very same century in which Paul lived other Jews like Philo of Alexandria and to a lesser extent the historian Flavius Josephus, writing for non-Jews, had also to adapt, and to borrow ideas. Paul naturally used the Greek Septuagint Version for Biblical quotations, and occasionally referred to the Greek classics. But he had a major dif-

---

* For this quotation see p.142, the second of four letters to the Corinthian community.

ficulty with matters like the Messianic, which were totally alien to Gentiles. Messiah was translated by the Greek Christ ('the anointed one'). So Paul should have written about Jesus as *the* Christ. But this would have caused complications. Paul had therefore to drop the definite article and treat Jesus Christ as if it was a composite name, or more exactly a name plus title like Claudius Caesar.

Pauline doctrine is thus very often Jewish teaching in a Greek dress, and to understand it we have to get behind the terms employed. This the Church Fathers failed to do. They could detect the similarities to pagan concepts and customs, but accused the Devil of having imitated the Christian verities by borrowing them in pagan practices. It is therefore imperative not to be confined to expounding Paul's teaching as it stands, but much more to get behind it, to seek for the elements, Jewish and pagan, which have created it.

But we also have to recognise that certain Pauline expressions, such as being 'in Christ', relate peculiarly to Paul's insistence that Gentiles by faith in Jesus are granted membership of Israel. Theology does not come into it.

Unfortunately, for exponents of Christianity, theology is paramount. And it is not Paul's personal and unique ideas which are the subject of inquiry, but the interpretation of them in terms of the theology of the Christian Councils of the fourth century.[*] Consequently we cannot and must not rely on any of the official versions of Paul's letters, or the translation of them. They are under the influence of later Christian doctrine. We do not possess the original manuscripts, and even in his own time Paul is witness that forgeries were in existence.[**] Therefore we have to be on the alert both for interpolations and mistranslations. The ordinary Christian reader of the New Testament is not aware of these interferences with the text, or of the abundant evidence available that supposedly saintly Christians were guilty of wilfully changing the text of vital ancient Jewish documents by inserting words which would give them a Christian doctrinal slant. The Church Fathers were propagandists, and many of them of

---

[*] The so-called Arian controversy councils, which were called over a dispute arising initially in the second decade of the fourth century in Alexandria and instigated by the elder Arius concerning the Divine Nature. The main councils were those of Nicea in AD 325 and Constantinople AD 381, with some dozen intervening synods and councils, centring, briefly, on whether the Son was of *one* or of *like* substance to the Father, and resulting in major credal statements.

[**] See *II.Thess*.ii.2, p.123, and *II.Thess*.iii.17, p.124.

the highest standing were ready to act criminally to get their views across.*

Even in the minor matter of the arrangement of Paul's letters the official versions are at fault. Outside the Bible it is the practice to present the letters of the famous as far as possible in chronological sequence. This enables such letters to be a means of exhibiting changes in ideas of the writers and bringing them into association with the authors' biographies. But Paul's letters are not set down in chronological order, and one of the later ones has been put first because it was directed to the Romans.**

The life and letters of Paul have to be taken together in any work that seeks to get at the changes in his views which were the outcome of his experiences. The translation of Paul's letters given in this volume is my own, taken from my work *The Original New Testament*, and it is made in accordance with the proper function of an editor and translator, and not in any theological interests. I am afraid it has to be said, though in no controversial spirit, that the most misleading and inaccurate English version of Paul's letters, as of the New Testament as a whole, is the so-called Authorised (or King James) Version, the one that is best known and still chiefly used by Protestants.

Another essential thing for the reader: he or she has to abandon adherence to a *lingua Christiana*, both descriptive and theological. Titles in Greek are perfectly able to be converted into English. It is wilfully misleading to allow it to be imagined that there is something uniquely Christian about words like Apostle, Bishop, Church, Deacon, etc. The reader will therefore find in my rendering, Envoy, Overseer, Community, and Supervisor, which directly translate the original Greek words.

In our account of Paul we have carefully to avoid anything that savours of Christianity as a new religion. In Paul's time it was not a religion. It was a Messianic movement claiming Jesus as the ultimate king of Israel in a period of Jewish history obsessed with the conviction that these were the Last Times when Israel would be delivered from her oppressors. Judaism, in those days, meant the Jewish way of life, not the views of any particular Party such as the Pharisees. Therefore, as regards Paul, discussion – often erudite – comparing Christianity with Judaism, as if both at that time were

---

* On this subject see also Schonfield, *Those Incredible Christians*, especially Chapter 9.
** Actually, to Jewish and non-Jewish *believers* in Rome. See Note 1, p.196.

specific religions, are entirely uncalled for. Judaism as a religion was the consequence of the destruction of Jerusalem and the Temple, and of all political Jewish independence. It was an interim faith developed by the rabbis as a means of sustaining Jewish spiritual solidarity for the duration of the Exile; and it grew out of, but was not in all matters identical with, the views of the Pharisees, who had been a small association of devotees concerned with bringing the common people back to their prophetic function as a holy nation. The synagogues were not temples: they were meeting houses for local spiritual and social needs, which the Pharisees sponsored.

What is of the greatest consequence is to bring Paul's life and letters into relationship with the contemporary world of his time, both Jewish and pagan, especially in the particular areas of his activities. Here both Greek and Roman, as well as Jewish, records are of great service; and we are now in a much stronger position thanks to the results of modern archaeological discoveries. The chronology of events has been helped, as well as a more intimate knowledge of the contemporary scene. And it was a grim time, with the Jewish homeland an occupied country under Roman domination, and a whole Mediterranean world run by harsh and even mad emperors like Caligula and Nero.

It hardly needs for me to say that I have read many books on Paul and his teaching, including the works *Paul and Palestinian Judaism* by E. P. Sanders (1977) and *The Mythmaker: Paul and the Invention of Christianity* by Hyam Maccoby (1986). But these are mainly concerned with theological matters, or influenced by them, whereas what is required is an objective historical approach, which I have pursued for the greater part of a long life. My books like *The Passover Plot* and *The Pentecost Revolution* have been very widely read. My interest may be said to have begun when I, a Jewish boy, was a pupil on the Classical side at St. Paul's School. A teacher I was on good terms with once spoke to me of Jesus as "our Saviour and your Messiah". These words epitomised the distinction between the Gentile and the Jewish followers of Jesus in the first century, and the distinction between a religious and a political approach remains to this day.

To get these things in historical perspective the right understanding of Paul is essential, which is why in this work I pay tribute to a much maligned and much misunderstood Jew, and a very courageous and dedicated man.

HUGH J. SCHONFIELD

1
Enter Paul

At the time Paul of Tarsus, self-styled Envoy of Jesus Christ to the Nations, was at the height of his activities, the Roman Empire also was at the height of its power and prestige. Paul himself was a Jew, who held the privilege of Roman citizenship, but claimed to be the appointed representative of the ultimate World Ruler, greater than Caesar and any other monarch.

The principal area of Paul's activities was north-east of the Mediterranean, the cities of Asia Minor and Greece. He had been born at its eastern end, in Tarsus of Cilicia. In appearance he was something of a Greek satyr of a man, attractive and superstitiously appealing because of his ugliness, especially as his face lit up and was transformed by the beauty of his smile.

One ancient record, the *Acts of Paul and Thecla*, offers a pen-portrait of Paul. He was to visit Iconium, and Onesiphorus with whom he would stay had been given a description of him by Paul's follower Titus. Onesiphorus could not fail to recognise his guest: 'He saw Paul coming, a man little of stature, thin-haired upon the head, crooked in the legs, of good state of body, with eyebrows joining, and nose somewhat hooked, full of grace; for sometimes he appeared like a man, and sometimes he had the face of an angel.'

Paul was a man with a very strong sense of mission, something which was part of his make-up long before he had any knowledge of Jesus. He was convinced that he had a special work to do in the world, and therefore it was essential to equip himself adequately. It was an asset that he had been born at Tarsus in Cilicia, 'no insignificant city', on the fringe of East and West, and had the dignity of Roman citizenship. It was even more consequential that in a heathen world his family were strict Jews, following the customs and convictions of the Pharisees.

On his own showing, Paul had some physical handicap, which may have disposed him to psychic experiences, and his appearance may also have been compensated for by mystical pursuits. According to the *Acts of the Apostles* he had a married sister in Jerusalem, probably older than himself, a fact which could have contributed to fulfilling his desire to go to the Holy City and study under the great Pharisee teachers of the time. Paul's father would strongly approve, and be proud of his son's ambition.

According to the *Acts*, Paul sat at the feet of Rabban Gamaliel, one of the leading contemporary Pharisees. And he relates, in his letter to the Galatian Communities, 'how I advanced in Judaism far beyond many students of my own age; for none was more keenly enthusiastic than I to master the traditions of my ancestors' (*Gal*.i.14).

It is essential for the reader to comprehend that Rabbinical Judaism by no means confined itself to moral and ethical matters, and the interpretation and application of the Law of Moses. It also devoted itself a great deal to psychic matters, and Jewish mysticism. There were two major branches of such studies, the one relating to the interpretation of the first chapter of *Genesis* (*Ma'aseh Bereshith*), and the other to the Heavenly Chariot in *Ezekiel* (*Ma'aseh Merkabah*).

We are able to infer that it was to the first of these to which Paul devoted himself, as we shall illustrate in due course. And having psychic experiences played no small part in convincing him that he had a special destiny of a Messianic nature well before he was aware of the claims of Jesus. We have to dig much deeper into Paul's personality if we are to understand the violence of his initial opposition to Jesus and his followers, and his subsequent 'conversion' and call to the distinctive function of Envoy to the Nations on the Messiah's behalf.

The date of Paul's birth is not known; but we can reckon that it must have been in the region of AD10. Paul, meaning 'short of stature' (Latin *paulus*), was probably not our hero's real name, though quite appropriate. He appears to have adopted it at the outset of his missionary activities after he was summoned to the presence of L. Sergius Paulus, Roman proconsul of Cyprus. Paul's Hebrew name was Saul, called after the first king of Israel who had been chosen from the tribe of Benjamin. The fact had been important to him, since he alludes to it in two of his letters (*Rom*.xi.1 and *Phil*.iii.4-5). To the Philippian Community Paul wrote: 'If anyone else thinks he can rely on the physical, I even more so, circumcised as I was on the eighth day, of the race of Israel, the tribe of Benjamin, a Hebrew sprung from Hebrews.' There is, however, the possibility that Paulus had already been the Roman name of Saul's father, which he inherited, and which he employed preferentially from the time of his encounter with L. Sergius Paulus.

The family must have been settled in Tarsus for some time for Paul to have inherited Roman citizenship. For a provincial such citizenship was a special privilege, conferred for services or for goodwill shown to the Imperial house, and it had usually to be purchased for a substantial sum. It is likely that Paul's father was in fairly good circumstances, and the Jewish custom required that he should teach his son a trade. Paul had proficiency as a weaver of tent-cloth, which was one of the products of Cilicia (Cilician goats' hair fabric known as Kilki material), in Latin *cilicium*.

From ancient records we can learn a great deal about Tarsus, and about the world in which Paul grew to manhood.

It was a strongly heathen world on the fringe of east and west, both in religion and culture, as well as being prominent in trade, since it had a protected harbour for shipping. In our introduction to Paul it is of consequence that we should familiarise ourselves with its atmosphere. It certainly was 'no insignificant city'. On some of its coins was stamped TARSUS METROPOLIS, FIRST, FAIREST AND BEST. On others the god Baal-Tarz, lord of the city, held out the emblems of his gracious gifts of corn and vine.

The approach to Tarsus from the Mediterranean was not in itself an impressive sight, unless one lifted one's eyes above the level of the humid Cilician plain, above the hills behind, to the distantly distinguished majestic outlines of the mighty snow-capped Taurus mountains beating against the sky. In the immediate foreground, while navigating carefully into the mouth of the River Cydnus, was only the low line of desolate shelving sandbanks. A short pull up-channel, however, the river opened out into a broad and placid lagoon, alive with vessels on its inner shore pressing close upon the bustling wharves and quays of Aulai, the dock area of Tarsus. The tang of the sea mingled with the indescribable odour of decaying fish and vegetables, Cilician pelts, and the multitudinous merchandise of many lands. Porters chanted their doleful repetitive refrains as in stalwart files they humped goods and supplies from ship to shore and shore to ship.

Penetrating the clutter of warehouses, taverns, and squalid dwellings, and the maze of narrow streets that gave on the waterfront, the River Cydnus held on its way through the city proper, clear of the stench of the port and its raucous din. Tarsus, fair though she might seem to many of her near half-million inhabitants, lay flat and sprawling in ungainly fashion, with only the more elaborate architecture of her civic, cultural and religious buildings to reflect her standing and accomplishments.

Philostratus reports the impression of the sage Apollonius of Tyana as he tasted the life of Tarsus close to the time of which we are writing:

> He found the atmosphere of the city harsh and strange and little conducive to the philosophic life, for nowhere are men more addicted than here to luxury: jesters and full of insolence are they all; and they attend more to their fine linen than the Athenians did to wisdom; and a stream called the Cydnus runs through their city, along the banks of which they sit like so many water-fowl. Hence the words which Apollonius addresses to them in his letter: 'Be done with getting drunk upon your water.' (*Life of Apollonius of Tyana*, Bk.I.vii, *Loeb Classical Library*).*

Tarsus came within the framework of the Roman province of Cilicia-Phoenicia-Syria, and so was linked politically with Judea. Greeks had migrated or had been settled there in successive colonising ventures: so had Jews, especially under the Seleucid kings. But Tarsus was little more Hellenic than Judaic: Persians and Assyrians before them had mingled their blood with the native stock. The homely language was the Aramaic of the Near East, though the *koine* – the international form of Greek – served for general intercourse.

Athenodorus, son of Sandon, Tarsian Stoic philosopher and teacher of the Emperor Augustus, had recently given the city a new constitution, which became operative shortly before Paul's birth. It was not completely autocratic; but it would be termed today capitalistic and reactionary, for the qualification for citizenship and the right of voting and election was landed proprietorship; and the inner councils of state were further reserved for those whose wealth or services had secured for them the privileges of Roman as well as local citizenship. The new constitution was designed as a safeguard against irresponsible demagogy, and would have the strong support of the Jews.

But there were limits to the participation of even qualified Jews in civic affairs, due to religious scruples. Few would go beyond these limits unless they were prepared to cut loose from the synagogue

---

* Philostratus, a Greek historian and Sophist, completed his life of the neo-Pythagorean philosopher Apollonius of Tyana in c. AD 217. Apollonius was born in c. 4 BC., and was said to have lived for nearly 100 years.

altogether. Both religion, which enjoined a strict code of behaviour, and the national consciousness, which looked towards Judea and Jerusalem, tended to a unity in community among the Jews of the Dispersion which kept them distinct from their neighbours though it did not mean unmindfulness of local duty and loyalty. There was special legislation for Jewish requirements under the Roman Empire, and when these enactments were violated the Jews would make common cause in defence of their rights.

The Romans recognized the Jewish groups of the Empire, as they did not recognize the migrant Greeks, as part of a nation – 'the nation of Jews' – as in a sense colonials of a country and government with which they were in amity. The Jews, compared with the factious Greeks, were regarded by the Romans as a law-abiding stabilising influence, and they favoured them correspondingly. The decrees and edicts which resulted were consequently the cause of much local friction and ill-will, especially on the part of the Greeks whose individualism was offended by Jewish solidarity, and who resented the austerity and morality of the Jewish faith, and the privileges which the Jews enjoyed.

Citizenship for the Greeks meant membership of a clan. This did not have to represent a tie either of race or blood. Anyone could enter into such an association by a religio-political conformity. But it did represent a kinship. As the Jews could not accept the religious implications they could not join a Greek tribe, unless they were apostate, and the Greeks consequently refused to treat them as kinsmen, and by the same token as full fellow-citizens. In a city like Alexandria, with a large Jewish population, the Jews could only obtain such title to citizenship as they had by constituting themselves as a distinct tribe, named after Alexander the Great as the tribe of Macedonians.

All the fruitful grounds for antisemitism were here present. The Jews were exempted by the Romans from military service. The Jews were permitted to have their own laws and customs. The Jews were granted liberty to keep the seventh day as a holiday, and were not required to appear before a judge on their sabbath. The Jews were allowed to send large offerings of money to the Temple at Jerusalem. The latter practice was elevated to a major grievance, and made much of by the Greek agitators.

Hostile sentiments freely expressed could easily, on occasion, lead to bloody riots, and even a Cicero could lend his oratory to swell the popular clamour by defending Lucius Valerius Gratus, who as governor of Asia Minor had confiscated the Jewish Temple-tribute.

We come now (he declaimed) to that famous cause of grumbling, the gold of the Jews... It is because of this chief part of the accusation, Lelius, that you have sought out this place and this crowd. You know what a numerous swarm they are (these Jews), how they stick together, how much power they exercise in the public meetings. I will speak low, just loud enough for the judges to hear me. I don't want to excite these people against me and against the best citizens. Seeing that Jews were exporting gold each year from Italy and from all the Provinces to Jerusalem, Flaccus prohibited this exportation from Asia. Who could not sincerely praise this measure?... Resistance to a barbarous superstition was a mark of energy on the part of Flaccus. To show contempt, in the interests of the Republic, for this mob of Jews who are so often turbulent in our meetings, that was a mark of a singular force. (Cicero, *Pro Flacco*)

But Roman imperial policy would have none of this. The Jews were a valuable corrective to lawlessness and disaffection, and their rights must be upheld by such decrees as the following:

Caesar Augustus, High Priest and Tribune of the People, ordains: Since the nation of the Jews has been found grateful to the Roman people, not only at this time, but in times past also, and chiefly Hyrcanus, the High Priest under my father Caesar the Emperor, it seemed good to me and my counsellors, according to the sentence and oath of the people of Rome, that the Jews have liberty to make use of their own customs, according to the law of their forefathers... and that their sacred money be not touched, but be sent to Jerusalem, and that it be committed to the care of the receivers at Jerusalem. And that they be not obliged to go before any judge on the Sabbath Day, nor on the day of preparation for it, after the ninth hour... And I give orders that the present decree be displayed in that most eminent place which has been consecrated to me by the Community of Asia at Ancyra. (Josephus, *Jewish Antiquities*, Bk.XVI.vi.2)

Life could not be easy for the Jewish population of Tarsus; and especially was it needful to stay off the streets on the annual festival of Baal-Tarz, when his image standing erect upon his lordly lion was borne through the city in a pyramidal shrine.

How different was the upbringing of Paul compared with Jesus!

13

For Paul Judaism needed continually to be stressed, for he was grow-ing to manhood in a land which was predominantly pagan. It was essential to emphasize the contrast and to cling tightly to Jewish cus-toms and practices. It was no wonder that the family favoured the Pharisee way of life. At the same time, as an ardent Jew in a Gentile environment it was a matter of concern that non-Jews should be weaned from their idolatry and brought to knowledge of the One God. Probably, in the synagogue the family attended, there were already Gentile proselytes and monotheists, 'strangers within the gates'. That Paul should ultimately be 'called' to become Envoy to the Nations on behalf of the Jewish Messiah chimed wholly with the circumstances of his youthful upbringing. That was his natural destiny.

With Jesus, in whose name Paul would ultimately rove the Roman Empire, the circumstances had been entirely contrary to those of Paul. He had grown up in a land predominantly Jewish, and never during his public life left it. He had no need, therefore, to emphasize Judaism as a religion, only to recall his people to the basic moral teachings of their faith. His emissaries were to go to the lost sheep of the House of Israel, and not into any Gentile's house or town.

The functions of Jesus and Paul were almost totally distinct, and indeed their concepts of the character of the Messianic. By a strange quirk of history they would be brought into an ideological partner-ship, which, however, would be the cause of great strain and stress, since the position of Jesus would be continued by his family and immediate associates.

2
Mission Messianic

Without the Messianic there can be no right understanding of the personalities either of Jesus or his professed servant and chosen envoy Paul. We have Christianity as a religion only because it is so hard for non-Jews to entertain the Messianic. They have to adapt to the sombre atmosphere of the impending climax of history which particularly affected the Jewish people in the first century of our era. Expressions such as the Last Times and the Kingdom of God reflected this sense of climax; and they had relationship to the ultimate destiny of Israel as God's instrument in uniting mankind in faith and in peace.

There had been a long build-up to the conviction of the imminence of the Messianic Age. It had been reflected in the visions of the Hebrew prophets both before and after the Babylonian Exile, and it had become part and parcel of the Jewish view of history, of human destiny. Association with Persian Zoroastrianism had promoted the idea of a long drawn out battle between the forces of Good and Evil in which the Good would ultimately triumph, and Jewish experiences, especially in the time of the Maccabbees, had reinforced Messianic expectations. As a consequence a new Jewish apocalyptic literature came into being, and much admonitory material in the names of Israel's ancient worthies. The faithful were on the watch for signs of the times, and Jewish sects like the Essenes and Pharisees sought to build up a faithful and devout remnant of Israel which would be deserving of the ultimate deliverance and be the instrument of mankind's redemption. Increasingly, there was awaited the advent of an ideal king of Israel, the anointed one (*Messiah*), who could lead his people into the New Age and overturn heathenism represented by an ultimate Great Power.

The message was spread not only in Jewish literature: it was communicated by Jewish interpolations of alien sacred books like the *Sibylline Oracles*. We may quote here two specimens:

But when Rome shall rule over Egypt, though still delaying, then shall the great kingdom of the Immortal King appear among men, and a holy king shall come who shall rule over the whole earth for all ages of the course of time. Then shall implacable wrath fall upon the men of Latium... Ah, wretched me, when shall that day come, and the judgement of Immortal God, the great King?

(Bk.III.45-56)

But when this destined day is fully come, a great rule and judgement shall come upon men. For the fertile earth shall yield her best fruit of corn and wine and oil... No sword shall come upon the land, nor shout of war... but deep peace over all the earth. King shall live as friend to king to the bounds of the age, and the Immortal shall establish in the starry heaven one law for men over all the face of the earth for all the doings of hapless mortals.

(Bk.III.742-760)

The Nativity stories relating to Jesus in the New Testament are part and parcel of the same conviction. They are peculiarly Jewish, peculiarly the outcome of the Hebrew reading of the objective of life on our planet; and they are typical of what was being believed by multitudes at the time when they were written. We do well to quote some of the statements, which are so Jewish in their content, in order to absorb the atmosphere of the period in which they were composed. And we do well to appreciate that we have to adapt ourselves to that atmosphere to discover the motivations behind certain Jewish personalities and events. The phenomenon of John the Baptist, for instance, was fantastic by any standard of judgement, but fitted perfectly into Jewish obsession with the End Time.

I quote here from the Gospels a few passages in my own translation, which is as accurate as possible.

From the annunciation to Mary (*Lk*.i.30-33):

But the angel said to her, 'Do not be alarmed, Mary. You have found favour with God. You will conceive in your womb and have a son, whom you are to call Jesus. He will be a great man, and be termed *Son of the Most High*, and the Lord God will give him the throne of his ancestor David. He will reign over the house of Jacob for ever, and his sovereignty shall be without end.'

Prophesy of Zechariah, father of John the Baptist (*Lk*.i.66-78):

Blessed be the Lord God of Israel,
For he has visited and ransomed his people,
And raised up for us a means of deliverance
Out of the house of his servant David,
As he said by his holy prophets of old;
Deliverance from our foes and all who hate us,
To maintain his mercy to our fathers,
And to call to mind his holy covenant,
The oath which he swore to our father Abraham,
Assuring that fearlessly, freed from foes,
We should worship him all our days
Purely and piously in his presence.
And you, child, shall be called 'Prophet of the Highest';
For you shall precede the Lord to pave his road,
To give intelligence of deliverance to his people,
Through the tender mercies of our God
Whereby a sunbeam from above has reached to us,
Lighting those in gloom and grim shadow,
Directing our feet to a path of safety.

An angel speaks to the shepherds at Bethlehem (*Lk*.ii.10-11):

Do not be afraid. I bring you word of a great joy which will be shared by all the people, that today in David's town a deliverer has been born to you, none other than the Lord Messiah.

It is noteworthy that as regards the Messiahship of Jesus (his being the Christ) his descent from King David is continually stressed. We are furnished with two versions of his genealogy. His father Joseph is referred to as Son of David (*Mt*.i.20), and it is insisted that he was born in David's town of Bethlehem.

The reason for this has not rightly been appreciated. The function of the Messiah was to bring his people back to their service for God, in order that Israel should lead the nations to God. Spiritually, David had been the ideal king of Israel and a true Son of God, who, more-over, as a youth, had ended Philistine domination by slaying the giant Goliath. Consequently a Davidic Messiah was specially anticipated by the Jews as an outcome of Roman domination. The armoured Roman legionary symbolised the new Goliath from the time of Pompey, and the Messiah was popularly expected by the Jews to be the means of ousting the Romans and restoring their own independence (*Acts* i.6). The two Jewish wars with the Romans in the first and second centuries of the Christian Era were inspired by Messianic faith, as were the anti-Roman propaganda activities of the Jewish Zealots, including many followers of Jesus. It was seen as an Act of Providence that Jewish emissaries from Israel had the benefit of Roman roads and transport.

The attitude of most Jews in territories under Roman rule was, however, very different, as we have noted. Rome for them was their protector from Greek and Syrian antisemitism, and guarantor of their religious liberties. The Romans, for their part, regarded the provincial Jews as a stabilising influence contributing to good order, and favoured them accordingly. Some were granted the privilege of Roman citizenship.

It is most important that we should appreciate from the outset the true cause of the difference in position of Paul and the Israeli Christians. It was essentially due to the difference in experience of the authority of Rome. For Paul Rome represented a benevolent authority which contributed to security and facility of travel and communication. For the Israeli Christians Rome was the tyrant, the enemy of the saints, who must be overthrown before the Kingdom of God could be established. Because of Paul's background in his youth he could receive the call to be Envoy to the Nations, and have Rome as the final objective of his evangelism. With the Israeli Christians, as with other Messianic Jews, the objective was the downfall and disruption of the Roman Empire to make way for the coming of the Kingdom of God. For them Rome was the fourth kingdom of Daniel's prophecy (*Dan*.ii.), the iron kingdom, to be destroyed by the Messianic stone as the stone from David's sling had destroyed Goliath. In those days 'the God of heaven will set up a kingdom, which shall never be destroyed.'

The author of *Luke–Acts*, biographer of Paul, does his utmost to reconcile these two positions and tone down the conflict between their advocates. As we have seen, he stresses the role of Jesus as the Davidic Messiah. At the same time, however, he is at pains to bring in the Good Centurion. In one case the Roman officer has a sick servant, and sends local Jewish elders to Jesus to beg him to come and cure him. These Jews entreat Jesus on the Roman's behalf: 'He deserves to be granted this request; for he loves our people, and had the synagogue built for us himself' (*Lk*.vii.4-5). In the other case we have the centurion Cornelius at Caesarea who sends for Peter, and who is described as 'pious and revering God with all his family, one who gave a great deal in charity to the people and looked continually to God' (*Acts* x.2).

There was, of course, a famous Roman official Petronius, legate of Syria (which included Judea), who in AD40-41 at the risk of his own life had refused to carry out the instructions of the mad emperor Gaius Caligula to have his statue set up for worship in the Jewish Temple at Jerusalem. The incident is reflected in the second letter of Paul to the Thessalonian Community, where the ultimate Antichrist 'opposes and elevates himself above everything regarded as a god or as an object of worship, so that he himself sits in God's Temple claiming to be God' (*II.Thess*.ii.4).

Fundamentally there was common ground in all Jewish Messianic convictions, namely that the ultimate Kingdom of God on earth would be the fulfilment of Israel's world mission. Where there were differences was in the circumstances by which the objective would be accomplished. The pious in Israel in Paul's time were urging that a faithful remnant would be the instrument of mankind's salvation, and its number would be augmented by the resurrection of the Hebrew saints of past ages. Paul would add to Israel those Gentiles who gave their allegiance to the king of Israel, and thus ceased to be Gentiles.

We shall, of course, have to return to these matters in the context of Paul's story. But in thinking about his personality and upbringing we have to apprehend that he was very spiritually-minded as a young man, with an ardent desire to bring the knowledge of the One God to pagan Gentiles. He also recognised that his possession of the privilege of Roman citizenship, as well as his experience of a non-Jewish environment, particularly qualified him for such service. What he needed was to enhance his Jewish religious equipment, and to be fully confident that he was a chosen vessel for God's use. It was imperative, therefore, that Paul should go to study at Jerusalem under the great Pharisee teachers of his time. And his father would be proud of his son's desire, and put no difficulties in his way.

3
Jerusalem Scene

This chapter and the next are of special importance, because they deal with matters of consequence affecting our understanding of Paul. We have to learn about Jerusalem and what was happening there, and about the kind of studies in which Paul was engaged. The New Testament records are of some service, but are largely inadequate and often inaccurate. New Testament scholars, unfortunately, have concentrated on Pauline teaching, seeing him particularly as the exponent of what was to become the Christian religion.

There is no source of information which enables us to know when Paul arrived at Jerusalem, whether this was before or after the crucifixion of Jesus as a rebel against Rome, claimant of the Jewish throne. Taking account of the time indications in the *Acts of the Apostles* it seems likely that it was shortly before.

Here it is important to impress on our minds that Paul was a stranger to Judea and to what had been happening there. As we have seen, he came from a region where Roman rule was greatly respected by Jews, and his family held the privilege of Roman citizenship. His whole upbringing had reflected the position that Roman authority was both humane and just. It would never have occured to him that it could be any different in the Land of Israel, that there Roman government was resented and abominated as heathen and sinister, justifying every kind of action that would bring it to an end. One might say of Paul (Saul of Tarsus as he then was) that he was extremely naive and idealistic.

As it happened, as far as Judea was concerned, there had for some time been a particularly unpleasant Roman official, acting as procurator, named Pontius Pilate. Judea was an Occupied Territory with a Jewish Government subservient to Rome, the Sanhedrin, mainly composed of a spiritual and aristocratic clique. The holy Temple of God at Jerusalem was overlooked by a heathen Roman garrison at Fort Antonia, and on the feast days the soldiers lined the roofs of the porticoes. The sacred vestments used by the High Priest on the solemn days in the Jewish year were held by the Romans, and handed out solely for each occasion.

Pontius Pilate was a jumped-up official whose regime had been characterised by Jew-hatred and utter ruthlessness. Philo of Alexandria, near the middle of the first century AD, had learned about him from the Herodian family, and described him in his *Embassy to Gaius* (the Roman emperor) as 'naturally inflexible, a blend of self-will and relentlessness, a man noted for vindictiveness and furious temper'. Very close to the time of his execution of Jesus for claiming Messianic kingship of Israel, Pilate had attacked the Samaritans among whom a prophet had appeared, killing and executing many of them (Josephus, *Jewish Antiq.* Bk.XVIII.85-87).

In the case of the Samaritans, they protested to Vitellius, the Roman legate of the Province of Syria, and Pilate's superior. He promptly sent his friend Marcellus to take charge of affairs in Judea and Samaria from Pilate, who was ordered to proceed to Rome to answer for his conduct. Vitellius later came to Jerusalem himself, and, among other acts, deposed Caiaphas (who had condemned Jesus) as High Priest. He hoped by these actions to conciliate the Jewish and Samaritan populace and prevent large-scale anti-Roman outbreaks.

Paul would in all probability have been aware of the efforts of Vitellius, which would have commended themselves to him. What he would not have been aware of was the strength of the Jewish liberation movement with its Messianic inspiration.

Opposition to Rome had developed at the dawn of the first century AD (Christian reckoning) shortly after the death of Herod the Great, who had made the Emperor Augustus executor of his will. It had begun when Herod's successor Archelaus had gone to Rome for ratification of his sovereignty. The Roman legate of Syria had sent a legion to garrison Jerusalem during his absence, and they were attacked by the Jewish populace at the feast of Pentecost. The Romans responded by setting fire to the porticoes of the Temple and plundering its treasury. But the revolt spread, and Varus had to suppress it with an army. Some two thousand of the prominent rebels were crucified.

Archelaus was deposed by the Romans in AD6, and the area of Judea, Samaria and Idumea was converted into an administrative

Roman region under a procurator responsible to the legate of Syria. The whole country thus became liable to tribute, for which purpose the new legate of Syria, Quirinius, ordered the taking of a census. By a poetic justice, according to Luke, it was this census which assured that Israel's Messianic Deliverer would be born in his ancestor David's city of Bethlehem.

The census provoked another anti-Roman outbreak headed by Judas of Galilee and his associate Zadok. They proclaimed that Israel acknowledged no other lord than God, and that this taxation reduced the Jews to the status of slaves. From that time there developed an underground movement of Jewish freedom-fighters. To Jews they were known as the Zealots, and some, because of the kind of daggers they used, as Sicarii. It is significant that two of the twelve envoys Jesus chose, Simon and Judas, were freedom-fighters, and some of the others were probably in league with them.

Thus already, even before the appearance of Pontius Pilate, there was a substantial history of Jewish resentment of Roman rule. Some of the Jewish aristocracy, including the chief priests, were also antagonistic to Roman rule; but they preferred to use the weapons of intrigue and diplomacy to undermine the authority of particularly noxious officials. They did recognize also that the Roman forces were a cushion against an armed rising by the Jewish populace against their government.

The Gospels refer to such incidents in the time of Pontius Pilate. 'Some people arrived to inform Jesus about the Galileans whose blood Pilate had mingled with that of their sacrifices'(*Lk*.xiii.1). 'There was one called Bar-Abbas, imprisoned with other insurgents who had committed murder during the rising' (*Mk*.xv.7). So it is extraordinary that Christians, because of their theology, should fail to see Jesus as the Messianic Jewish Deliverer.

As an expression of what the Messiah was expected to do we are given a prophecy 'by the Holy Spirit' uttered by the father of John the Baptist: that God would raise up a means of Israel's deliverance out of the house of David, 'deliverance from our foes and all who hate us'. Christians do not see Jesus in this capacity at all. So why speak of him as the Christ (i.e. the Messiah)? Before we can interpret events aright we have to get into the first century atmosphere in Israel, and discard the Church's non-Jewish one of subsequent centuries.

Not only with the historical circumstances, but also with the aspect of Jerusalem itself, we have to get back into the first century. The

22

Church of later times failed wholly to recognise – for instance in imagining the Via Dolorosa as the road taken by Jesus to his crucifixion – that Jerusalem had undergone several destructions, first with the war with the Romans in AD66-70. After the second destruction in AD135 during the revolt of the pseudo-Messiah Bar-Cochba, the city had been rebuilt by the Romans on a smaller scale and with a different axis and layout under the name of Aelia Capitoline. The city Paul knew was totally unlike the one we know today, and has much to tell us that can assist our understanding of Paul and of Christian beginnings.

The Jerusalem of those days was built on a group of hills, with a valley in its midst which represented both a physical and ideological division. On the eastern side was Mount Zion and the original city of David, linked to the north, the Temple Mount, by a spur known as the Ophel where were the priests' quarters. Outside the city on the east was the Kidron Valley, and immediately beyond was the Mount of Olives. The west and north-west of the city was Graeco-Roman as reconstructed and developed by Herod and Great. Its whole atmosphere was alien to pious Jewish sentiment. On his visits to Jerusalem from Caesarea on the coast, the Roman procurator could reside in Herod's palace. Closer to the Temple area at the north-west were the homes of the chief priests and Jewish aristocracy, and a viaduct over the valley gave direct access to the Temple Mount. In the vicinity of what may be called Government Hill, the Sanhedrin had its meetings, while down in the intermediate valley, known as the Tyropoeon, and on its slopes, was the part of the city where Jews from many lands congregated, with numerous synagogues to serve their needs.

It was in the quarter for foreign Jews that Paul would have had his home when he came to the city from Tarsus. And we are introduced to it in the *Acts of the Apostles*. The propaganda of the associates of Jesus had made its impact here, and many had joined the Messianic Movement. There had been an appointment of supervisors to deal with the distribution of food because of complaints by the foreign-born Jews (Hellenists) that their widows had been discriminated against. Several of these supervisors were foreign Jews. We learn of Stephen, Philip, Prochorus, Nicanor, Timon, Parmenas and Nikolaus, a proselyte to Judaism from Antioch (*Acts* vi.5).

Stephen, it would appear, was an active propagandist for the Messiahship of Jesus, but encountered the resistance of certain members of two synagogues for foreign Jews; one was the synagogue for African Jews (Libyans, Cyrenians and Alexandrians), while the other was for Jews from Cilicia and Asia. Of the second Paul would have been a member.

Stephen would be stressing the Messiahship of Jesus, inevitably linked with the overthrow of the Roman government. And this would naturally antagonise Jews coming from territories like Egypt and Asia Minor, who were Hellenists and who regarded Rome as their protector. Stephen was denounced to the Sanhedrin on totally false charges, and evidently it had Paul's approval.

We cannot attribute any authority to Stephen's speech in self-defence in the *Acts*. Like so many speeches, in *Luke–Acts* and *John* particularly, attributed to Jesus and others, including Paul, these are the creations of the writers and have no historical validity. It was customary in those days for authors to invent such speeches either in terms which they thought appropriate to the circumstances or for particular propaganda purposes. Classical literature is full of instances. The reader has to get used to the fact that many speeches in the New Testament, which he has regarded as faithful and reliable are actually fictitious and do not even depend on tradition or any record.*

One has the feeling, in the case of Stephen however, that what he represented was particularly offensive to Paul to make him so irate as on his own showing he was. In an autobiographical passage, writing many years later to the Galatian believers, he tells 'how I ruthlessly hounded down God's Community and ravaged it' (*Gal.*i.13). For a declared Pharisee to seek authority to do this from a Sadducean High Priest was such an extraordinary circumstance that only the strongest personal feelings amounting to dementia could have induced Paul to take such a step.

We have the evidence, which we shall shortly relate, that Paul was a mystic, and that in Jerusalem he plunged deeply into Jewish occultism. What was it that drove him to this? Was it his unattractive appearance which turned him to an inwardness? And did that inwardness nominate him for some unique world mission? We can, of course, only speculate. But it needs to be considered very seriously that Paul's initial hostility to Jesus, and therefore to his followers, was that Jesus was achieving the function which Paul believed to be his own.

---

* On this subject see, for example, Schonfield, *The Pentecost Revolution*, Ch.2, and Ch.9.

4

Behind the Curtain

The young Paul was evidently a man of moods, with a strong sense of dedication, believing himself called to a special destiny. He was also very passionate, apt to be strongly emotional and explosively violent. With all that we can learn of him he was anything but normal. He was also a brooding type, with an inwardness which was partly the consequence of his outward drawbacks. He had a permanent form of suffering, his 'thorn in the flesh', which did not make for mental and physical comfort. But he was a determined man, with a strong will-power, driven by his star, yet fundamentally a loving and wishfully gregarious person. Altogether a character of whims and contrasts.

When we consider Paul, as we have already illustrated, we have also to see him in the setting of the contemporary scene with its peculiar Last Times atmosphere, particularly affecting the Jewish people. Only in such an age could Messianic concepts be a dominant factor, something very hard for Gentiles to comprehend. Israel, struggling under a pagan yoke, yet nourished the persuasion of its world mission as a divinely elected nation, 'a kingdom of priests', whose true calling was to be 'a light to the Gentiles... for God's salvation to the ends of the Earth' (*Isa*.xlix.6).

'How odd of God to choose the Jews', punned an eminent Christian divine. Odd or not, the story of Israel is from the beginning the story of such conviction. To Abraham, the father of the nation, God had said repeatedly that 'in his descendants shall all the nations of the earth be blessed.'

John the Baptist, Jesus, and many other Jews of the first century AD testify to this sense of Jewish mission to Mankind which was so strong a feature of the period. The experiences of persecution in the time of the Maccabees had underlined this conviction of dedication, and

25

many events that had followed down to Paul's day. About a century earlier, in the *Letter of Aristeas*, the Jewish High Priest Eleazar had pointed out that the function of the laws of Moses was to preserve Israel in a priestly purity, for which reason the Jews were known abroad as 'men of God'. The fellowship of the Essenes had been the outcome of the need felt to achieve a priestly purity and dedication, and that of the Pharisees was similarly inspired at a popular level.

But as well as the emphasis on the external evidences of devotion to the Divine Plan for Mankind, there was a strong attachment to the spiritual and the occult. That Judaism in the first century AD was purely legalistic has been for centuries a falsehood disseminated by the Church. There was also a deep devotion to the mystical; and it was to this that Paul was drawn, and to which he refers when many years later he wrote to the Galatians of 'how I advanced in Judaism far beyond many students of my own age; for none was more keenly enthusiastic than I to master the traditions of my ancestors.'

Those who are knowledgeable about Jewish occultism can readily appreciate the particular field of study to which Paul applied himself. As we have seen, there were two main areas of involvement. One of these was known as *Ma'aseh Bereshith*, which dealt with the mysteries of the Creation Story in *Genesis*, while the other was called *Ma'aseh Merkabah*, and dealt with the significance of the Heavenly Chariot described by the Prophet Ezekiel. *Pardes* (paradise -- the Garden) belonged to the mystery of the Creation, and we can ascertain from Paul's letters that it was to this branch of Jewish occultism that he devoted himself. It also dealt with the implications of the origins of Man.

It was laid down in the *Mishnah* that 'men are not to expound unlawful unions with a company of three nor the Lore of Creation with two, nor that of the Chariot (in *Ezekiel*) with one; but if a man do so, he must be a very wise man, and one who has much knowledge of his own. Everyone who meddles with the four things that follow, it were better for him that he had not come into the world, namely, what is Above and what is Below, what is Before and what is After. And everyone who does not revere the glory of his Maker (i.e. the nature of God) it were better for him that he had not come into the world.' (*Mishnah, Chagigah*.ii.)

There were very grave dangers in probing into the hidden mysteries. The ancient rabbis distinguished seven heavens, and corresponding to them seven degrees of initiation. The third heaven was *Pardes*. In what is perhaps an autobiographical passage, Paul would write much later:

> If I must continue to boast, undesirable as that is, I will come to visions and revelations of the Master. I know a man in Christ who fourteen years ago – whether in the physical or astral state, I do not know, God knows – was caught up as far as the third heaven. I know that this man – whether in the physical state or otherwise, I do not know, God knows – was caught up into 'the Garden' [Paradise] and heard ineffable words which no human is permitted to utter. Of someone like this I will boast, but about myself I will not boast, only of my disabilities. Even should I want to boast, I should be no fool, for I state the truth. But I will refrain in case anyone should think more of me than what he sees and hears. But with the transcendence of the revelations, in case I should be too elated, there was given me a spike in the flesh, an emissary of Satan to prod me (*II.Cor*.xii.1-7).*

But the lore of the Creation had other elements. It was considered, for instance, that when Adam was created 'in the image of God' he was of gigantic proportions, with his head reaching to the heavens. But when he sinned God made him small (*Chag*.fol.12a). There is an allusion to this in Paul's letter to the Ephesians (iv.13): 'until we all reach unity of faith and knowledge of the Son of God, the Perfect Man, the measure of the stature of the full-grown Christ.' Since Adam was the Son of God (*Lk*.iii.38), the Jewish mystics conceived that in heaven there must be the reflection of God in a manlike figure, the *Adam Kadmon* (the Archetypal Man). This is echoed in the Son of Man in heaven of the *Book of Enoch*. There was a danger in this teaching, since it might be inferred that there were two Powers in heaven, God and His likeness, the Son of God, identified with the Messiah.

Primitive Jewish Christianity did conceive of the Messiah on earth as the incarnation of the Heavenly Man, who had entered into Jesus at his baptism, thus making him the Second Adam. The rabbinical occultists were teaching that the Spirit (Wind) of God which fluttered over the Primeval Waters (*Gen*.i.2) was the Spirit of Messiah.

We shall see in due course how such mystical teachings would influence Paul's conceptions, especially in relationship to evangelising the Gentiles. He had great difficulty in seeking to expound such

---

* See the third of four letters to the Corinthian community, p.162.

ideas to converts from paganism, and indeed to this day Christians quite misunderstand them in their theology. It is necessary to repeat that Paul had to write to the Corinthians, 'It was impossible, brothers, for me to speak to you as spiritually-equipped people, only as physically-equipped, as infants in Christ. I had to feed you with milk rather than solid food, for you were not equal to it. Neither are you equal to it yet, for you are still at the physical stage' (*I.Cor*.iii.1-3). Even the author of *II.Peter* had to write of Paul's letters that in them 'there are certain things by no means easy to understand, which the unskilled and unstable twist to their own ruination as they do the rest of the Scriptures' (*II.Peter* iii.16).

Delving into the great mysteries, as Jewish sources convey, was a very dangerous pursuit, which could result in death or insanity even for advanced scholars. How more positively disturbing could they be expected to be for an immature student? It is hardly surprising that the conduct of Paul in his opposition to the followers of Jesus, his personal witch-hunt with an insane violence, exhibits all the marks of a period of dementia.

We cannot be positive of what lay behind the outbreak reported in the *Acts*. It is said there that Saul, 'still giving vent to dire threats against the followers of the Master, went to the High Priest and begged him for letters to Damascus, for the synagogues there, so that should he find any of this persuasion, whether men or women, he could bring them in bonds to Jerusalem' (*Acts* ix.1-2). Why Paul should wish to go to Damascus is not stated. But that region, as we learn from the Dead Sea Scrolls and rabbinical sources, was a place of refuge for Jewish sectarians and persecuted people. There the True Teacher of the Essenes had proclaimed his New Covenant.

Paul's state of mind could conceivably have been due to an inner conviction that he himself had been given the vocation of Messianic messenger to the Gentiles. This came through to me very strongly in studying Paul's letters many years ago, and I stated my findings at the time.[*]

The principal sources of Messianic prophecy were *Isaiah* and the *Psalms*, as is confirmed by those references held to apply to Jesus. Paul uses these books more than any others, quoting or alluding to *Isaiah* about sixty-five times and to the *Psalms* about forty-two times. So if Paul sought evidence of his Messianic vocation as a young man

------

[*] See Schonfield, *The Jew of Tarsus* (1946).

28

we may infer that he turned to such records. One of them reads:

> And He said, 'It is a light thing that thou shouldest be My servant to raise up the tribes of Jacob ... I will also give thee for a light to the Gentiles, that thou mayest be My salvation unto the ends of the earth.' Thus saith the Lord, the Redeemer of Israel and his Holy One, to him whom man despiseth, to a servant of rulers; kings shall see and arise, princes also shall do homage, because of the Lord that is faithful, and the Holy One of Israel, and He shall choose thee (*Isa.*xlix.6-7).

Saul was very conscious of his unattractive physical appearance. To such a sensitive soul such words could only be intended for his consolation, indicating that his very defects were a sign of his Messianic appointment. In writing very much later to the Galatians he could still speak of 'when it had pleased God, who separated me from my mother's womb and called me by his mercy, to reveal his Son to me that I should proclaim him to the Gentiles' (*Gal.*i.15-16).

But if Isaiah had predicted Paul's mission, the Psalmist also could have done so in a Messianic passage which ran: 'Ask of Me, and I shall give thee the Gentiles for thine inheritance, and the uttermost parts of the earth for thy possession' (*Ps.*ii.8). Might not that word 'ask' (Heb. *Sheal*) refer to him *Shaul* (Saul)? It could be read: 'Saul is from Me, and I will give thee the Gentiles for thine inheritance.' Such a word-play was quite in accord with current methods of exegesis.

It would not be alien to the circumstances if Paul had harboured this inner conviction of his destiny, and it would help to explain his vision on the road to Damascus. His was a very abnormal personality, stimulated and intensified by his penetrations 'behind the curtain'. In the circumstances, what could be closer to Paul's self-consciousness than the language of the Second Isaiah[*] about the Suffering Servant of God?

> He hath no form nor comeliness; and when we shall see him, there is no beauty that we should desire him. He is... a man of sorrows and acquainted with grief; and we hid as it were our faces from him... and we esteemed him not (*Isa.*liii.2-3).

---

[*] i.e. chapters xl - lv in the *Book of Isaiah*. Against the traditional view of the unity of authorship, most modern scholars regard the evidence for the tripartite division of *Isaiah* as conclusive. (See I. W. Slotki, *Isaiah, Soncino Books of the Bible*, Introduction, x)

5

Damascus

There is a great deal of mystery about Paul's expedition to Syria to arrest followers of Jesus there. The principal area of the activities of Jesus had been Galilee. Why then should the Syrian area in the region of Damascus be substituted?

To answer this we have to appreciate that there is very much that is hidden from us about Christian beginnings, especially in Israel. At Jerusalem, from a dramatic beginning at the festival of Pentecost, there is rapidly built up an organisation with requirements that members should embrace voluntary poverty by selling their possessions. They would become known as 'the Poor' (Hebr. *Ebionim*, Ebionites). At their head would be a triumvirate with a form of Council as the governing body. Pentecost, according to the *Acts*, would be the occasion of an annual assembly to which representatives of communities would report on their activities. The information in the *Acts* and Pauline letters reflects a structure so like that of the Essenes, as we have now discovered from the finding of the Dead Sea Scrolls, that it can hardly be a matter of coincidence. There must have been some association or relationship. The immediate envoys of Jesus from Galilee were humble persons with no experience of intricate organisation, who could not have invented the system.

An Essene relationship is also suggested by the men in white (the Essene apparel) who were at the tomb of Jesus at the time of the 'resurrection', assumed in some traditions to be angels.

We now know from the Essene literature that when their organisation had been created by one known as the Teacher or Master of Righteousness in the time of the Maccabees, they had entered into a New Covenant (same as New Testament), and this of all places was in the region of Damascus. In Paul's time the Essene communities were continuing to function in Syria, and they would give refuge to Jewish refugees from persecution. When the war with the Romans broke out in Israel in AD66, we learn from Nazorean sources that many Jewish followers of Jesus fled to the north, to the saints in Syria under the leadership of a cousin of Jesus, Simeon son of Cleopas. So it could perfectly well have happened that some followers of Jesus had done so earlier when danger threatened.

Some day, perhaps, there may be a find of Judaeo-Christian manuscripts, and we shall learn much more of the true story which underlies the accounts in the *Acts*.

When close to Damascus with the agents of the chief priests, Paul had been smitten in some way that temporarily blinded him. It could have been a lightning discharge of electricity or some kind of stroke. We can only quote the circumstances as related in the *Acts*.

He heard a voice saying to him, 'Saul, Saul, why are you hunting me?' 'Who are you, lord?' he asked. 'I am Jesus, whom you are hunting. Now rise, and go into the city, and you will be told what to do.' Saul's companions stood there speechless, hearing the voices but seeing no one.

When Saul rose from the ground, and had opened his eyes, his sight had gone. So they led him by the hand, and conducted him to Damascus. For three days he was unable to see, and neither ate nor drank.

Now there was a disciple in Damascus called Ananias, and the Master said to him in a vision, 'Ananias!' 'Here I am, Master,' he replied. 'Rise,' said the Master, 'and go to the street called Straight Cut, and inquire at the house of Judas for Saul called the Tarsian. He is praying there, and has beheld a man called Ananias coming and laying his hands on him so that he may regain his sight' (*Acts* ix.4-12).

The story continues that Saul did regain his sight, was baptised, and immediately began to proclaim Jesus in the synagogues of Damascus as Son of God, arguing that here indeed was the awaited Messiah. The consequence was that 'the Jews plotted to kill him'. To prevent his escape from Damascus, the Jews kept watch on the gates day and night; but he did escape by a ruse, being let down the city wall in a basket by the followers of Jesus. Returning to Jerusalem he attempted to join the believers there, but they were afraid of him and did not credit that he was a disciple (*Acts* ix.18-26).

31

The account sounds quite credible. But we need to remind ourselves that very largely the material in the *Acts*, as in the Gospels, is what may be described as historical fiction. The speeches and much of the story-line is the work of the author, utilising for his purpose certain reports to which he had access. All the Gospels and the *Acts* were written in other lands than Palestine, for the benefit of non-Jewish Christians, and later than the Jewish War with the Romans which ended in AD 70, and in which much that was authentic was lost. Consequently the Gospels often tell things differently from each other and contradict each other in important particulars. Similarly, where there is a possibility of comparison, as in the story just related, we find Paul in autobiographical passages in his letters saying something quite different to what is related in the *Acts*.

First of all it was not 'the Jews' who were trying to kill Paul and prevent his escape from the city. Paul himself says: 'At Damascus the ethnarch of King Haretath picketed the city of the Damascenes to hem me in; but through a loophole I was let down the wall in a basket, and so escaped his clutches' (*II.Cor.*xi.32-33).* So it was the Arab governor of the city who was concerned.

Similarly, Paul relates that he did *not* immediately return to Judea and try to join the disciples of Jesus. He himself says:

I did not take immediate steps to consult any earthly authority, neither did I go up to Jerusalem to interview those who were envoys before me. Instead I went away to Arabia and returned again to Damascus. Not until three years had elapsed did I go up to Jerusalem to report to Cephas (i.e. Peter), and I remained with him fifteen days. But I met none of the other envoys except James, the Master's brother. These are the facts I am giving you. Before God, I am telling no lie! After that I went to the regions of Syria and Cilicia, and remained unknown to the Christian communities of Judea. They only heard that 'he who formerly persecuted us now proclaims the conviction he once attacked,' and they praised God for me (*Gal.*i.16-24).

Consequently, while we have to use the *Acts of the Apostles* for a great deal of Paul's career, we have always to remember that much in it is artificial and also slanted. Some elements, preserved by Paul's companion in later life whom he speaks of as 'dear Dr Luke', may be regarded as more reliable than others, but still fictionalised. And

---

* See the third letter to the Corinthian community, p.162.

wherever practicable we need to check with other information available.

The reader, who may believe that the Bible is one hundred per cent authentic, will perhaps be shocked. But for purposes of historical research we have to apply to the New Testament records the same canons of judgment that we employ for non-Biblical documents. The writer does not wish to allude to this matter again; but it is hoped that the reader will bear it continually in mind as we proceed.

We are left in doubt as to whether it was Paul's first or second time in Damascus that he was forced to escape from the city. But a point of dating crops up. It was from AD37 to 40 that the Roman emperor Gaius Caligula ceded the government of Damascus to Haretath (Harith IV) king of Nabataean Arabia, and the city reverted to Roman rule on Haretath's death.

After his *volte face*, Paul on his own testimony first went into Arabia from Damascus and was there for about three years. What was he doing in this time? He could well have been with an Essene community for a three-year probationary period. We have already indicated that in the first period of the Christian Community there was a very close association between them and the Essenes, and it would be quite natural, when the persecution broke out in the south, that a number would have fled for asylum to the 'Saints' in the north.

We do not as yet have the means to explore the relationship or to ascertain what actually happened. But it could be significant that, when writing to the Corinthians about his escape from Damascus, Paul immediately continued with stress on visions and revelations of Messiah which someone – some fourteen years previously – conceivably himself, had experienced.

It is worthy of consideration that in those three years in Arabia Paul laid the foundations of his Christology. From his rabbinical studies of the Mysteries of the Creation, he had already acquired knowledge of the incarnation in Adam of the Archetypal man. He would now, very excitingly, be able to erect on this – with the help of the faith of the Saints – the notion of Jesus as the heavenly Son of Man incarnate, the Second Adam. *The Book of Enoch* had already identified the Messiah with the heavenly Son of Man, which was why Jesus had employed this description of himself.

But the description also favoured Paul's conviction that it was his own destiny in a Messianic capacity to be 'a light of the Gentiles' to convey 'God's salvation to the ends of the earth'. That conviction was not banished by what was revealed to him: it was enhanced. While Jesus as the Messiah was now in heaven until his second advent, Paul saw himself as representing him on earth in the intervening period for the express purpose of 'proclaiming him to the Gentiles' (*Gal*.i.16). He concludes his letter to the Galatians with the dramatic words: 'From now on let no one deal me any more blows, for I carry the scars of Jesus on my body.'

What made Paul's acceptance of Jesus as the Messiah possible fundamentally was the 'revelation' that Jesus had certified Paul's conviction that he should carry out the mission that he had long believed was peculiarly his own. This not only distinguished Paul from the other envoys who had been the immediate followers of Jesus in his lifetime and who were aware that his mission had been 'to the lost sheep of the house of Israel' (*Mt*.x.6), it put him in direct conflict with them. That conflict would continue until Paul's death, though naturally the author of the *Acts* does his best to tone it down.

From the viewpoint of the immediate followers of Jesus, the claims of Paul were pretentious and arrogant. He had never companied with Jesus, yet presumed to know his mind better than his closest associates. And indeed we cannot fail to agree, on the evidence, that Paul's sense of mission amounted almost to a mania, which partly had physical causes. He is so very humble, and yet mentally quite the reverse. The bombastic aspect comes out in the prologue to Paul's letter to the believers at Rome:

Paul, servant of Jesus Christ, a chosen envoy, assigned to the proclamation of God's News, which he had previously announced by his Prophets in the Sacred Writings, concerning his Son, Jesus Christ our Master, born in the physical sense of the line of David, but potently demonstrated to be God's Son in the sanctified spiritual sense by resurrection from the dead. By him I have obtained favour and envoyship to procure loyal submission to his authority on the part of all nations, among whom you likewise are summoned by Jesus Christ (*Rom*.i.1-6).

6
Antioch

Paul's spiritual and mystical experiences with the Saints in Arabia were of the greatest importance to him. He had the deepest need to get himself sorted out, to adjust to his new understanding. It is only in modern times that we have recovered some of the literature of the originators of the Essenes. In one of their books (*Zadokite Document*, VII, also called the *Damascus Rule*), could be read this passage:

> *As God said, 'And I will cause to go into exile Siccuth your king and Chiun your images, the star of your god, which ye made for yourselves, beyond Damascus'* (*Amos* v. 26-27). The books of the Law are the tabernacle (*succoth*) of the king, as He said, '*And I will raise up the tabernacle of David that is fallen*' (*Amos* ix.11). 'The king' is the congregation, and 'Chiun your images' are the books of the Prophets, whose words Israel has despised. And 'the star' is the Student of the Law, who came to Damascus, as it is written, '*There shall come forth a star out of Jacob, and a sceptre shall rise out of Israel*' (*Num*.xxiv.17). 'The sceptre' is the prince of all the congregation.[*]

Could Paul have read these lines? Not only was he a student of the Law, who had come to Damascus, but he was reported to have had a vision on the way there at *Kochaba* (the village called *Star*).[**]

After his initiatory period of three years with the Saints in Arabia, Paul had felt the need to confer with the leaders of the Nazoreans. On his own showing, as we have seen, he travelled to Jerusalem and

---

[*] Schonfield, *Secrets of the Dead Sea Scrolls*, p.47. For this form of exegesis and word-play in the Hebrew original see further, T.H.Gaster, *The Scriptures of the Dead Sea Sect in English Translation*, pp.79-80, and Notes, p.110-111.

[**] On this tradition, see Schonfield, *The Pentecost Revolution*, Chapter 29: 'Meeting Place', especially p.293f.

stayed for some days with Peter, and also met Jacob (James), the brother of Jesus, who was now head of all the followers of the Messiah. Then he departed for his native land of Cilicia to clarify his perspective. There would be many questions about Jesus which he would have been able to put to a member of the Messiah's family and to his closest associate. How much Paul told them about himself we are in no position to learn. But we can be certain that he would inform them of his concern to bring the knowledge of God to the Gentiles.

In the narrative of the *Acts*, it is Peter who is the first to communicate information about the Messiah to non-Jews, though in his case it was to the centurion Cornelius and his household who were already 'strangers within the gates', God-fearers. News of this was something of a shock to the Jewish followers of Jesus who, like him, were very strict about associating only with Jews. But when Peter related what had taken place they praised God saying, 'So to the Gentiles too God has granted repentance that they should live' (i.e. in the Messianic Age).

Peter and Paul are of course the heroes of the *Acts*, whose non-Jewish author was concerned to portray the evangelization of the Gentiles, and how this had come about. He reveals how the persecution of the Nazoreans, which had started with the death of Stephen and had involved Paul, made a direct contribution to this end.

'Now those who were dispersed as a result of the persecution, that broke out over Stephen, travelled as far as Phoenicia, Cyprus and Antioch, proclaiming the Message to none but Jews. Some of them were Cypriots and Cyrenians who, when they came to Antioch, declared the Message (i.e. about Jesus as Messiah) to Greeks as well, proclaiming the Lord Jesus. The Lord's hand was with them, and a great number believed and came over to the master' (*Acts* xi.19-21).

When the news of this reached the Jerusalem Community they dispatched Barnabas to Antioch. Barnabas (actually a contraction of Bar-Nadabas, meaning 'the Encourager', Son of Encouragement) was the nickname of a Levite called Joseph who hailed from Cyprus.

To continue the quotation from the *Acts*: 'Barnabas, having arrived and seen the evidence of God's mercy, was delighted, and encouraged them all with firm resolve to remain loyal to the Master; for he was a good man, of great spirituality and faith. A substantial body was now associated with the Master. So Barnabas set off for Tarsus in quest of Saul, and when he had found him he brought him to Antioch. For a

36

whole year they were jointly entertained by the community and instructed a considerable number of people. It was at Antioch too that the disciples first received (or 'first gave themselves') the designation of *Christiani*.' To remind ourselves, Christ, of course, is the Greek translation of the Hebrew word Messiah (anointed one). So the Christiani were in fact Messianists. The term in no way signified a new religion.

We also have to appreciate that the Greeks at Antioch who came over to the following of the Messiah were not pagans. They had abandoned idolatry for the worship of the God of Israel, and attended services in the synagogues. But they had not become naturalised Jews by the males undergoing circumcision and taking Hebrew names. They were respected as 'strangers within the gates'. There was no idea at this time to proclaim Jesus to the heathen. But all Jews, whether they were followers of Jesus or not, could instruct Gentiles in the knowledge of the One God. We have clearly to recognize the distinction. It was a matter of change of religion to come over from heathenism to Judaism. But to accept Jesus as Messiah (Christ), king of the Jews, had political implications. The latter did of course involve the former, at least in the first century of the Christian Era. It was only subsequently that Christianity became a religion in its own right which ascribed deity to Jesus, and separated itself from Judaism. The *Acts* makes it very clear that all Jewish adherents of Jesus, including Paul himself (*Acts* xxi.19-26), remained Jews by religion.

What is not mentioned by the author of the *Acts*, or directly referred to by Paul himself, is why at Antioch at this time there should be so many Gentiles interested in Jewish matters and attending the synagogues there. Chronology here is of the utmost importance. Wherever possible it is essential to bring Christian events into relationship with contemporary circumstances which help throw light on them.

We have already seen that when Paul escaped from Damascus it was when the representative of the Arab ruler King Haretath was governor of the city. This was from AD37 to 40. In AD40, Roman rule replaced that of the Nabateans. The emperor concerned was Gaius Caligula, who now became notorious for his mad project to have a statue of himself erected for worship in the Jewish Temple at Jerusalem.

The Roman emperors had adopted the device of asserting their deity, as Son of Jupiter, as a means of binding their foreign subjects to them. Gaius Caligula, however, was the first of the Caesars to take his deity literally. And it was one of his governors in the east, Lucius Vitellius, legate of Syria, which included Judea and whose seat was at Antioch, who played up to the emperor's aberration. Returning to Rome at the end of his term of office he adored the emperor by prostrating himself before him, and would only appear in his presence with his head veiled. The Roman historian Suetonius, who reports this, also tells how Gaius 'began to arrogate to himself a divine majesty. He ordered all the images of the gods, which were famous either for their beauty or for the veneration paid to them, to be brought from Greece, so that he might take their heads off and substitute his own ... He also instituted a temple and priests, with choicest victims in honour of his own divinity. In his temple stood a statue of gold, the exact likeness of himself, which was daily dressed in garments corresponding with those he wore.' (Suet. *Lives of the Twelve Caesars, Gaius* xxii)

In AD39 Gaius appointed Petronius legate of Syria in succession to Vitellius. The province of Syria included Judea, and the Roman procurator of Judea served under the legate. To Petronius the emperor entrusted the task of having his statue made. It was to be transported to Jerusalem and erected for worship in the Jewish Temple. Skilled Phoenician craftsmen were employed at Sidon to make the effigy, and a force of two legions with auxiliaries was assembled at Ptolemais (Acco) as escort for the statue in case of any Jewish resistance. In AD 40 all was ready, and the Jewish authorities were invited to send representatives to Ptolemais where they were informed of what was going forward. They were horrified, and conveyed the dire news to every part of Israel. The response was immediate. From all over the country thousands of unarmed Jews, men, women and children, converged on Ptolemais. Petronius was startled, realising that to enforce the emperor's design would demand the slaughter of thousands of the population. He moved to Tiberias, and there too he was besieged by wailing multitudes.

The circumstances, as I have related them elsewhere in my book *The Pentecost Revolution*, must here be repeated. Petronius was in a quandary. Members of the Herodian family urged him to write to Gaius telling him of the position. They suggested that he point out that because the populace had forsaken the countryside the crops would not be sown, and therefore it would be impossible to meet the payment of the Roman tribute. Apart from the reluctance of Petronius to make war on a whole nation, which was not in arms, this contention seemed to make enough sense to justify him in writing to the emperor to change his mind. We should observe here that with the Jews the year AD 40-41 was a Sabbatical Year when no crops were sown in any case.

The letter was forwarded to Gaius with the utmost speed, but the reply that came back insisted that Petronius proceed with the installation of the statue. His friend, the Jewish prince Agrippa, pleaded with him. And Gaius was so far moved as reluctantly to give way as regards erecting his statue in the Temple itself. It is not certain whether the emperor had got as far as writing to Petronius to this effect before he received a further despatch from his legate, which so enraged him that he changed his mind again. Josephus relates that Petronius had been so affected by the pleas of the Jews that he took a risk which might well result in his own death.

The response of Gaius was to accuse Petronius of taking bribes from the Jews and to recommend him to commit suicide for flouting his orders. Philo declares that it was the intention of the emperor to have another statue made in Rome, which would be conveyed to Judea on the ship by which he himself would travel after visiting Alexandria (*Embassy to Gaius*, 337-8).

But on the 24th January, AD41, Gaius was assassinated in Rome, and news of this reached Petronius twenty-seven days before the arrival of the emperor's latest letter, which bad weather had delayed in transit for three months. This circumstance was ascribed by the Jews to God's direct intervention on behalf of His people, and to honour Petronius for protecting them. The probability was that had the design gone forward not only would hundreds of thousands of Jews have perished in their homeland, but massacres would have followed in Egypt, Asia, Greece and Italy. As it was there were some incidents; but the death of Gaius and the prompt action of his successor Claudius prevented their development.

From the strange way in which things had worked out there were numerous Gentiles who now concluded that the Jews must be under a special providence. Consequently there was a notable inducement at this time for many to become God-fearers and attend worship in the Jewish synagogues.

The New Testament documents, written for non-Jews, do not refer directly to this astounding event, but there are incidental reflections of it. One of these is in a speech of Jesus about the Last Times: 'When, therefore, you see the "Abomination of Desolation" announced by the Prophet Daniel stand in the holy place (let the reader understand the allusion), then let those who are in Judea escape to the Mountains' (*Mt*.xxiv.15). Similarly, Paul himself writes of the final enemy of the Saints in his second letter to the Thessalonians, 'the Doomed One who opposes and elevates himself above everything regarded as a god or as an object of worship, so that he himself sits in God's Temple claiming to be God' (*II. Thess*.ii.3-4). In the *Book of Revelation,* the Beast (Imperial Rome) supports the Emperor Beast, 'telling those who dwell on earth to make an image of the Beast... He was also permitted to animate the image of the Beast, so that the image of the Beast could speak, and he causes such as refuse to worship the image of the Beast to be slain' (*Rev*.xiii.14-15).

It is little wonder, then, that the circumstances relating to Gaius's statue, and the outcome, should have had a profound effect on the citizens of Antioch, where Petronius had his seat as legate of Syria. The city, the third metropolis of the Roman Empire, had a substantial Jewish population, noted for their gifts to the Temple at Jerusalem. Josephus, who mentions this, goes on to make the curious statement that the Jews of Antioch 'were constantly attracting to their religious ceremonies multitudes of Greeks, and these they had in some measure incorporated with themselves' (*Jewish War*, VII.45).

All the conditions were present at Antioch for a great impetus to be given to the proclamation of Jesus as the awaited Messiah, with special interest being shown by the God-fearing Gentiles.

7

Go Forth

Because more than nineteen centuries have elapsed since the period we are describing it is very difficult for the reader of today, especially for those who are Christians, to enter into the Last Times atmosphere of the first century AD. So much has happened since, so much has changed, as we know so well, that we are virtually incapable of crediting the convictions and the sense of immediacy that overwhelmed the consciousness of prophecy-minded Jews and Christians of those days. For them the world was on the eve of a total transformation, heralded by significant signs and portents.

The affair of the statue had offered a tremendous confirmation that time was running out before the climax of the ages would be reached. Consequently there was an enormous urge to forge ahead with what needed to be done. A primary task, clearly, was to spread the Messianic word to all areas of Jewish Dispersion.

The incident of the statue was followed by predictions of an imminent great famine. The *Acts* reports: 'Now at this period prophets came down from Jerusalem to Antioch. One of them called Agabus rose and indicated under inspiration that a severe famine would soon afflict the whole empire. Thereupon the disciples determined, as the means of each of them permitted, to send a contribution for the benefit of the brothers resident in Judea. This they carried out, forwarding it to the elders by Barnabas and Saul' (*Acts* xi.27-30).

Jesus, near the end of his activities, when seated with his disciples on the Mount of Olives overlooking Jerusalem, is said to have forewarned them of what to expect. 'Take care,' he told them, 'that no one misleads you. Many will come using my title, saying "I am he," and will deceive many. But when you hear of wars and rumours of wars do not be perturbed. This is bound to happen; but it is not the End yet.

For nation will rise against nation and kingdom against kingdom. There will be earthquakes in various places; there will be famines. These are the beginning of the [Messianic] pangs' (*Mk*. xiii.5-8).

When Barnabas and Saul returned to Antioch from Jerusalem they took with them John known as Mark. The *Acts* here continues:

> Now there were at Antioch with the community there both prophets and teachers. There was Barnabas, and Simeon nick-named Niger, Lucius a Cyrenian, Menahem a foster brother of Herod the tetrarch, and Saul. As they were performing their religious rites and fasting, the holy Spirit said, 'Set apart for me Barnabas and Saul for the task I have assigned to them.' So when they had all fasted and prayed, they laid their hands upon them and let them go. Thus commissioned by the holy Spirit they came down to Seleucia, and from there sailed to Cyprus. Landing at Salamis they proclaimed God's Message in the Jewish syna-gogues, with John acting as their attendant (*Acts* xiii.1-5).

But also at about this time Peter and other envoys of the Messiah would have set forth on their own journeys. There may be a reference to this in Paul's statement that Peter had been entrusted with the News for the Circumcised (*Gal*.ii.7). In the *Preaching of Peter*[*] it is said that Jesus had also told his disciples that after twelve years they were to go out into the world. And tradition has it that Peter reached Rome in the reign of Claudius. Paul mentions that Peter was accom-panied, at least initially, by his wife, and that among the envoys of Jesus were some of his brothers, who also had their wives with them (*I.Cor*. ix.5).[**]

In a fragment of a Gospel in Coptic[*] it is stated: 'They went forth by three to the four regions of heaven and proclaimed the Gospel of the Kingdom in the whole world, the Messiah working with them by the word of strengthening and the signs and wonders which accompanied them. And so have men learnt of the Kingdom of God in all the earth and in the whole world of Israel for a testimony for all nations that are from the rising of the sun unto the going down thereof.'

The Christian Gospels wish it to be understood that from the beginning there was a design to communicate knowledge of Jesus to

---

[*] *The Preaching of Peter* and a fragment of a Gospel in Coptic were translated by M. R. James, *The Apocryphal New Testament* (Oxford, 1969 reprint).

[**] See beginning of first letter to the Corinthian community, p.135. See also Note 2, p.138.

all mankind, Jews and Gentiles alike. But the evidence makes it clear that this was not the case. The aim was to reach the Jews of the Diaspora with the word that the Promised Messiah had appeared. To this end, according to tradition, the Apostle Matthew had compiled in Hebrew a collection of proof-texts from the Old Testament which pointed to Jesus as Messiah and were accompanied by illustrations of how his experiences had fulfilled them. We may assume that a copy of such a document was in the hands of Paul and Barnabas.

The knowledge possessed by the Antioch community, supplemented by the information brought back by Barnabas and Paul from Jerusalem, was of a character that could only be construed as evidence of the nearness of the Kingdom of God which would be established on earth. As we have seen in the extract from the *Acts* above, the prophets and teachers at Antioch therefore felt it imperative to betake themselves to fasting and prayer to determine their course of action. The outcome was assent to the wishes of Barnabas and Paul to proclaim Jesus to Jews of the Diaspora. Having been solemnly invested with authority, the two envoys departed for Seleucia, the port of Antioch, and sailed for Cyprus. The year was about AD 48, or possibly AD 49.

It was natural that Barnabas should wish that his native island of Cyprus should be included in the itinerary, and this, no doubt, accounts for a beginning being made there. The story of the tour is represented in chapters xiii and xiv of the *Acts*.

Landing at Salamis they gave out their message in the local synagogues, with John acting as their attendant, and afterwards crossed the island to Paphos. There they encountered a Jewish magician named Bar-Jesus, who was in the retinue of the Roman proconsul L. Sergius Paulus. The proconsul wished very much to hear the message of the envoys. It is related that Bar-Jesus sought to oppose this, and that Paul invoked his temporary blindness.

Sergius Paulus thus became the first pagan Gentile to be told about the Messiah. There is no report of his conversion, but certainly the incident created a precedent. It would seem that soon after this Saul of Tarsus began to call himself Paul, possibly from this incident. We do not know whether John Mark was very upset by it, but when the envoys reached the mainland at Perga in Pamphylia he parted from them and returned to Jerusalem.

The envoys travelled on to Pisidian Antioch, and as usual gave out their message in the synagogue, this time on two successive Sabbaths because of the interest of the congregation. The second Sabbath it is said that quite a crowd of pagan Gentiles turned up to listen, which, according to the author, roused Jewish resentment. We read how Paul and Barnabas bluntly told them, 'It was essential initially to proclaim God's Message to you; but since you spurn it and do not deem yourselves worthy of Eternal Life, perforce we turn to the Gentiles. The Lord has instructed us to this effect, "I have set you for a light to the Gentiles, to serve for salvation to the ends of the earth" (*Isa*.xlix.6). When the Gentiles heard this they rejoiced and praised God's Word; and those who were meant for Eternal Life believed' (*Acts* xiii. 44-48).

Paul had always believed, so far as we can judge, that he was destined to bring the knowledge of the One God to the Gentiles. But he had not known that he would achieve this as the Messiah's chosen envoy. We have to recognize, however, that in the narration of how and why things happened we are in the hands of a converted Gentile, who would incline to colour his story in the interest of his convictions.

Paul and Barnabas continued their journey to Iconium, where again they first visited the synagogues. They had considerable success and remained for some time; but eventually they were forced to leave, and travelled to Lystra and Derbe, cities of Lycaonia. Here a man lame from birth was healed by faith. Paul was instrumental in this instance. The story in *Acts* continues:

When the populace saw what Paul had done they shouted in the Lycaonian tongue, 'The gods have come down to us in human form.' Barnabas they called Zeus, and Paul Hermes, because he was the spokesman. Thereupon the priest of the temple of Zeus-more-ancient-than-the-city brought oxen and garlands to the gates, proposing with the populace to offer sacrifice. But learning of this the envoys Barnabas and Paul, rending their garments, rushed into the crowd crying, 'Men, what are you about? We are the same kind of human beings as yourselves, preaching to you to turn from these errors to the Living God, who made heaven and earth, and the sea, and all they contain. In bygone ages he let all the nations go their own way. Yet even so, by his beneficence, he did not leave himself unattested, giving you rain from heaven and fruitful seasons, satisfying your hearts with food and good cheer.' But even by saying this they with difficulty prevented the people from sacrificing to them.

The author of the *Acts* again reports the hostility of the Jews in

44

Antioch and Iconium, some of whom had travelled to Lystra in the wake of the envoys to stir up the populace against them. Paul was stoned and left for dead, but was quite capable the next day of travelling to Derbe. They then returned to Lystra, Iconium and Pisidian Antioch, says our author, 'confirming the disciples, encouraging them to maintain their allegiance, and telling them, "We have to enter the Kingdom of God by the hard road"'.

Virtually retracing their steps they finally arrived back at Syrian Antioch and reported their experiences to the community there, 'and how He had opened the door of faith to the Gentiles'.

This statement suitably introduces the question of what was to be the status in the Nazorean Movement of Gentile God-fearers who acknowledged Jesus as Messiah, the king of Israel. The true circumstances have been very much misrepresented, and are still not understood by the vast majority of Christians.

8
Crisis

At this stage of affairs the *Acts* relates: 'Now certain persons came down from Judea and instructed the brothers, "Unless you are circumcised in conformity with the Mosaic ordinance you cannot be saved." And when there arose no small conflict and controversy with them on the part of Paul and Barnabas, it was decided that Paul and Barnabas with some others of the community should go up to the envoys and elders at Jerusalem about this question' (*Acts*.xv.1-2).

This is not strictly correct, and tones things down. The emissaries in fact came from James (Jacob), the younger brother of Jesus who was now head of all believers in the Messiah, and Paul and Barnabas were ordered to report to Jerusalem to explain their conduct in admitting uncircumcised Gentiles into full fellowship, as if they were actually Israelites.

Jacob, as it is preferable to call him, had, it was claimed, been chosen by Jesus himself to take his place during his absence. One of the fragments of the *Gospel of Thomas*, found in Egypt, says that at the end the disciples of Jesus came to him and asked him, 'When you have left who will be great over us?' To this he replied, 'In the place to which you will go (i.e. Jerusalem) you will go to Jacob the Just, for whose sake heaven and earth came into being.' In any case it was thought fit and appropriate that he should act as the Messiah's Regent.

No one was more suitable in the prevailing circumstances, when there was great tension in Jewish circles, both because of the occupation of the Holy Land by a pagan power and the anticipations that these were the Last Times before the Day of Judgment. Unlike his brother Jesus, who 'came eating and drinking' with the well-to-do,

46

Jacob was a saintly ascetic, of whom it was related that he spent long hours on his knees in the Temple praying for the sins of his people. He was adored by the Jewish populace as both saint and champion, and very naturally he set the tone for the Jewish followers of Jesus. Redeemed Israel, according to the Jewish Prophets and Jesus, was to be the means of establishing the Kingdom of God on earth. Consequently, as was being emphasised in Essene and Pharisee circles, it behoved Israel to live up to being 'a kingdom of priests and a holy nation' by the strict observance of the laws given to Israel for this very purpose. Jesus, for this very reason, had said:

'I tell you positively, until heaven and earth pass away not one iota, not a single stroke, shall be removed from the Law until it has completely been put into effect. So whoever would relax the most insignificant of commandments, and teach men so, shall be treated as insignificant in the Kingdom of Heaven. But whoever both observes and teaches them shall be treated as of consequence in the Kingdom of Heaven. I tell you, therefore, unless your devoutness exceeds that of the scribes and Pharisees, you will never enter the Kingdom of Heaven' (*Mt*.v.18-20).

It was the function of the Messiah to set his people an example by himself being a model Jew, and Paul believed this as much as the other envoys of Jesus and all loyal Jews. But he was carried away by his desire to win Gentiles for Jesus and make them Israelites by faith rather than in fact, which would be so much more difficult. More will need to be said about this later, and the device Paul adopted.

What stood out just now for the Nazorean government at Jerusalem was that Paul and his associates were compromising the status of Israel and the People of God, obedient to His Law, by breaking down the Middle Wall of Partition. This was the barrier in the Temple which separated the Court of the Gentiles from the Court of Israel, which bore the inscription in Hebrew, Latin and Greek, warning Gentiles that they must not pass this barrier on pain of death.

We are required to capture the extreme sensitiveness of the situation. These times were – so to speak – Israel's last chance of fulfilling its world mission before the great cataclysm, by conforming strictly to its priestly responsibilities. Christians understand the severity of discipline of monastic orders; but they seem unable, or unwilling, to grasp the concept of a 'national' priestly discipline. This was to enable Israel to be an example to the nations.

47

It stood to reason, therefore, that every non-Jew who became a member of the People of God, and gave allegiance to its Messianic sovereign, understood the responsibilities of his new status which embraced the observance of God's laws. This was especially the case at the climax of the ages. Near the close of the century the author of the *Apocalypse of Baruch* cries: 'For we are named One People, who have received One Law from One; and the Law which is among us will aid us, and the Supreme Wisdom within us will help us' (xlviii.24). In the Christian *Revelation* the Dragon incarnate in Rome directs his attack on 'those who observe the Commandments of God and hold the testimony of Messiah Jesus' (*Rev*.xii.17). The followers of Jesus saw themselves in the vanguard of the struggle. As the Party of the king of Israel, soon to return from heaven, it was up to them in particular to set an example to the whole nation of devotion to the Law.

We have two versions of what took place at Jerusalem when Paul and Barnabas appeared before the Nazorean Council presided over by Jacob. One is in the *Acts* and the other in Paul's letter to the Galatians. Both were written later than the circumstances they describe. The former much later, but more representatively and circumstantially. Paul's own account is harsh and bitter, written under the influence of his failure to achieve his purpose, the conferment on Gentile believers in Jesus of Israelite status.

Let us here use his own words.

Some fourteen years later [i.e. than Paul's previous visit] I again went up to Jerusalem with Barnabas, and also took Titus with me. I went there by a revelation and reported to them the terms of the News I proclaim to the Gentiles. This was privately to those of repute, in case I should strive or had been striving to no purpose. But there was no forcing of Titus, who accompanied me, to be circumcised, Greek though he was, despite the infiltrated false brothers who had crept in to spy out the liberty we enjoy in Christ Jesus in order to enslave us. Not for an instant did we strike our colours, so that the true character of the News might be preserved to you. As for those of repute – whatever they were makes no difference to me: God takes no one at face value – they imposed on me nothing additional. Quite the contrary. When they saw that I had been entrusted with the News for the Uncircumcised, as Peter for the Circumcised ... and when they realised the privilege that has been granted me, then James, Cephas and John, the re-puted 'Pillars', extended to myself and Barnabas the right hand of fellowship. We were to go to the Gentiles, they to the Circumcised. Oh yes, they did add one thing more, we were to remember the Poor, which personally I was only too ready to do (*Gal*.ii.1-10).

Paul knew what he was up against, and in fact things had not gone in his favour. What he had sought to achieve was the recognition by the Nazorean government that Gentiles who accepted Jesus as Messiah, the king of Israel, were automatically to be regarded as Israelites, without the obligation to accept the regulations governing Israel. This was refused. Such Gentiles, provided that they observed the so-called Laws of Noah[*] applicable to the righteous of all nations, would be received as 'Strangers *within* the Gates', as friends and brothers, but not as fellow-Israelites.

The *Acts* reports how the Council's decision was delivered by the brother of Jesus as President:

> My verdict is, that those of the Gentiles who turn to God be not molested, but that we write to them to abstain from whatever is polluted by idols, from sexual impurity, from eating strangled animals, and from blood. For Moses from ancient times has had his preachers in every town, being publicly read in the synagogues every sabbath (*Acts* xv.19-21).

There was no getting round this verdict, since it was official. But Paul continued in his letters to argue (as in *Rom*.xi) that Gentiles who accepted Jesus were part of Israel. The consequence was that friction resulted between Barnabas and Paul, and they parted company. Paul went off to Syria and Cilicia, while Barnabas, taking Mark with him, sailed for Cyprus.

The *Acts* tells us that Paul found a new young assistant named Timotheus (i.e. God-fearer), a name appropriate to one who was the son of a Greek father and a Jewish mother. And since Paul would be visiting Jewish communities he had Timotheus circumcised. But Paul kept to the ruling of the supreme Nazorean Council, and to every group of adherents to Jesus the verdict of the Council was delivered. Paul was no schismatic, and whenever practicable presented himself to report to the Council at Jerusalem at the annual Pentecost gathering, which the Nazoreans held just like the Essenes. On one occasion he would

---

[*] There are two lists extant of these primeval laws, derived from God's words to Noah, and applicable to the sons of Noah from whom the nations descended. Of the seven laws in both lists, five are identical (see Schonfield, *The Jew of Tarsus*, p. 157).

49

not visit the adherents of Jesus at Ephesus, and sent to the elders of the community there to meet him at Miletus 'for he was anxious if at all possible to reach Jerusalem by Pentecost' (*Acts* xx.16).

However much Paul was in disagreement with the Jerusalem Council's verdict he strictly adhered to it at this time. The *Acts* states that as he and his associates passed through the cities 'they delivered the stipulations for the communities to observe which had been decided upon by the envoys and elders at Jerusalem. Thus the communities were strengthened in their allegiance and increased in membership daily' (*Acts* xvi.4-5).

The first period of Paul's activities as a follower of Jesus virtually ends here. What follows in the *Acts* is a much more detailed account of Paul's experiences, reproducing in places a first-hand account of what transpired, written by a member of his entourage. We do not know whether this was 'dear Doctor Luke', as Paul calls him, or someone else.* But, whoever it was, the presence of this element invests the narrative with a greater sense of authenticity.

On Paul's second journey, which began, it would appear, after a fair interval, the *Acts* says that in addition to Timotheus he had with him Silas (Silvanus), described as a prophet who, with Judas Bar-Sabbas, had been sent from the Council at Jerusalem to confirm their ruling on the admission of the Gentiles to Nazorean communities.

---

* The so-called Diary Document, a contemporary record consisting of notebook extracts written in the first person plural, beginning at *Acts* xvi.10 (see next page). Some think the writer was Timotheus or Silas, but this is inconclusive (see Schonfield, *The Jew of Tarsus*, p.166f.)

9

The Second Tour

Paul's second tour would embrace a large part of Macedonia where a good many Jews were settled. He had attempted to travel into Bithynia, but had been prevented, and with his associates had come down to Troas (Trojan-Alexandria). There, the *Acts* relates, Paul had a vision in which a certain man of Macedon appeared to him and appealed, 'Cross over to Macedon and aid us.' Philip of Macedon, known as the Man of Macedon, would seem to be indicated. He had been the father of Alexander the Great, a benefactor of the Jews. Here follows in the *Acts* a direct quotation from the Diary Document.

> In accordance with the vision Paul had seen we at once endeavoured to get to Macedonia, deducing that God had summoned us to proclaim the News to them. Putting to sea from Troas, therefore, we ran a straight course to Samothrace, and the day following to Neapolis, and thence to Philippi, which is the top-ranking city of Macedonia, a Roman colony. We spent some time in the city, and on the Sabbath day we went outside the gate to the river bank where we had reason to believe there was a Jewish oratory [i.e. *Bet-tefilah* in Hebrew, in Greek *Proseuche*]. There we sat down and spoke to the women who attended it. There was one woman who listened called Lydia, a worshipper of God, of the city of Thyatira, who was in the purple cloth trade. The Lord opened her mind to receive what Paul said, and when she was immersed with her household she begged, 'If you are satisfied of my loyalty to the Master you must come and stay with me.' We were absolutely forced to accept.
>
> Once as we were going to the oratory a slave-girl possessed by an oracular spirit [lit. 'a pythonic spirit', a form of ventriloquism] met us, who made her masters a good living by fortune-telling. She persisted in following Paul and ourselves crying,

51

'These men are servants of the Most High God, who tell you the way of salvation.' For several days she carried on like this, until in desperation Paul turned round and told the spirit, 'In the name of Jesus Christ I order you to leave her!' Out it went that very instant.

The account reproduced in the *Acts* continues in much the same vein; but it is quite impossible to determine whether the author of the Diary Document is being quoted directly, or whether the author of the *Acts* is utilising this source for his narrative. But the existence of the source does allow us to place a great deal of confidence in the reliability of the narrative. Of course, the author of the Diary Document and the author of the *Acts* could be one and the same person. In the circumstances it would seem fairest, as well as being more graphic, to reproduce in translation from the Greek from this point the actual text of the *Acts* down to what in the English Bible corresponds to chapter xvii.15.

When her masters saw that their prospect of gain was gone, they seized Paul and Silas and dragged them to the magistrates' court, and brought them before the praetors. 'These men,' they said, 'Jews of course, are making serious trouble for this city of ours, advocating practices which as Romans we are not permitted to entertain, much less engage in.'

The crowd was solidly against the envoys, so the praetors gave orders to have them stripped and beaten with rods. When numerous strokes had been given them, they threw them into prison, cautioning the jailer to guard them securely. Having had a warning like this, he threw them into the inner prison, and secured their feet in stocks.

Around midnight Paul and Silas were at prayer praising God, with other prisoners listening to them, when all of a sudden there was such a great earthquake as to shake the foundations of the jail. Immediately all the doors sprang ajar, and the fetters of all the prisoners were freed. Roused from his sleep, and seeing the doors of the prison standing open, the jailer drew his sword, and was about to kill himself thinking the prisoners had escaped, when Paul shouted, 'Don't harm yourself! We are all here.' Calling for lights he burst in, and all of a tremble fell down before Paul and Silas. Taking them outside he said, 'Oh sirs, what must I do to assure my safety?'

'Put your trust in the Lord Jesus,' they said, 'and both you and your family will be preserved.'

Then they gave him and his family God's Message. He took immediate care of them at that time of night, bathed their stripes, and was himself immersed with all his family in their new found faith in God.

When morning came the praetors sent lictors with the message, 'Release those men.' The jailer broke this news to Paul. 'The praetors have sent word that you are to be released. So now you are quite free to go.'

But Paul sent word back to them, 'After flogging us in public uncondemned, men who are Romans of course [echoing the sneer 'Jews of course' of verse 20], they threw us into prison. Now they are throwing us out again secretly. Oh no! Let them come officially and fetch us out.'

The lictors reported these words to the praetors, who were dismayed when they heard they were Romans. Hurrying to the prison, they entreated them, and bringing them out begged them to leave the city.

On coming out of the prison they went to Lydia's house, and having seen and encouraged the brothers they took their departure.

Following the road through Amphipolis and Apollonia they came to Thessalonica, where there was a Jewish synagogue. As was Paul's custom they went in, and for three successive Sabbaths they discoursed from the Scriptures, expounding them, and explaining how the Messiah had to suffer and to rise again from the dead, and that 'this Jesus I am telling you about is the Messiah.'

Some of them were convinced and adhered to Paul and Silas, with a large number of Greek proselytes and not a few influential ladies. But the Jews in their jealousy got hold of some worthless loafers, and forming a mob set the town in an uproar. They concentrated on one Jason's house with the intention of bringing the envoys before the court; but failing to find them they dragged Jason and some other brothers before the politarchs [i.e. the city prefects], clamouring that 'these subverters of the Empire [lit. the world] have now reached here, and Jason has harboured them. All of them are violators of Caesar's decrees, and declare there is another king, one Jesus.' They alarmed the people and the politarchs when they heard this; but after taking sureties from Jason and others they let them go.

At once the brothers sent away Paul and Silas by night to Beroea, where on arrival they went straight to the Jewish synagogue. The Jews there were more civil than those at Thessalonica: they received the Message with every consideration, examining the Scriptures daily to ascertain whether it was correct. Consequently many of them believed, and not a few ladies and gentlemen of quality.

When the Jews of Thessalonica were aware that God's Message was being proclaimed by Paul at Beroea as well, they came there too to sway and stir up the populace. At once the brothers sent Paul away to the coast, though Silas and Timotheus stayed on at Beroea. Those who were escorting Paul accompanied him as far as Athens, and there left him, taking back his instructions to Silas and Timotheus to rejoin him as quickly as they could.

There are very important indications in this passage of the Diary Document to a development in Jewish affairs, though this is not stressed as it should be and, we would hope, would have been in a more comprehensive record. As it stands, the impression is conveyed to the Christian reader that the Jews are enemies of the Christian Gospel. But that is not all the true significance of the passage. What the words convey to an impartial investigator is that the Jews of Thessalonica identified the preachers with Zealot agents from Judea who at this time were travelling through the Roman Empire collecting funds for armaments and fomenting anti-Roman activities in order to bring about the destruction of the Empire.

The incident of the attempt of Gaius Caligula to have his statue set up for worship in the Temple at Jerusalem had contributed to Zealot developments. And the new emperor Claudius found himself confronted with a menace, which it was very difficult to counter.

The period we have now reached is around AD 49-51, and we need to turn aside here to take note of the widespread Zealot campaign. It was fostered by the practice, which the Romans had never interfered with, of the Jewish Council at Jerusalem having the facility of sending its emissaries to the Jewish communities in all parts of the Empire for the regulation of religious matters. Both the followers of Jesus and the Zealots had been able to take advantage of this practice in visiting the synagogues of the Diaspora, and indeed it cannot be excluded that very often the Zealots and the Nazoreans were in collusion.

Of course this did not apply to envoys like Paul, who was both proud of his Roman citizenship and spiritually had his head in the clouds. He appears to have been quite unaware of why his message encountered so much Jewish opposition, and did not realise at all that at this time the Jews of the Empire were deeply concerned that the protection they enjoyed was being seriously jeopardized by visiting Jewish extremists.

10

The Militants

The Emperor Claudius had found himself confronted with a serious problem in the Jewish homeland. There was a growing risk of revolt, which he had sought to avoid by pacific measures. The most important was to withdraw a Roman procurator from Judea and appoint Prince Agrippa as king.* Agrippa had sought to consolidate his position by action against the Jewish elements hostile to his regime, the Nazoreans and Zealots. For the former there was now only one rightful king of the Jews, and that was Jesus.

We learn from the *Acts* that Agrippa ordered the arrest and execution of Jacob (James) the son of Zebedee, one of the 'tempestuous' brothers whom Jesus himself had nicknamed *Boane-ragsha* ('Sons of Storm'). Agrippa had gone on to take the stronger step of arresting Peter. The measure of Peter's popularity with the Jewish patriots is shown by the statement that it was thought necessary to have the prisoner chained to two guards, with two others in attendance, the four being changed for each three-hour watch.

Despite these precautions the escape of the prisoner was contrived, which indicates how very efficient and effective was the Jewish nationalist 'underground'. The *Acts* naturally introduces a miraculous element to describe the rescue, which we need not quote. But as I have stated elsewhere: 'Peter's rescue so alarmed the king that after having the guards interrogated, probably under torture, he gave orders that they be put to death. Such a drastic punishment would hardly be called for if the prisoner had been regarded as no more than a preacher of somewhat unorthodox religious views. The rescue revealed not only a security weakness, but the possibility of organised conspiracy which put the king's life in peril. Some of the Jewish members

---

* Herod Agrippa I, a grandson of Herod the Great, was king of Judea from AD 41 - 44.

of his retinue might be in league with the seditionists. Hastily, therefore, Agrippa removed himself from Jerusalem to the safer environment of Caesarea. There the population was predominantly Gentile, and the king had at hand a substantial body of troops.'

In spite of this move Agrippa died shortly after at Caesarea. The circumstances are differently reported by the *Acts* and by Josephus, and it is very possible that he was poisoned.

The Roman government was now becoming increasingly aware of what it was up against. The Jewish patriots were clearly ready to carry the war into the enemy's camp through agents sent out to Jewish communities of the Diaspora. Among these agents we can by no means exclude the Nazoreans, the envoys of King Jesus. A letter has been discovered, sent by Claudius to the Jews of Alexandria, warning them not to entertain Jewish itinerant preachers from Syria if they did not wish to be treated as abettors of 'a pest which threatens the whole world'.

From Suetonius we learn that Claudius 'expelled the Jews from Rome, who were continually making disturbances at the instigation of Chrestus' (Suet. *Claudius*, xxv). Dio Cassius, however, says that the Jews were too numerous to expel from the capital without danger, but that Claudius closed the synagogues (Dio Cass. *Roman History*, lx.6). Probably it was only the foreign Jews who were actually expelled from Rome. The *Acts* mentions that among them were Aquila the tentmaker and his wife Priscilla. Aquila was a native of Pontus in Asia Minor, and Paul met the couple at Corinth after they had left Italy (*Acts* xviii.2).

The methods of the Jewish militants were devious. As we have seen, they sought the aid of the Diaspora Jews, chiefly by soliciting financial contributions with which weapons could be purchased and shipped to Judea. But they also sought to play upon the superstitions of the native populations of the Empire. One chosen means was by adding passages to manuscripts of the *Sibylline Oracles*. To quote one such passage:

God's revelation of great wrath to come in the Last Time upon a faithless world, I make known ... On thee some day shall come, O haughty Rome, a fitting stroke from heaven, and thou the first shall bend the neck, be levelled to the earth, and fire shall utterly consume thee, bent upon thy pavements. Thy wealth shall perish, and on thy site shall wolves and foxes dwell, and then shalt thou become all desolate as though thou hadst not been ...

Near at hand is the End of the World, and the Last Day, and judgment of immortal God on behalf of those who are both called and chosen. First of all inexorable wrath shall fall on Rome. A time of blood and wretched life shall come. Woe, woe to thee, O land of Italy, great barbarous nation... And no more under slavish yoke to thee will either Greek or Syrian put his neck, barbarian or any other nation. Thou shalt be plundered and shalt be destroyed for what thou didst, and wailing aloud in fear thou shalt give until thou shalt all repay (*Sibylline Oracles*, Bk.VIII).

Unless we have a sense of the spiritual and political antagonism of the Jewish populace in Israel for the rule of Rome at this time, we shall misunderstand the significance of the activities of the Nazoreans and Zealots. The Romans and their representatives were not blind to the operations of the Jewish 'Underground', which included many of the followers of Jesus. And the circumstances naturally made the foreign Jews resident in the cities of the Empire fearful for their own safety, since the authorities might well hold that they were hand-in-glove with the Jewish freedom fighters.

The letter of Claudius we have quoted, and the expulsion of the foreign Jews from Rome, speak for themselves. Paul and the other Envoys (Apostles) of Jesus were always in danger in the cities of the Empire, since they were believed to be acting treasonably. Unfortunately the Church with its teaching has totally failed to grasp what even in the New Testament is expressly stated.

The charge which eventually was brought against Paul was not a religious one: it was political. 'We have found this man a plague-carrier, a fomenter of revolt among all the Jews of the Empire, a ring-leader of the Nazorean sect' (*Acts*.xxiv.5).

Inevitably Paul, as envoy to the Gentiles, was caught up in the activities of the Jewish freedom-fighters, in the various means they employed to sow dissension in the Roman Empire and enlist the co-operation both of the Diaspora Jews and the non-Jewish subject peoples. But Paul had his head so much in the clouds as a visionary, and with his sense of his own special destiny, that he quite failed to grasp the state of affairs in which he was involved from this time onward. Busy with proclaiming the outcome of the Resurrection of Christ (in Greek *anastasis Christou*), he was incapable of comprehending that this might be construed in the sense of promoting a 'Messianic uprising'.

But in those days Rome was the arch-enemy of the Saints in Israel, of all persuasions. So we read in the *Apocalypse of Baruch*:

Its power will be harsh and evil far beyond those kingdoms which were before it, and it will rule many times as the forests of the plain, and it will hold fast the times and will exalt itself more than the cedars of Lebanon. And by it the truth will be hidden, and all those who are polluted with the iniquity will flee to it, as evil beasts flee and creep into the forest. And it will come to pass when the time of its consummation that it should fall has approached, then the principate of My Messiah will be revealed... and it will root out the multitude of its host (xxxix.5-7).

Paul was not without his own strong apocalyptic sense, for example, when he wrote to the Christians at Thessalonica about the Antichrist, 'the Lawless One... whom the Lord Jesus will consume with the breath of his mouth and annihilate with the radiance of his presence' (*II.Thess*.ii. 8). But it was all very visionary, and did not impinge very much on the actual political scene.

For the Jewish followers of Jesus, including his surviving personal associates, the Revelation of Jesus Christ and the Revolution of Jesus Christ were inextricably intermingled in a manner in which Paul, the missionary mystic, was quite unable to assimilate. We shall find him unrealistic in another way. He could not apprehend how his sentiments about the Mosaic Law would open wide the door of immorality for converts from the Gentiles, predominantly women and slaves.

The Christian reader has continually to bear in mind that in the lifetime of Paul, and indeed in the century after his death, no such thing as a distinct Christian religion existed. In Paul's faith the converted Gentile had become a worshipper of the God of Israel and a member of the People of Israel.

To put ourselves in the atmosphere of the time we are describing we have to concern ourselves far more with Jewish history than with Christian theology. As it happens we can be well-informed of the significance of the circumstances in which Paul found himself caught up, since in the very next century they were to be repeated. This was in advance of the second Jewish revolt in the time of the Emperor Hadrian, and when again the impetus was Messianic.

This time, by a preconcerted plan, the Jews of the Empire did break out into open rebellion almost simultaneously in such widely different areas as Egypt and Cyrene, Cyprus and Mesopotamia, choosing the occasion when the Emperor Trajan was engaged in his second Parthian campaign. Even though the Romans finally got the upper hand after sanguinary battles, their partial success encouraged the Jewish Zealots to further efforts. They now had a notable advocate in the famous Rabbi Akiba, who personally visited the Jewish communities in Parthia, Asia Minor, Cilicia, Cappadocia, Phrygia and Galatia, in truly apostolic fashion. In Media, Akiba dwelt on the sufferings of Job, pointing out how these were the prelude to better things.

In Akiba's missionary journeys, preaching his gospel in the synagogues, proclaiming the advent of the Messiah (Christ) afterwards revealed as Bar-Cochba (Son of a Star), collecting funds for arms and equipment, organising revolt, we see the kind of activity in which Paul was believed to be engaged, and how easy it was for the provincial Jews to receive the impression that he was a Zealot agent. The fame of Akiba, and the changed attitude of the Jews towards Rome in his time, secured him a more ready and responsive hearing, though even then many were opposed to the message and its object. In Paul's day the majority of the Jews of the Empire had seen no reason to revolt, and every reason why they should not. Paul, of course, while he was proclaiming a Messiah, was not organising rebellion, though he was thought to be, and some of the Nazoreans, like the Zealots, actually were.

11
Athens and Corinth

Paul's stay in Athens was a remarkable experience. He was in the cultural centre of Greece, and the city with its magnificent buildings and temples offered much to please and inspire. It also offered opportunity for high level religious and philosophical discussion. There were Jewish residents in the city with their own synagogue, which was also attended by Greek proselytes to Judaism. But the local Jews would not have been very strong propagandists, since in Greek circles there was a great deal of antisemitism. This reticence in proclaiming the One True God was unacceptable to Paul. 'Therefore,' the *Acts* relates, 'he held forth in the synagogue to the Jews and proselytes, and daily in the market-place to those who were present.'

On one such occasion, we are told, certain of the Epicurean and Stoic philosophers encountered Paul. "What is this garbage-picker driving at?" said some. To which others replied, "He seems to be a propagator of foreign divinities." So they took him along and brought him before the Areopagus [i.e. the Council of Public Morals and Welfare] with the request, "May we be informed of the nature of the new doctrine you are preaching? You are bringing some very queer notions to our attention, and consequently we should much like to know precisely what they signify."

The *Acts* reproduces the speech Paul was said to have delivered, and it is worth quoting, even if the authenticity cannot be relied on.

Standing before the Areopagus, Paul spoke as follows:

Athenians, I cannot help but notice how intensely religious you are. For as I went about and looked at your various objects of worship I even came across an altar on which was inscribed, 'To a God Unknown'. It is He with whom I am acquainting you, the One you unwittingly revere.

61

The God who made the universe and everything in it, being as He is Lord of Heaven and Earth, does not reside in artificial temples, nor is He tended by human hands as though he stood in need of anything, since He is the giver of Life, breath and substance to all. From one man he produced every section of the human race, which occupies the entire surface of the Earth, and fixed the exact dimensions and boundaries of their settlement, that they should seek after God; for if they would but grope for Him they would find Him, for in fact He is not far from each one of us. Indeed, 'by Him we live, and move, and have our being', as some of your own poets have also stated, 'for we are truly His offspring'.* Being then God's offspring, we ought not to conceive the Divine Nature as capable of representation in gold, silver, or stone, modelled by art and human ingenuity.

The ages of ignorance, however, God overlooked; but now he calls upon all mankind everywhere to repent, since He has set a day on which He will judge the world with justice by the Man he has appointed, furnishing everyone with concrete proof of this by raising him from the dead.

The sequel states that, 'when they heard of the resurrection of the dead some scoffed, while others said, "Perhaps you will tell us about this some other time." So Paul left their presence. But some joined him and believed, including Dionysius the Areopagite, a woman called Damaris, and a few others.'

A scribe's note suggests that Paul's interrogators supposed that he was propagating a male and a female divinity, Jesus and Anastasis (Resurrection).

At Athens Paul had a full taste of Gentilism, its sophistry, idolatry and superstition, and he did not like it one little bit. All his Jewish-ness came to the surface. Far from being divine, Paul's Jesus is Man clearly distinguished from God.

As soon as he could, Paul left the city. The rewards of his preaching had been dramatically meagre, and significantly, among the letters of Paul to Christian communities, there is none addressed to the Athenians.

Paul travelled next to Corinth, and it is to be observed that when he wrote later to the Christian community there his experiences at Athens were still in his mind.

---

* Quotations from the poets Epimenides (sixth century BC) and Aratus (c. 315 - 240 BC) respectively. See also *Hymn to Zeus* by Cleanthes (c. 331 - 232 BC).

He exclaims:

What becomes of the sage, the scribe, the scholar of this world? Has not God made nonsense of the world's wisdom? For since in God's wisdom the world failed to know God by wisdom, it pleased God to save those who believe by the folly of preaching. For while the Jews demand a sign, and the Greeks require wisdom, we preach a crucified Christ, an obstacle to Jews and nonsense to Gentiles. But to those who are chosen – Jews and Greeks alike – a Christ who is the power of God and the wisdom of God. For God's *folly* is wiser than men, and God's *weakness* is stronger than men.

As regards this choice, take yourselves, brothers. There are not many sages among you in the world's sense, not many persons of consequence, not many highborn. Instead, God has selected what is foolish in the world to shame the wise, and what is weak to shame the mighty, and what is of base origin and treated with contempt has God chosen, and even what is non-existent to bring to an end the existing order, that not a single human being should boast in God's presence (*I.Cor.* i.20-29).*

After Paul's lack of success in Athens it was with some loss of confidence that he came to Corinth. As he wrote later to the believers there: 'When I came to you, brothers, I did not come disclosing to you the Divine Secret with imposing speech or wisdom; for I was determined to be conscious of nothing while among you but of Jesus Christ, and of him as crucified. And so it was in weakness, and in fear, and in great trepidation, that I arrived among you; and my speech and proclamation was with no persuasive words of wisdom, but with spiritual and phenomenal demonstration, so that our conviction should not rest on human wisdom but on divine power' (*I.Cor.* ii.1-5).

Paul was to stay at Corinth for about eighteen months in AD 50-51, the longest time that he was to spend anywhere in the course of his travels. It was a memorable period, reflected not only in the account in the *Acts*, but also in the subsequent letters to the Corinthian believers. In the Biblical manuscripts this correspondence is presented in two letters; but in fact the two are an amalgamation of four, as exhibited in my edition and translation. To no other body of Christians

---

* See the second of four letters to the Corinthian community, p. 141.

did Paul write so considerably and so intimately; and consequently these letters are more revealing of Paul's personality and convictions than any other records.

We have already described how at this time the Jewish Zealots were extremely busy with their anti-Roman propaganda, and this circumstance would also affect the Jews at Corinth. Indeed, Paul's first encounter there was with Aquila and his wife Priscilla, who, as we have seen, were among the Jews Claudius had expelled from Rome on account of Messianic agitation. Both Paul and Aquila were tentmakers by trade, and they teamed up at Corinth and worked together.

As was Paul's custom, he made it his first business to proclaim the Messiahship of Jesus to fellow Jews, and the *Acts* reports that it was no different in Corinth. Every Sabbath he discoursed in the synagogue, and convinced both Jews and Greeks. 'When Silas and Timotheus came down from Macedonia Paul was deeply engaged with the Message, adducing evidence to the Jews that Jesus was the Messiah. But when they ranged themselves against him, and became abusive, he shook out his clothes, and told them, "Your blood be on your own heads! I am guiltless. From now on I go to the Gentiles." So he changed his venue, and went to the house of a proselyte called Titus Justus, which adjoined the synagogue. But Crispus, president of the synagogue, believed in the Master, as did his whole family, and many of the Corinthians who listened believed and were immersed.'

As will be seen, Paul did *not* immediately go to the Gentiles. He continued his teaching at the home of a full Gentile proselyte to Judaism. Such proselytes were described in Hebrew as *Ger-zedek*, and often took the surname of *Zedek* (Latin Justus). Crispus the president of the synagogue was personally baptised by Paul. (*I.Cor.*i.14.)

According to the *Acts* Paul continued his activities at Corinth for a year and a half, as we have noted. And if we are to judge by Paul's letters to the Corinthian believers in Jesus, this was to prove to be a period when a radical change took place in the representation of the Messianic Faith. This was because of the native beliefs and superstitions of the local people, and their low moral level. Paul had virtually to devise a new religion for them, part Jewish, part pagan, which they were capable of comprehending. To a large extent he had to count on psychic phenomena, speaking with tongues, and so on, to get through to the minds of those he was seeking to reach. Paul did not have an intention to create a new religion, but inevitably this proved to be the outcome of his efforts to get through to the minds of his hearers. Being himself psychic and very deeply a mystic, the changes and ideas he was to introduce he regarded as direct instructions from the Jesus, who was in heaven, and who had chosen him as his earthly mouthpiece.

In the letters to the Corinthians Paul dwells much on 'the Hidden Wisdom of God contained in a Mystery'. This, as we shall in due course explain, derived from the training in Jewish occultism he had received, and which had enabled him to accept Jesus as the Heavenly Son of Man. This acceptance had chimed with his own personal sense of mission to win Gentiles for God, so that he could claim, in justification of being the odd man out compared with the Twelve, that Jesus spoke to him from heaven, while they depended on what Jesus had said on earth.

The reader of the New Testament requires to be concerned much less with theology and far more with psychology and the End of the World atmosphere which these records reflect.

We are required to apprehend that what would in due course become Christian religion with many additions in doctrine and practices had much of its origin in Paul's problem with the pagan Corinthians; and this would include the conversion of the last Passover meal Jesus had celebrated in Jerusalem into the quasi-pagan Communion service celebrated on Sundays. It was at Corinth that this rite began to be practised, as one of Paul's revelations from the Jesus in heaven. And it is to be noted that the formula in *I.Cor.*xi.23-25[*] is reproduced by the author of *Luke–Acts* (cf. *Lk.*xxii.19).

As Paul – once again – wrote subsequently to the believers at Corinth: 'It was impossible for me to speak to you as spiritually-equipped people, only as physically-equipped, as infants in Christ. I had to feed you with milk rather than solid food, for you were not equal to it. *Neither is your faith to become a substitute for the Table of Serapis and other heathen gods.'*[**]

---

[*] See p. 149f.

[**] See Note 20, p.138. It is perhaps of interest to note here that in early Christian times there were Christians in Egypt who worshipped Serapis, and people who called themselves bishops of Christ who were in reality devotees of Serapis. Temples dedicated to Serapis existed throughout the Hellenistic world (see RGG Vol. 5, 1961, article *Serapis*). See also Schonfield, *The Passover Plot, Part II*, Ch.1 *Messianism and the Development of Christianity*: 'It was bound to happen that for many Christians of non-Jewish origin King Messiah would become the Lord Christ, like the Lord Serapis, Saviour and Son of God...' Paul would have to contend with such problems, as Schonfield here intimates in italics.

In the next chapter it will be necessary to come to grips with Paulinism, which was now taking a more positive shape. But to communicate Paul's own convictions to the ignorant and superstitious Corinthians was quite impossible. And here we may quote Paul's own words again:

Take yourselves, brothers. There are not many sages among you in the world's sense, not many persons of consequence, not many highborn. Instead, God has selected what is foolish in the world to shame the wise, and what is weak to shame the mighty, and what is of base origin and treated with contempt has God chosen ... So when I came to you, brothers, I did not come disclosing to you the Divine Secret with imposing speech of wisdom ... (*I.Cor.* i. 26-27).*

The new set-up at Corinth, half-Jewish half-pagan, was naturally anathema to the local Jews, who turned for redress to the new Roman proconsul of Achaia, L. Junius Gallio (July AD 51 to June 52), who was the brother of the famous Seneca. So we read in the *Acts*:

During Gallio's term as proconsul of Achaia, the Jews took common action against Paul, and brought him before the tribunal, saying, 'This man is seducing the people to become proselytes without reference to Jewish Law.'

As Paul was about to reply, Gallio said to the Jews, 'If this was a matter of misdemeanour or criminal offence, Jews, I would quite properly sustain your cause. But if it is a question of esteem and reputations, and of law as it concerns yourselves, that is your affair. I would rather not be a judge of such things.' And he barred them from the tribunal. Then all those present seized Sosthenes, president of the synagogue, and beat him in front of the tribunal; but Gallio had no responsibility for this (*Acts* xviii.12-17).

There could be no objection on the part of Jews to proclaiming the Jewish faith to non-Jews. But Paul was not making converts to Judaism: he was proclaiming a faith of his own invention which, while it called for belief in the One God of Israel, did not require acceptance of the laws governing Israel, or even the laws governing Gentile God-fearers.

---

* See p. 141.

12
Paulinism

At this point in our story Paulinism begins clearly to emerge and to be defined. It rested on three platforms: 1) The relationship between Jesus and God; 2) The relationship of Paul to Jesus; and 3) The relationship of Paul's Gentile converts to Israel.

But before we can consider these matters we need to have Paul's sense of immediacy. We are now looking back over nearly two thousand years in which a Christian religion would develop to a time when all followers of Jesus were convinced of his imminent return to Earth. In no more than a decade, perhaps, the opportunity to participate in his kingdom would be gone. Christianity, as a religion in its own right, did not come into the picture, and Paul was not planning to create it. What concerned him was that as many people as possible should be saved from the Coming Wrath. Paul's experience at Corinth emphasized this.

'Though I am in every sense a freeman, I have made myself everyone's slave so as to win over far more. So I have been a Jew to Jews to win over Jews. I have been subject to law to those under law – not being under law myself – to win over those under law. I have been alien to law to those without law – though not alien to God's law and legally bound to Christ – to win over those without law. I have been subject to limitations to those with limitations (i.e. in matters of diet, etc.), to win over those with limitations. To everyone I have been as they are, that at all events I should save some' (*I.Cor.*ix.19-22).[*]

The Christian reader has to forget his own Christian theology, and not seek to impose it on Paul. He has to be free to identify himself with Paul's peculiar convictions, alien as these will be to his own concepts.

---

[*] See p. 136

The Relationship between Jesus and God

The Gentile Church, because of its unjewishness, found it impossible after the first century AD to comprehend the mystery of the Messianic in relation to Jesus, and relegated his Jewish followers to the rank of heretics. In fact they had preserved much of the original Nazorean position, which had been that of Jesus himself, and this had derived from the teaching of the Jewish mystics. Some of this teaching has been disclosed in Chapter 4, where we dealt with the mystery of the Creation, as Paul himself came to know it.

The Jewish mystics declared that where it is stated in *Genesis* that 'the Wind [Spirit] of God ruffled the surface of the [primeval] Waters', the outcome was the emergence of life. In that act was anticipated the whole of history, all that was to happen on Earth in future time. Therefore, said the Jewish sages, the Spirit was that of Messiah, who signifies the meaning and purpose of what we are pleased to call history. The Messianic relates to our world, not to any other state of existence.

Similarly with the creation of Adam. He is the planting on our world of the presence and activity of God, made in the image and likeness of God. Adam was conceived by the Jewish mystics as of towering height with this head reaching the sky. But when he sinned his stature was reduced to what it is now. But what of the Spirit Adam, the Heavenly Archetype? He represented the Messiah Above, the Son of Man of the *Book of Enoch*, based on the prediction of *Daniel* about the Son of Man who would come to Earth after appearing in a cloud before the Ancient of Days, and receiving from him 'dominion, and glory, and a kingdom, that all people, nations, and languages, should serve him' (*Dan*.vii.13-14).

Of this Son of Man we read in *Enoch* xlviii: 'Before the sun and the signs were created, before the stars of heaven were made, his name was named before the Lord of Spirits. He will be a staff to the righteous... and the light of the Gentiles, and the hope of those who are troubled of heart. All who dwell on earth will fall down and bow the knee before him and will bless and laud and celebrate with song the Lord of Spirits.' Of Him, it was held, the Psalmist had written: 'The Lord said unto my lord, "Sit thou at my right hand, until I make thy foes thy footstool"' (*Ps*. cx.1).

The Nazoreans would hold, and Jesus himself, that the Archetypal Man above had entered into Jesus below at his baptism, thus making him both Messiah and Son of Man. And the words he heard were those of *Psalm II*: 'Thou art My son; *this day* have I begotten thee. Ask of Me, and I shall give the heathen for thine inheritance, and the uttermost parts of the earth for thy possession.'

It was not at his birth but at his baptism that Jesus was made Messiah (Christ). That is why, in his new capacity, Jesus suffered temptation in the wilderness. The oldest Gospel, that of Mark, has no Nativity story.

Jewish *Genesis* mysticism, as studied by Paul, would have had no difficulty in seeing the relationship between the Adam Above and the Adam Below. And it is significant that the stress on this is found in Paul's letters to the Corinthian converts. 'For since by man came death, so by man also came resurrection from the dead. For as in Adam all die, so in Christ (i.e. the Messiah) will all be brought to life, though each in his proper order, first Christ, followed at his coming by those who belong to Christ, then the remainder when he has handed over the Kingdom of God (to the Father) after abolishing all other government, authority and power' (*I.Cor.* xv. 21-24).*

Paul goes on to say: 'Just as it is stated, "The first man (Adam) became a living soul" (*Gen.* ii.7), so the last Adam became a vitalising spirit... The first man was "dust from the earth", the second man was from heaven.'

The Heavenly Man doctrine of the Jewish mystics is applied again to the Messiah by Paul in his letter to the Philippians, in a passage Christian theologians have not rightly understood. Paul writes: 'Let your disposition, indeed, be that of Christ Jesus, who though (as Son of Man) he had godlike form, did not (as Adam did, *Gen.* iii.5) regard it as a prize to be equal to God, but divested himself, taking the form of a servant. Appearing in human likeness, and disclosed in physical appearance as a man, he abased himself, and became subject to death, death by the cross. That is why God has so exalted him, that at the name of Jesus every knee, heavenly, earthly and infernal, should bend, and every tongue acclaim Jesus Christ as lord, to the glory of God the Father' (*Phil.* ii.5-11).

The Heavenly Man who would incarnate in Jesus did not commit the crime of Lucifer, who had said (*Isa.* xiv.14): 'I will ascend above the heights of the clouds; I will be like the Most High.' And it was Lucifer (Satan) who had tempted Adam through Eve.

The disciple of Paul who is the author of *Luke–Acts* makes it

* See p. 154

very clear in the Nativity story that Jesus would be descended from King David, but would be called Son of God (*Lk*.i.35). He is 'a man proved to be from God' (*Acts* ii. 22), who is seen by the martyr Stephen as 'the Son of Man standing at God's right hand' (*Acts* vii.56).

Thus through Jesus, the Heavenly Adam 'to the fight and to the rescue came' by incarnating in him. For Paul's Messianic teaching much is due to Jewish mysticism, the concept of the *Adam Kadmon*, the Archetypal Man, which in turn owed its inception to Persian Mithraism. Paul could utilise various aspects of contemporary Mithraism, notably in the Lord's Supper, in appealing to Gentiles.

The Relationship of Paul to Jesus

It is unfortunate that scholars and theologians have concentrated on Pauline doctrine without sufficient consideration of Paul the man, a very extraordinary and complex man with a belief in his own divine calling and mission. He had been named Saul, who had been the first Messiah ('anointed one') as king of Israel. He was an ugly man, as the records show, and evidently suffered from some physical ailment. As indicated in Chapter 4 above, he may well have applied to himself the image of the Suffering Servant in *Isaiah*, liii. That personality 'had no form nor comeliness; and when we shall see him there is no beauty that we should desire him.' His occult Jewish studies may well have intensified his delusions about himself.

The sudden emergence in Jerusalem of the exuberant movement giving allegiance to Jesus as the Davidic Messiah must have come as a great shock to the young Saul of Tarsus, partly unhinging his mind. It seemed as if again David was replacing Saul. Only a severe mental disturbance could have brought on his violent antagonism to the followers of Jesus, and induced him, a Pharisee, to seek authority from a Sadducean High Priest, to conduct a pogrom against the Nazoreans and make wholesale arrests. The House of Annas must have been delighted to have the services of someone in the opposite camp to do their dirty work for them. Saul had already been weakened in mind and body by his occult studies, and it is not surprising that on the road to Damascus he should have had some kind of fit or attack.

The story of Paul's conversion is told graphically in the *Acts*, with how much reliability it is impossible to say. But it is very evident that he did surrender to the authority of Jesus, yet in a way that did not eliminate his convictions about his own destiny.

Paul was at a great disadvantage compared with the disciples who

had companied with Jesus and received his teaching; and it is
significant that in his letters he does not at all employ the well-
known sayings of Jesus. As Paul writes: 'Even if we have known
Christ in the physical sense, we do so now no longer' (*II. Cor.* v. 16).*
He glories in the claim that he personally was directly instructed
by the Jesus in heaven, who had chosen him specially as his envoy
to the Gentiles. The opening of his letter to the believers at Rome is
in grandiose terms:

> Paul, servant of Jesus Christ, a chosen envoy, assigned to the
> proclamation of God's News, which He had previously an-
> nounced to His Prophets in the Sacred Writings, concerning His
> son, Jesus Christ our Master, born in the physical sense of the
> line of David, but potently demonstrated to be God's Son in the
> sanctified spiritual sense by resurrection from the dead. By him
> I have obtained favour and envoyship to procure loyal submission
> to his authority on the part of all nations, among whom you like-
> wise are summoned by Jesus Christ (*Rom.*i.1-6).

Paul now had what might be called a Jesus fixation. He had become in the most direct sense the earthly reflection of the heavenly
Christ, thus reconciling his status with his earlier beliefs in his own
special destiny. Great pride is linked with great humility in his new
imagination. He writes to the Galatians:

> God forbid that I should boast of anything but the cross of our
> Lord Jesus Christ, by which the world has been crucified to me,
> and I to the world! It is neither circumcision nor uncircumcision
> that counts for anything, but a new creation. To all who toe this
> line, peace and mercy be upon them, and upon the Israel of God.
> From now on let no one deal me any more blows, for I carry
> the scars of Jesus on my body (*Gal.*vi.14-17).

Paul's Gentile converts and Israel

Paul was a Jew, and remained one at heart all his life. For him there
was only One God and there was only one People of God, Israel. His
religion was that of Moses, and the Prophets, and the Messiah. All
other religions were superstition and idolatry. Paul had no aim to
create a new Christian religion in which Jesus was worshipped as
Divine. For him, in any case, as we have seen, the end of the existing

---

* See the fourth letter to the Corinthian community, p. 170.

world order was imminent. Apart from any need, there was no time for such a development. What was vital was to bring into the worship of God and allegiance to Jesus as many Gentiles as possible.

Initially, as Envoy to the Gentiles, Paul's primary concern was to claim that all Gentiles who believed in the God of Israel and gave their allegiance to Jesus as king of Israel thereby ceased to be Gentiles and automatically became Israelites. This claim was rejected by the communities' highest authority at Jerusalem, the Council consisting of the Envoys chosen by Jesus, and other eminent Jews, under the Presidency of Jacob (James) the Messiah's brother. To qualify for membership of the People of God it was fundamental to observe the Laws of God given to Israel. What could be granted was that Gentiles who worshipped God and accepted the Messiah would be received as colleagues, 'strangers within the gates', provided they observed the less stringent Laws of Noah.

Paul was nominally forced to accept this ruling. But it was galling to him because it placed his converts in a lower category than Jewish believers. Progressively, therefore, he rejected it, especially as it put a substantial impediment in the way of his winning many Gentiles for Christ.

According to a Jewish teaching, where it says of the Messiah (*Isa.* ix.6) 'the government shall be upon his shoulder', this was interpreted as 'he has taken the Law upon himself to keep it'. Obviously the king of Israel should be the exemplary observer of the Law of Israel. Paul therefore argued that all who were 'in the Messiah' should be reckoned as Israelites, since they were covered by the Messiah's observance of the Law. Gentiles by 'being in Christ' had experienced a new creation. They had become Israelites by adoption. 'If anyone is in Christ (the Messiah) he is a new creation. The old relationships have gone, replaced by the new' (*II.Cor.* v. 17). And again: 'You are all Sons of God by faith in Jesus Christ, for those who have been identified with Christ by immersion have assumed Christ's personality. It is impossible for there to be Jew or Greek, slave or freeman, male or female; for in Jesus Christ you are all one and the same person. If you are *in* Christ you *are* 'the Seed of Abraham', heirs in accordance with the promise' (*Gal.* iii.26-29). The argument is fully developed in *Galatians*.

Another line of argument used by Paul develops the Seed of Abraham contention (*Rom.* iv). Abraham was reckoned as righteous because he believed in God, and before he received the sign of circumcision. So one can believe without the sign of circumcision and be accounted righteous. 'Abraham received the mark of circumcision as a ratification of the rectitude arising from the faith he had while uncircumcised ... For it was not by law that the promise was made to Abraham, or to his seed, that he should be "heir of the world", but by rectitude deriving from faith ... Necessarily it is based on faith, so as to be a matter of favour, that the promise might be secured to all the seed, not only that which is based on the Law, but also to that which is based on the faith of Abraham, who is our common ancestor, as it is stated (*Gen*.xvii.5), "I have made you father of many nations"' (*Rom*. iv.11-17).

At one point, because of his antagonists, Paul bursts out: 'In whatever way anyone may make sweeping claims – I am keeping up this fool talk – so can I. Are they Hebrews? So am I. Are they Israelites? So am I. Are they the Seed of Abraham? So am I. Are they the agents of Christ? Mad as it sounds, I am even more so. My labours have been harder, my terms of imprisonment longer, my floggings beyond all bounds, my risks of death more frequent' (*II.Cor*. xi.21-23).

The conclusion Paul reached by his Biblical erudition was that by act of faith, rather than by law, believing Gentiles have been accorded Israelite status. 'Bear in mind,' he writes to the Ephesians, 'that you were once Gentiles in the physical sense, who are termed the uncircumcision by those termed in respect of an operation in the flesh the Circumcision, because at that time you were without benefit of Christ, aliens to the body politic of Israel, and strangers to the covenants of promise. But now in Christ Jesus you who were once far off have been brought near by the blood of Christ' (*Eph*. ii.11-13).

Paul clinches his arguments in his letter to the believers at Rome. He uses the symbol of an Olive Tree to represent Israel. Because of failure by some Jews to recognise Jesus as Messiah these branches have been broken off. In their place believing Gentiles as branches of a wild olive tree have been grafted into Israel in substitution (see *Rom*. xi).

Whoever follows Pauline teaching must accordingly agree with him that all who accept Jesus as king of Israel, whether Jews by birth or Gentiles, are now the loyal People of Israel. Consequently non-Jewish Christians are not in fact Gentiles: they are now Israelites. The Land of Israel is *their* homeland. One wonders what would happen if Christians of today believed Paul.

13
Ephesus

At this point in the narrative of the *Acts of the Apostles* there would appear to be some condensation. After remaining for some time at Corinth, Paul sailed for Syria accompanied by Aquila and his wife Priscilla. On the way, at Cenchreae, he had his head shaved as he was under a vow. Paul left his friends at Ephesus, but only paused himself for a few days in which he attended the synagogue and gave out the Good News of the Messiah. The *Acts* says that the Jewish community begged him to stay longer, but he declined, telling them, 'I must by all means keep the approaching festival at Jerusalem. But, God willing, I will return to you.'

Ephesus was a very important city, capital of the Roman province of Asia. Its temple of Artemis (Diana) was one of the wonders of the world. Therefore it was a valuable target for Pauline propaganda. Yet Paul would not stay at this juncture because of a Jewish festival, though he would seem to have left Aquila and Priscilla there. What festival would this have been?

In our understanding of the Jewish followers of Jesus, they had adopted from the Essenes a great deal of their organisation and practices, including an annual assembly at the festival of Pentecost to which representatives of the various communities would report of their activities. As an accepted agent of the Nazorean Council, Paul was obliged to report if at all practicable to James (Jacob) the brother of Jesus and the Nazorean leaders. If he did not, there was the risk that he would be disowned, not only as an official envoy (apostle) but altogether. Paul could not take this risk; and since he already had a number of enemies in the Nazorean camp it was essential for him to appear to plead his cause.

Even though Paul regarded himself as the unique Envoy to the

Gentiles, he never neglected at any time to make it his first duty to proclaim the Messianic message in the synagogues wherever he went. Also, from the Nazorean communities he created, he demanded that they should set aside funds which at each Pentecost he would convey to Jerusalem as their gift to 'the Poor'. This too would stand in his favour with the Council.

'Paul set sail from Ephesus,' states the author of the *Acts*, 'and on arrival at Caesarea went up to Jerusalem to pay his respects to the Community. Then he went down to Antioch, and after allowing himself a certain time there he left again, covering successively the Galatian region and Phrygia, confirming all the disciples.'

While Paul was travelling we learn that 'there arrived at Ephesus a Jew called Apollos, a native of Alexandria, a learned man well-versed in the Scriptures. He had some knowledge of the Faith of the Master, and being an enthusiast he spoke and taught very much to the point the matters relating to Jesus, though acquainted only with John's rite of immersion. He spoke very boldly in the synagogue, and Priscilla and Aquila, having listened to him, made friends with him and explained God's way to him more exactly. And when he wished to cross over to Achaia, the brothers, who were very taken with him, wrote to the disciples to make him welcome. On his coming he proved a valuable ally to those who by God's mercy had believed; for he confuted the Jews most forcefully by common consent, demonstrating from the Scriptures that Jesus was the Messiah.'

When Paul kept his word and returned to Ephesus he devoted three months, says the author of the *Acts*, to speaking about the Kingdom of God in the Jewish synagogue. It would seem that this course had been impressed on him as an outcome of his reporting to the Nazorean Council at Jerusalem. The statement is particularly interesting because for multitudes in the Jewish homeland the theme of the coming Kingdom at this time was related to the freedom of Israel from the Romans, and the Divine destruction of the Roman Empire. We will be taking account of this in the next chapter, and it is of prime importance for a true history of Christian beginnings. What was going on was not unknown to the Jews throughout the Roman Empire. They were familiar with Jewish agents and preachers seeking to gain their support and collecting funds for armaments. Paul, wrapped up in his own mission, was blind to the point almost of insanity to what was going on, and did not rightly identify the true cause of the opposition he encountered from the Provincial Jews, dependent on Rome for their

75

protection from Greek antisemitism. Christian clerics, in their expositions, continue largely to share the same blindness.

Paul transferred his place of instruction, we are told, to the lecture hall of Tyrannus where he gave a daily discourse. And we quote:

> This went on for two years, so that all who lived in Asia (Asia Minor), Jews and Greeks alike, heard the Master's message. God effected extraordinary miracles through Paul's instrumentality, so that even handkerchiefs and loincloths were taken away for the sick after physical contact with him, and by this means they were freed from their diseases and the evil spirits left them.

The *Acts* goes on:

> Then certain Jewish travelling exorcists attempted to use the name of the Lord Jesus on those possessed by the evil spirits, saying, 'I adjure you by Jesus whom Paul proclaims!' But the evil spirit replied, 'I know Jesus, and I am familiar with Paul, but who do you think you are?' And the man in whom the evil spirit dwelt leapt on them, and overpowered them both, so that they fled from that house lacerated with their clothes in ribbons.
>
> This became known to all the inhabitants of Ephesus, Jews and Greeks alike, and they were seized with fear, and the name of the Lord Jesus was magnified. Many of those who believed came and confessed, and made a clean breast of their practices. Several, who were practitioners of magic, made a bonfire of their books in the sight of all. The value was computed and was found to come to fifty thousand pieces of silver.

Whatever may be the factual merits of this narrative, it is at least in keeping with the historical conditions; for Ephesus was pre-eminent for addiction to curious arts. Here at the gate of Asia was piled up the magical merchandise of the East, charms and amulets, scrolls of conjurations, Ephesian Scripts, rigmaroles of queer Hebrew and Chaldean names to impress the superstitious Greeks. It was a lucrative trade at all levels, exploited to the full by unprincipled Hebrews like the fortune-telling gypsy wife of whom the satirist Juvenal writes:

> Leaving her hay and basket,
> The trembling Jewess whispering begs her bread,
> Interpreter of Salem's law, and priestess
> Of trees, and faithful go-between of heaven.
> She fills the hand too, but with smallest coin.
> Those Jews will sell you any dreams you please. (Satire VI)

While Jews, Egyptians, and orientals of diverse races pandered to the superstition and licentiousness of Roman, Greek, and the native population of Asia Minor, and made rich profits thereby, the blame attaches less to them, perhaps, than to the credulous, novelty-hunting and decadent people who encouraged them. In our own time in the West there are still an abundance of the credulous devoted to 'Light from the East', and who eagerly, and often for mercenary gain, become devotees of Asian cults.

There is on record the letter which a non-Jewish sage of those times wrote to the Ephesians. This was the famous Apollonius of Tyana. He told them:

> You are devoted to holy ceremonies no less than to honouring the Emperor. In general I cannot condemn your custom of inviting and being invited to feasts; but I do condemn the people who by night and by day share the home of the goddess [Artemis], otherwise I should not see issuing thence thieves and robbers and kidnappers, and every sort of wretch or sacrilegious rascal; for your temple is just a den of robbers (Philostratus, *Epistles of Apollonius*, lxv, Loeb Classical Library).

And here, appropriately, we may quote a lengthy passage from the *Acts* which forms the climax to Paul's second stay in Ephesus. The narrative is both graphic and entertaining.

> Just at this period there was a serious disturbance over the Faith [lit. That Way]. It was due to a certain Demetrius, a silversmith, who provided a good living for his craftsmen making shrines of Artemis [Diana]. Calling them together, and others engaged in similar employment, he addressed them as follows:
>
> 'Men, you fully appreciate that our livelihood depends on this employment. You will also have observed and noted that this fellow Paul with his persuasions has affected a whole lot of people, not only of Ephesus but of pretty well all Asia, saying that what human hands have made are no gods at all. This means not only that we run a grave risk of loss of reputation, but also that the temple of the great goddess Artemis, whom all Asia and the Empire reveres, will count for nothing and her sway will be ended.'
>
> When they heard this they got wildly excited and yelled, 'Up with Artemis of the Ephesians!'
>
> The city was filled with confusion, and by common consent

they rushed to the theatre, carrying along with them the Macedonians Gaius and Aristarchus, Paul's travelling companions. Paul would have gone in there to the people, but the disciples would not let him. Some of the Asiarchs too, who were his friends, sent him word begging him to keep out of the theatre. Some there were shouting one thing, and some another; for the assembly was completely confused, the majority not having the slightest idea for what cause they had congregated. Among all the crowd they decided it must have to do with Alexander, because the Jews were pushing him forward. Alexander then waved his hand for silence, anxious to defend himself to the people. But no sooner were they aware that he was a Jew than they broke into a chorus of yelling for some two hours on end, 'Up with Artemis of the Ephesians!'

When the city recorder had got the crowd calmed down, he said, 'Ephesians, where is there a single individual who does not know the city of Ephesians as custodian of the temple of mighty Artemis, and of the heaven-sent statue? Since these facts are indisputable, you ought to keep calm and do nothing outrageous; for you have brought these men here who are neither sacrilegious nor insulters of your goddess. If, therefore, Demetrius and the craftsmen with him have a grievance against anyone, the courts are open and there are proconsuls: let them mutually prefer their charges. If you wish to take the matter further, it will be dealt with in the assembly provided by law. For we run the risk of being accused of riot over today's uncalled-for proceedings; for we cannot offer the slightest justification for this concourse.' With this he dismissed the assembly.

When the general commotion had subsided, Paul sent for the disciples, and having exhorted them and said farewell he left for Macedonia (*Acts* xix).

14
Saints and Sinners

It is essential at this juncture that we should be fully conscious and informed of the state of affairs in the Jewish homeland. For these had a profound effect on the believers in Jesus as Messiah. A Last Times atmosphere was now paramount, reinforced by the deteriorating conditions. Largely here we have to rely on the accounts given by the historian Josephus, who, though he was anxious to let the Romans off as lightly as possible and pin blame for the circumstances on the Jewish spiritual and political extremists, paints a picture which is substantially dependable.

In the middle of the first century AD there were multitudes in Israel who were convinced that the tribulations they were experiencing were the pangs of Messiah, and that before long he would manifest himself, drive out the Romans, and set up his kingdom. The appearance in these Latter Days of several individuals claiming to be the Messiah testifies to this conviction. In contemporary apocalyptic and didactic writings predictions abounded.

Popular response largely took two forms. One of these was the accentuation of religiosity based on the conviction that the tribulations of Israel were due to failure strictly to observe the requirements of the Law (the Torah). The other was a militancy directed against the heathen occupying power and its Jewish supporters, and the well-to-do who followed the ways of the Gentiles. A great many were in both these categories, constituting the body known as the Zealots, some of whom were assassins, so called from their daggers Sicarii.

It was an unhealthy atmosphere, with groups and sects watching each other, watching the Roman officials and Roman forces and those in Israel who co-operated with them, watching the Samaritans, who had their own Messianic hopes of triumphing over the Jews.

In the Temple at Jerusalem itself there was the barrier warning Gentiles that they must not pass it on pain of death, and many would extend this prohibition to the whole country. It must become a Holy Land from which all aliens with their idolatry were excluded. Hippolytus* refers to these extremists (*Philosophumena*, Bk.ix. 26): 'Some of them observe a still more rigid practice in not handling or looking at a coin which bears an image, nor will they even enter a city at the gates of which statues are erected. Others again threaten to slay any Gentile taking part in a discourse about God and His Law if he refuses to be circumcised ... Others again will call no man lord, except God, even though they be tortured and killed.'

Only a short time before Paul was to come to Jerusalem the Samaritans had been the cause of what might have proved a major disaster for the Jews, and which had aroused all their most intolerant feelings. I have described the circumstances in my book *The Pentecost Revolution*, from which I may quote:

> It began with an attack by the Samaritans on the village of Ginae, the modern Jenis, on a band of Jewish pilgrims from Galilee travelling to Jerusalem for one of the festivals ... One or more of the Galilean pilgrims had been killed by the Samaritans, and complaint was immediately made to the Roman governor Cumanus. For some reason he refused redress to the Jewish notables who appealed to him, which not only incensed the Galileans but aroused the ire of many of the inhabitants of Jerusalem. The Zealots were evidently behind the next move to enlist the support of the guerrilla bands under the command of a famous nationalist rebel Eleazer Bar-Deinaeus, who for many years from his mountain fastnesses had carried out numerous raiding expeditions and had successfully evaded capture by the Romans. With the co-operation of Eleazar, and led by him and a certain Alexander, a punitive attack was made on several Samaritan villages in the Acrabatene area, south-east of Shechem, whose inhabitants were ruthlessly massacred and their houses burnt down.
>
> When the news reached Cumanus he took cavalry of a Roman corps recruited in Samaria, and perhaps infantry as well, and marched against the aggressors, slew many and captured others – though not Eleazar himself. The gravity of the situation

---

* Early third century Church Father who died c. 236, a pupil of Irenaeus (c.130 – c.200).

was such at this point that the Jews were closer to open rebellion against Rome than they had ever been before, and the alarmed Sanhedrin sent representatives to calm things down... Many of the people yielded to the entreaties of the magistrates and dispersed; but Josephus remarks that from this time revolutionary outbreaks in various parts of the country were continuous. Tacitus, the Roman historian, paints an even more alarming picture of the situation than Josephus. He speaks of a number of Roman soldiers killed by the Jews, and of strong action which had been taken to prevent a full-scale war.

Quadratus, the legate of Syria, was forced to intervene after hearing the charges on both sides, and crucified a number of the prisoners taken by Cumanus, both Jews and Samaritans. Finally the chief representatives of the two nations, together with Cumanus and tribune Celer, were sent to Rome to answer to the emperor. A decision was given by Claudius against the Samaritans as the primary cause of the trouble, and Cumanus was held responsible for resorting to force before investigating the circumstances. He was accordingly sentenced to banishment, while Celer was sent back to Jerusalem, there to be dragged round the city and publicly beheaded. By these judgments a temporary peace was achieved. Antonius Felix, who was only a freedman, was appointed as the new governor of Galilee, Samaria and Judea.

From this time forward, however, conditions in the Jewish homeland would progressively deteriorate as fanatics and militants, often united, deprived the country of peace. The conviction gained widespread credence that the circumstances represented the Great Tribulation which should precede the ultimate Messianic Age.

Devotion to the Mosaic Law, the Torah, was naturally intensified as a passport to salvation, as much among the many thousands of Jewish followers of Jesus as among the Pharisees and Essenes. The Nazoreans, in fact, were highly approved of and applauded by the Jewish populace, and more especially as their leader Jacob (James), younger brother of Jesus, was a very pious ascetic. His personality would become almost as legendary as that of Jesus.

The Church historian Eusebius would write of him: 'Now Jacob, the brother of the Lord, who, as there were many of this name, was termed the Just by all, from the days of our Lord until now, received the government of the Church with the Apostles. This Apostle (Jacob) was consecrated from his mother's womb. He drank neither wine nor fermented liquors, and abstained from animal food. A razor never came upon his head; he never anointed himself with oil or used a public bath. He alone was allowed to enter the Holy Place (in the Temple). He never wore woollen, only linen garments. He was in the habit of entering the Temple alone, and was often to be found upon his knees and interceding for the forgiveness of the people; so that his knees became as hard as a camel's ... And indeed, on account of his exceeding great piety, he was called the Just (i.e. *Zaddik*) and Oblias (i.e. *Ophlaam*), which signifies justice and the People's Bulwark, as the Prophets declare concerning him' (*History of the Church*, II.xxiii).

Jacob (James) was not only a Nazirite as well as a Nazorean. Jerome says that he was so venerated by the Jewish populace that 'they would crowd around him and strive to touch the hem of his garment.' There was even the myth that he was empowered to wear the high priestly diadem, and permitted to enter the Holy of Holies in the Temple once a year, as did the High Priest on the Day of Atonement.

Christians are never instructed that in the first century of the Christian era the head of all believers in the Messiahship of Jesus, whether Jews or non-Jews, was his brother Jacob. To him and his Council Paul, in common with all Nazorean emissaries, was required to make report, customarily at the Jewish festival of Pentecost. At the very outset of Paul's activities he had been informed by Jacob that converted Gentiles would be acknowledged as brothers provided that they observed the Laws of Noah. But they would not be regarded as fellow-Israelites unless they became subject to the Law of Moses. This was an impediment to his activities which Paul was determined to overcome, and he was now about to travel to Jerusalem to make a supreme effort. He would be taking with him as evidence representative Gentile believers in Jesus as Messiah. He could not have chosen a worse time.

It is doubtful whether Paul had any idea of the critical situation at Jerusalem, the intensity of anti-heathen feeling which had developed, the emotional fanaticism and indulgence in atrocities by extremists. The whole Jewish nation seemed to be in the grip of a Last Days complex, with passions and outbreaks which could turn in a moment to mob violence. And many of the extremists were followers of Jesus, to whom Paul and all he represented was anathema. And, as we shall see, they did nothing to save him, as they had saved Peter, when he fell into the hands of the authorities.

The story of what took place is largely covered by the Diary Document, the graphic and substantially reliable source reproduced in the *Acts* in lengthy extracts.

15

Journey to Jerusalem

The *Acts* picks up the narrative at the point where Paul, having left Ephesus, decided to travel to Jerusalem via Macedonia.

In attendance on Paul were Sopater son of Pyrrhus of Beroea, Aristarchus and Secundus of the Thessalonians, Gaius of Derbe and Timotheus, and Tychicus and Trophimus of Asia. These going on ahead awaited us at Troas.

After the festival of Unleavened Bread we sailed from Philippi, and in five weeks' time we reached them at Troas, where we spent a week. Then on the day after the Sabbath, when we were together for the communal meal, Paul discoursed to them prior to setting off on the morrow, and prolonged his address until midnight.

There were a number of lamps burning in the upstairs room where we were gathered, so a youth called Eutychus sat in the window [i.e. because of the fumes]. As Paul's discourse went on and on, he grew drowsy and fell fast asleep. Drooping in his sleep he fell three floors down, and was picked up for dead. Paul went down, and threw himself upon him, and taking him in his embrace said, 'Do not lament. He is still alive.' He went upstairs again, broke bread, ate, carried on conversation for quite a time until dawn, and was then leaving, when the lad was carried in conscious, and they were enormously relieved.

We ourselves, having gone ahead to the ship, sailed for Assos, with the intention of taking Paul on board there in accordance with his instructions. He proposed himself to travel overland. When he met us as Assos we embarked him and came on to Mitylene, and from there set sail and arrived the following day off Chios. The day after we hove to at Samos, and on the next day we reached Miletus. This was because Paul had decided to sail past Ephesus, so that he would not have to linger in Asia; for he was anxious if at all possible to reach Jerusalem by Pentecost. From Miletus he sent to Ephesus, however, to summon the elders of the community. When they arrived he addressed them as follows:

'You are well aware how I have constantly acted in your interests ever since I first set foot in Asia, serving the Master with all humility and tears, and with the trials that came my way through the hostile schemes of the Jews.[*] I have never concealed anything that might be of benefit to you, whether in preaching to you or teaching you, both in public and private, most earnestly entreating Jews and Greeks alike to turn to God and have faith in Jesus our Master.

'Well, now I feel constrained to go to Jerusalem, not knowing what I shall have to face there. I only know that in city after city the Holy Spirit has solemnly assured me that imprisonment and severe trials await me. But I set no value whatever on life for myself, only that I may finish my course and the commission I received from the Lord Jesus to witness expressly to the News of God's mercy.

'I know full well that all of you among whom I have gone, proclaiming the Kingdom of God, will never see my face again. See to it that you tend the Master's community, which he has acquired with his own blood. I know that after I have gone home grievous wolves will get in among you who will not spare the flock; and even from yourselves men will arise talking twistedly to draw away disciples. So be on your guard, remembering that night and day for three years on end I never ceased tearfully warning each one of you.

'Now I commit you to God and to the Message of his mercy, which can fortify you and give you inheritance among all who are sanctified. I have coveted no one's silver, gold, or belongings. You are well aware that these hands have provided for my own needs and those of my associates. I have given you a complete demonstration how thus by your own toil you should assist the incapacitated, bearing in mind those words uttered by the Lord Jesus, "It is a finer thing to give than to get." '

---

[*] The Jews were in fact acting in self-defence as we have seen, believing Paul to be an anti-Roman Zealot agent. See pp. 54f., 60, 75-76.

When he finished speaking he knelt down with them all and prayed. A fit of weeping seized them, and they fell on Paul's neck and embraced him, grieving most over what he had said, that they were never going to see his face again. Then they escorted him to the ship.

When we sailed, after tearing ourselves away from them, we came on a straight course to Cos, the next day to Rhodes, and then to Patara. Finding a ship bound for Phoenicia, we went on board and sailed with her. After sighting Cyprus, and leaving it on our left, we sailed on to Syria and coasted down to Tyre; for there the ship was to discharge her cargo. Having located the disciples we stayed there a week; though they warned Paul by the Spirit not to go on to Jerusalem. We left, however, when our time was up, and were escorted on our way by them all, with their wives and children, until we were outside the town. Then, after kneeling in prayer on the beach, we said good-bye to one another; and we went on board while they returned home.

Completing the voyage from Tyre we arrived at Ptolemais. We paid our respects to the brothers and remained a day with them; but on the next we left for Caesarea, where we went to the house of the evangelist Philip and stayed with him. He had four maiden daughters who were prophetesses. In the course of our lengthy stay a prophet called Agabus came down from Judea and visited us. Taking Paul's girdle he bound his own hands and feet, and declared, 'Thus says the Holy Spirit, the man to whom this girdle belongs, the Jews in Jerusalem will bind and deliver him into the hands of the Gentiles.'

When we heard this, both we and the local disciples begged Paul not to go up to Jerusalem. But he replied, 'Why do you cry so, and weaken my resolve? For the sake of the Lord Jesus I am quite ready not only to be bound but even to die at Jerusalem.'

Failing to persuade him, we gave it up and said, 'The Lord's will be done.'

Some days later we made our arrangements to go up to Jerusalem. Several of the disciples from Caesarea went along with us to conduct us to Mnason, a Cypriot, one of the earliest disciples, with whom we would obtain lodging. Having duly reached Jerusalem, the brothers gave us a most friendly welcome. The next day Paul and ourselves had an audience with James [i.e. the brother of Jesus]. All the elders were present. And when we had paid our respects to them, Paul gave a full description of all God had done among the Gentiles by his agency.

The document in the first person plural breaks off at this point, and is not resumed for a considerable time. But it is highly probably that part of the intervening narrative derives from this source. The style of the author of the Gospel in the name of Luke, and of the second treatise the *Acts of the Apostles*, is very similar to that of the Diary Document so freely quoted in the latter. So there are reasonable grounds for believing that one individual was responsible for them all, and that this person was the Doctor Luke mentioned by Paul in some of his letters. *Luke–Acts*, however, was composed at a very much later date than the Diary Document, and after a number of Gospels had been in circulation (*Lk*.i.1-4) and also the works of the historian Josephus.

We have to appreciate in dealing with *Luke–Acts* that the intention of these documents is conciliatory. Their aim is to reconcile the Jewish and Gentile expressions of Christianity, which had become almost totally divided, to modify the conflict between Peter and Paul, and in general to produce a record of Christian beginnings which could be acceptable as church history suitably adorned with miracles and ethics in the manner of the times. We have to be specially grateful for the Diary Document as a source because it is so unpretentious, so readable and graphical, so that the reader experiences the life of the period and the personalities who participated in it. It is therefore well worth staying with our author for his account of what befell Paul at Jerusalem.

It remains to be said that the speeches and dialogues are in the main fictitious, especially where the author could not have been present. It was customary with the ancient historians, to make their work more graphic and realistic by inventing what is said by the various individuals, employing language suited to the persons and to the occasion.

16
Paul the Prisoner

In this chapter we are reproducing in my own translation the narrative which corresponds in the Bible to chapters xxi to xxiii of the *Acts*. We are not in a position to get at the facts; but we can recognize that in the story-line there is a substantial amount of verisimilitude. And certainly the narrative makes graphic reading. The author now takes over from the Diary Document he has been quoting.

> When the elders had listened to what Paul had to say they praised God, and then said to him, 'You must take into consideration, brother, how many ten thousands there are of Jews who have believed [i.e. in the Messiahship of Jesus]. Naturally they are staunch upholders of the Law [i.e. of Moses]. But they have been informed about you that you teach all Jews in Gentile lands to apostasize from Moses, telling them not to circumcise their children or conform to the customs. What is this going to mean? Many are bound to learn of your arrival. Here then is what you must do. We have four men under a mutual vow. Take over these men and undergo purification with them and pay their offering costs so that they can shave their heads [i.e. having let it grow long under a Nazirite vow].* Everyone will then realise that there is no foundation whatever for what they have been informed about you, and that on the contrary you yourself conform to and observe the Law. So far as Gentiles who have believed are concerned, we have communicated our decision that they should avoid what is dedicated to idols, blood, eating strangled animals, and sexual impurity.'

---

* The men had taken a Nazirite vow, and Paul assisted them in their absolution from it. See *Num.* vi; Mishnah, *Naz.* ii. 3.

Then Paul the very next day took over the men, and [confirming his Judaism] being purified with them entered the Sanctuary, giving notice of when the completion of the purification period would take place on which the sacrifice should be offered for each one of them.

When the seven days were almost up some Jews of Asia caught sight of him in the Sanctuary and roused all the people, crying as they seized him, 'Help, Israelites! Here is the fellow who goes around turning everyone everywhere against our people, and the Law, and this Place [i.e. the Temple]. He has even brought Greeks into the Sanctuary and desecrated this Holy Place.' [They had previously seen Trophimus the Ephesian in the city with him, and imagined Paul had brought him into the Sanctuary].

The whole city was set in uproar, and the people came rushing together. Those who had seized Paul dragged him outside the Sanctuary, and at once the gates were closed.* They were attempting to kill him when word reached the military tribune that all Jerusalem was seething. Instantly he took troops and centurions and ran to them, and as soon as they saw the tribune and the troops they stopped striking Paul.

Coming up, the tribune took him in charge, and ordered him to be bound with two chains, and inquired who he was and what he had been up to. Some of the crowd said one thing and some another; and as he could not discover the truth because of the commotion, he ordered Paul to be conveyed into the fort. When the steps were reached it was found that he had to be lifted up by the soldiers because of the pressure of the crowd; for the mass of the people surged close behind yelling, 'Away with him!'

When they were about to enter the fort, Paul said to the tribune, 'May I have a word with you?'

'Do you speak Greek?' he replied. 'Aren't you then the Egyptian who recently started an insurrection and led those four thousand assassins out into the wilderness?' [see Josephus, *Jewish War*, Bk.II. 261-263].

'I am actually a Jew,' said Paul, 'from Tarsus in Cilicia, a citizen of no insignificant city. Please allow me to address the people.'

---

* There was a barrier separating the Temple proper from the outer Court of the Gentiles. Notices warned Gentiles that they must not pass beyond it on pain of death. See p. 47.

Receiving permission, Paul stood at the top of the steps and waved his hand for silence. When there was sufficient quiet he addressed them in the Hebrew language, 'Brothers and fathers, give me a chance to explain myself to you.' Hearing him speak to them in Hebrew they quietened down still more.

'I am a Jew born in Tarsus of Cilicia,' Paul continued, 'but brought up in this city at the feet of Gamaliel, strictly trained in our ancestral Law, being zealous on God's behalf, just as all of you here are. I was one who hunted down this persuasion to the death, binding and delivering to prison men and women alike, as the High Priest and the whole Sanhedrin can bear me out.' [Here follows an account of his vision on the road to Damascus, and its outcome, *Acts* xxii. 5-21.]

Up to this point they listened to him, but then they cried out, 'Away with this fellow from the earth! He's not fit to live.'

As they shouted and tore their clothes, and flung dust in the air,* the tribune ordered him to be taken into the fort and examined by flogging, to discover the reason why they were so vociferous against him. As they were making him fast with straps, Paul said to the centurion in charge, 'Is it right for you to flog one who is a Roman and uncondemned?'

When he heard this the centurion went to the tribune and reported it. 'What do you propose to do?' he asked. 'This man is a Roman citizen.'

Going along, the tribune said to Paul, 'Tell me, are you a Roman?'

'Yes,' he replied.

'I had to pay a pretty penny for my citizenship,' said the tribune.

'But I had it by birth,' said Paul.

Those who were going to interrogate him at once stood away from him; and even the tribune was uneasy when he was aware that he was a Roman citizen, and that he had been responsible for binding him.

The next day, concerned to get at the truth of why Paul was denounced by the Jews, the tribune freed him, and requested the High Priest and the full Sanhedrin to meet, and brought Paul down to confront them. Paul peered at the Sanhedrin and said,

---

* As a sign of mourning for the dead.

'Brothers, I have lived with a perfectly clear conscience before God to this day."

Here the High Priest Ananias* ordered those who stood beside Paul to strike him on the mouth.

Then Paul said to him, 'God will strike you, you white-washed wall.** Do you sit there to judge me in accordance with the Law, and illegally order me to be struck?'

Those who stood beside him cried, 'Do you abuse God's High Priest?'

'I did not know he was the High Priest, brothers,' Paul said, 'for it is stated [*Exod*.xxii.28], "You must not speak evil of the ruler of your people."'

When Paul was aware that one part of the Sanhedrin were Sadducees and that the others were Pharisees, he cried out, 'Brothers, I am a Pharisee of Pharisee stock. I am being judged for the expectation of the resurrection of the dead.'

By saying this he set the Pharisees at loggerheads with the Sadducees, and there was a split in the Assembly. For the Sadducees say there is no resurrection, nor any angel or spirit, while the Pharisees affirm both propositions. A first-class row ensued, with some of the Pharisee scribes hotly contending, 'We find nothing criminal in this man. If a spirit has spoken to him, or an angel ...' The conflict here became so furious that the tribune, afraid lest Paul would get torn to pieces, ordered a company down to extricate him from them and escort him back into the fort ...

When day came, some of the Jews made a compact, and took an oath neither to eat nor drink until they had killed Paul. These going to the High Priest and elders said, 'We have taken a most solemn oath to taste nothing until we have killed Paul. You should therefore, with the Sanhedrin, represent to the tribune that he should bring him down to you as you propose to investigate his case more thoroughly, while we will be in wait to kill him before he reaches here.'

Paul's sister's son, who was close by, heard about the ambush, and went into the fort and informed Paul. Paul then called one of the centurions and said, 'Take this young man to the tribune.

---

* Ananias son of Nedebaeus was murdered by the Jewish revolutionaries in AD 66.
** Possibly just a saying, or it could suggest that Paul, having 'peered' at the Sanhedrin, had only a blurred impression of a splash of white of the white-robed person presiding, suffering as he did from defective vision.

He has something to tell him.' So he took him along to the tribune and said, 'The prisoner Paul sent for me, and asked me to bring this young man to you as he has something to tell you.'

The tribune then took him by the arm, and retiring with him in private enquired, 'What is it that you have to say to me?'

'Some of the Jews,' he said, 'have agreed to ask you to bring Paul down to the Sanhedrin tomorrow as they propose to go into his case more thoroughly. But you must not consent, for more than forty of their men will be lying in wait for him. They have taken an oath not to eat or drink till they have killed him. And now they are in readiness awaiting your assurances.'

The tribune then dismissed the youth, cautioning him 'not to tell a soul what you have disclosed to me.' Next, having summoned two of his centurions, he issued instructions: 'Have two hundred men ready to go to Caesarea, also seventy cavalry and two hundred light infantry, this evening at nine o'clock sharp. And have a baggage train brought round to convey Paul safely to the Governor Felix.' He also wrote a letter to this effect:

'Claudius Lysias presents his compliments to His Excellency the Governor Felix.

'This man had been apprehended by the Jews, and they were about to kill him when I arrived with a force and extricated him. On learning that he was a Roman citizen, and wishing to ascertain the reason he was being accused by them, I brought him down to their Sanhedrin. There I found him to be accused of questions affecting their law, but not of anything meriting death or imprisonment. On information received of there being a plot against this man, I have at once sent him to you, and likewise advised his accusers to lay before you their charges against him.'

Then in accordance with their instructions the soldiers took Paul and escorted him by night to Antipatris. But the next day they returned to the fort, leaving the cavalry to go forward with Paul. On reaching Caesarea they delivered the letter to the governor, and also surrendered Paul to him. When the governor had read the letter he asked Paul from which province he came, and being told that it was Cilicia he said, 'I will hear you as soon as your accusers arrive,' and remanded him in custody in Herod's praetorium.

17
Remand at Caesarea

We continue here to follow the text of the *Acts of the Apostles*, chapters xxiv and xxv. But again we would remind the reader that this source of information is not history but a dressing-up of the historical circumstances with suitably composed speeches for the personalities concerned.

Five days later the High Priest Anaias came down with some of the elders and an advocate Tertullus. These laid information against Paul with the governor.

When Paul had been summoned, Tertullus opened the case for his accusers as follows:

'Thanks to you, Your Excellency Felix, profound peace is our lot, and law and order has been restored to our nation under your wise guidance. This we freely and fully acknowledge with deep gratitude.'

The present author takes leave to break in here to point out that these flattering words, appropriate for the advocate's case, are contrary to the reality of the situation at the time.

The Roman historian Tacitus wrote of Felix: 'He was a man who, from low beginnings, rose to power, and with the true genius of a slave exercised the tyranny of an eastern prince' (*Hist.* Bk.V. 9). In his *Annals* Tacitus said of him: 'Pallas had a brother known by the name of Felix, who had for some time been governor of Judea. This man did not think it necessary to prescribe any restraint on his own desires. He considered his connection with the emperor's favourite as a licence for the worst of crimes... Felix inflamed the discontent of the [Jewish] people by improper remedies; and Ventidius Cumanus, to whom a part of the province was committed, was ready to cooperate in any wicked project' (*Annals* XII.54).

Josephus, the Jewish historian, in his *Jewish Antiquities*, paints a grim picture of Jewish affairs under Felix and his successor Festus, and it is worthy of serious consideration that the author of *Luke–Acts* depended a great deal on the works of Josephus for circumstances and incidents in his own compositions. It is possible that the reference to Jewish Zealots who had vowed to assassinate Paul (see previous chapter) was based on the Jewish *Sicarii* (dagger men) who, as Josephus says of this period, "would mingle at the festivals with the crowd of those who streamed into the city from all directions to worship, and thus easily assassinated any that they pleased" (*Antiq.* XX.187).

We resume here the speech attributed to Tertullus the advocate against Paul.

'In order not to weary you unduly, therefore, I beg for your consideration in putting our case with the utmost brevity.

'We have found this man a plague-carrier, a fomenter of revolt among all the Empire, a ringleader of the Nazarene sect. When we apprehended him he was also attempting to desecrate the Sanctuary, as you can ascertain for yourself by investigating these several charges we bring against him.'

The Jews concurred, affirming that the facts were as stated.

Then, at a nod from the governor, Paul made his reply.

'Knowing that you have had many years' experience in governing our nation, I speak in my own defence with every confidence, since you can ascertain that barely twelve days have elapsed since I went up to worship at Jerusalem. They neither found me in the Sanctuary arguing with anyone, nor haranguing a crowd either in the synagogues, or up and down the city. They can offer no shred of evidence to support the charges they now bring against me.

'I will admit to you that I serve the God of our fathers in accordance with the persuasion, which they term a sect, believing whatever has been recorded in the Law and the Prophets, and having hope in God – which indeed they themselves share – that there will be a resurrection of the just and also of the unjust. Because of this I am personally at pains always to have a clear conscience towards God and man.

'Now after an interval of several years I arrived to make charitable gifts to my nation, and also to offer sacrifices, engaged in which activities some Jews of Asia found me in the Sanctuary

94

when I had undergone purification, with no sign of a crowd or commotion. They should have been here before you to accuse me if there had been anything against me. As they are not, let those who are here speak of what wrong-doing they discovered when I stood before the Sanhedrin, or about the one thing I cried out as I stood among them, "Concerning the resurrection of the dead I am being judged by you today!"'

Here Felix, who had very accurate knowledge of the Way, adjourned the proceedings, saying, 'When Tribune Lysias gets down I will decide your case.'

While instructing the centurion to hold Paul, he was to permit him his liberty, and not to prevent his own people looking after him.

Shortly after this Felix was again in Caesarea with his wife Drusilla, who was a Jewess, and sending for Paul listened to him on the subject of faith in Christ Jesus. As he discoursed about righteousness, self-control and the coming Judgment, Felix became uncomfortable and said, 'You had better go now. When I have time to spare I'll call for you again.'

He rather hoped that Paul would make him a gift of money, which was why he sent for him fairly frequently and conversed with him. But when two years had passed Felix was succeeded by Porcius Festus. Anxious to stand well with the Jews, Felix left Paul still a prisoner.'

Porcius Festus was Roman procurator for the period AD 60-62. What there is no hint of in the *Acts* is why at this juncture Felix should have been recalled by the Emperor Nero. It appears, however, that there had been serious trouble at Caesarea, and the leaders of the Jewish community there had gone to Rome to accuse Felix.

For some time there had been a worsening of relationships between the Jewish and Gentile inhabitants of Caesarea. As I have written elsewhere: 'The Jews contended that they had the precedence, because Caesarea had been created by Herod the Great, while the Syrians asserted that before that there had been no Jewish inhabitants of what had formerly been called Strato's Tower. Mutual abuse led to stone-throwing and the prospect of even more serious strife. Finally Felix intervened with his troops, directing their attack particularly against the Jews as the primary instigators of the conflict. He only desisted when a number of the Jewish citizens of worth and substance begged him to do so. The plea was perhaps accompanied by a considerable financial "sweetener".'

The situation had been so bad in fact that Josephus, who had described it in his *Jewish War*, claimed in his *Antiquities* that the events at Caesarea had 'kindled the flames of war.' When Festus had arrived he was almost immediately embroiled with the Jewish revolutionaries in Judea, and had to send a force against what Josephus calls 'an impostor' who had led a mob into the wilderness 'promising them salvation and rest from troubles.' The Festus of the *Acts*, like Felix, is a very controlled and judicial individual.

There is no hint in the *Acts* of the gravity of Jewish affairs at this juncture, and the culpability of the Roman procurators. The text relates that representations were made to Festus in Jerusalem by the chief priests to have Paul brought back to Jerusalem. But this was refused, and they were told to bring any charges against him at Caesarea. This they did, and the *Acts* continues:

> Festus, anxious to stand well with the Jews, said to Paul, 'Are you willing to go up to Jerusalem to be tried before me there regarding these matters?'
>
> Paul replied, 'I am standing now at Caesar's tribunal, where I should be tried. I have not injured Jews, as you can see quite plainly. If I am at fault and have done something that merits death, I am not trying to beg myself off from dying. But if there is no foundation for these charges they bring against me, no one is entitled to gratify them. I appeal to Caesar.'
>
> Then Festus, after conferring with the Council, answered, 'You have appealed to Caesar. To Caesar you must go.'

18
Paul before Agrippa

There is a final incident reported in the *Acts* before Paul was to make what would prove to be his last journey. This was the courtesy visit to Festus at Caesarea made by Agrippa, king of Chalcis, and his sister Berenice. Agrippa was the son of Agrippa I, former king of Judea, who had died at Caesarea in AD 44 after a very short reign.

The narrative of the *Acts* is now resumed, and is reproduced:

When they had been there a few days Festus broached the subject of Paul to the king. 'We have a man here,' he said, 'left a prisoner by Felix, against whom the head priests and elders made representations to me when I was in Jerusalem. They asked for his condemnation: but I told them it was not customary in the case of Roman citizens to grant an individual such a favour before the accused has had an opportunity to face his accusers and offer his defence to the charge. Consequently, when they came here with me, without any delay I took my seat next day on the tribunal, and ordered the man to be produced. But when his accusers stood forward they did not bring against him a single charge of any of the crimes I had supposed. They only had against him certain questions affecting their own religion, and a certain Jesus who had died, and who Paul affirmed was alive. As I was quite out of my depth with an investigation dealing with such matters, I asked him whether he would go to Jerusalem and be tried there. But when Paul appealed for his case to be reserved for the verdict of Augustus, I ordered his remand until I could send him to Caesar.'

'I should rather like to hear the man myself,' said Agrippa to Festus.

'You shall hear him tomorrow,' he replied.

The next day Agrippa and Berenice came in state, and entered the audience chamber accompanied by the military commander and the city notables. Festus ordered Paul to be brought in.

Festus then spoke. 'King Agrippa, and all who have honoured us with their presence. Here you find a man for whom I have had the whole pack of Jews down on me both in Jerusalem and here, yelping that he ought not to live any longer. But when I was aware that he had really done nothing meriting death, and when he appealed to Augustus, I decided to send him. I find myself, however, with nothing definite to write to our lord. I have therefore brought him before you and especially before you, King Agrippa, so that after this examination I might know what to write; for it seems senseless to me to be sending a prisoner without at the same time specifying the charge against him.'

Then Agrippa said to Paul, 'You have our leave to speak for yourself.'

So Paul extended his arm and began his defence.

'I count myself fortunate, King Agrippa, that it is before you today that I am to answer all the charges Jews have brought against me, particularly because I know you to be so well-versed in all Jewish customs and questions. I beg you, therefore, to accord me a patient hearing.

'With my early life, which was spent entirely among my own nation at Jerusalem, Jews are fully familiar. Being acquainted with my antecedents they could testify, if they would, that I lived in accordance with the strictest sect of our faith as a Pharisee.

'So here I stand trial for that Hope,* which was God's own promise to our fathers, and to which by their devotional zeal night and day our twelve tribes expect to attain. It is for harbouring this very Hope, Sire, that Jews are accusing me. Why should one regard it as incredible that God raises the dead? I used myself to think it necessary to act in the utmost opposition to the authority of Jesus the Nazarene, which moreover I did in Jerusalem, and locked up many of the saints in prison with the warrant I had from the head priests. When they were sent to their death I pressed the vote against them, and had them punished repeatedly in all the synagogues, and compelled them to revile Jesus. Being

---

* The Messianic Hope of the Redemption of Israel and the institution of the Kingdom of God on earth.

mad with them beyond measure, I even hunted them to towns across the border.

'Travelling while so engaged to Damascus, with a warrant and commission from the head priests, I saw, Sire, while on the road at midday, a light from heaven stronger than the sun's glare shining about me and those who accompanied me. We all fell to the ground, and then I heard a voice saying to me in Hebrew, "Saul, Saul, why do you hunt me? You only hurt yourself kicking against the good." "Who are you, lord?" I asked. The Master said, "I am Jesus whom you are hunting. Get up now, and stand on your feet. I have appeared to you personally to take you in training as my assistant, and as witness that you have seen me, and of what I shall make clear to you later. I am setting you apart from your people, and from the Gentiles to whom I am going to send you, to give them the power of distinction, that they may turn from darkness towards the light and from the authority of Satan to God; that they may receive forgiveness of their sins and inheritance with the sanctified by their loyalty to me."

'There could be no question, King Agrippa, of disobeying the heavenly vision, and accordingly, to those in Damascus first, then to the inhabitants of Jerusalem, the whole country of Judea, and afterwards to the Gentiles, I preached repentance and turning to God, and the performance of deeds indicative of repentance. As a consequence the Jews seized me in the Sanctuary and attempted to murder me. Aided, however, by God's providence, I continue to stand – just as I am doing at this moment – witnessing to high and low, uttering no single word beyond what the Prophets foretold would happen, yes, and Moses himself, that the Messiah would suffer, that he would be the first to rise from the dead, and thereafter bring light to our people and to the Gentiles.'

When he had reached this part of his defence, Festus interjected, 'You are raving, Paul! All this study has disturbed your reason.'

'I am not mad, Your Excellency Festus,' Paul rejoined. 'I am speaking plainly matters of fact and sense; for the king, before whom I can express myself freely, well understands these things. I am persuaded that none of them has escaped his notice, for they were not done in a corner.

'King Agrippa, do you believe the Prophets? Of course you do.'

99

Said Agrippa to Paul, 'In next-to-no-time you will be persuading me to turn Christian.'

'I pray God,' Paul replied, 'that whether in next-to-no-time or a long time, not only you but all who hear me today will become as I am, except for these chains.'

Then the king rose, followed by the governor, Berenice, and the assembled company. When they had withdrawn they discussed the matter among themselves. "The man has done nothing,' they agreed, 'to deserve death or imprisonment.'

'He could have been released,' said Agrippa to Festus, 'had he not appealed to Caesar.'

So much for the narrative of the author of the *Acts*. It is of course fictional, though well-contrived, and conveys the period atmosphere. There are errors in what is put into Paul's mouth. For example, that there are any predictions in the Books of Moses relating to the Messiah, and to the effect stated.

But if we had omitted these records we might have been accused of negligence. The author is a very competent and convincing novelist. He sets his scenes well, and where required takes us behind them; and the contrived speeches are broadly in character.

There can be no certainty, however, that what is offered to us rests on any reliable foundation, and as we have already pointed out, the Roman personalities have been whitewashed in order that the references to these dignitaries would give a good impression, favourable to the Roman government, should they come into the hands of the authorities. We have always to bear in mind that when the Christian records were written, Christianity was not a religion licensed by the Romans. On the contrary, the Christians were regarded as revolutionaries and enemies of the Empire. To confess to being a Christian could be grounds for capital punishment.

It is notable that in the New Testament documents the Jews are almost invariably put in the worst possible light. This was not only due to green enmity towards the Jews, but to the circumstances that the Jews in their homeland had revolted against the Romans in AD66, and their fight for freedom had to be suppressed with all the might of the Roman armies, carrying fire and sword to the whole country. The resistance movement continued to be active in various parts of the Roman Empire for decades until a second revolt under Bar Cochba in the next century.

19

The Last Journey

The record of Paul's journey to Rome is contained in the Diary Document which the author of the *Acts* was able to utilise with dramatic effect. It is the longest extract from that source, and so vividly written that we can feel ourselves to be present. The tale is one of courage in disaster, and at the same time presents us with a picture of what life was like in the first century of our era. At the outset we learn that Paul was accompanied by one or more of his friends. He was not strictly a prisoner, since there had been no case made out against him, and he had not been condemned. He was in custody, but could enjoy certain privileges.

When it was decided we should sail for Italy, they entrusted Paul and some other prisoners to a centurion called Julius of the Augustan cohort. Going on board a ship of Adramyttium which was to sail, calling at the Asiatic ports, we put to sea. Aristarchus, a Macedonian of Thessalonica, accompanied us.

The next day but one we touched at Sidon, Julius treating Paul very decently, liberating him on parole to visit his friends to benefit by their attentions. Putting to sea again, we ran under the lee of Cyprus because of adverse winds, and driving on through the sea of Cilicia and Pamphylia we made the port of Myra in Lycia. There our centurion found an Alexandrian boat, bound for Italy, and transferred us to her.

For some days, battling against the wind, we made poor progress, and with difficulty reached a point off Cnidus, and had to sail under the lee of Crete off Cape Salmone. We had a hard job to weather it and reach a place called Fair Havens, next to which was the town of Lasea.

After being held up here for a considerable time, and navigation having become very risky because the Fast Day* had already gone by, Paul advised them: 'Gentlemen, it is my conviction that the voyage will bring strain and stress not only to cargo and vessel but to ourselves as well.' But the centurion preferred to follow the advice of the navigator and the captain rather than Paul's recommendation. The harbour was by nature unsuitable for laying up, so the majority favoured putting to sea again and having a good try to reach and lay up at Phoenix, a harbour of Crete facing south-west and north-west. So when a moderate wind from the south sprang up they weighed anchor, hugging the coast of Crete, thinking they would achieve their object.

But not long after there swept down from the island a violent norther** known as Euraclyon. When it caught the ship, and finding ourselves unable to turn her into the wind, we let her drive along. Running under the lee of a small island called Clauda, we struggled hard to haul in the ship's boat; and when it was aboard they brought into commission their cable supports to undergird the vessel. Then, apprehensive of being thrown on the Syrtis quicksands, they let down sail and drifted.

Next day, as we were in great distress, they cleared the decks, and the day following we threw the ship's gear overboard with our own hands. For days on end neither sun nor stars were visible, while the storm raged with unabated fury and all remaining hope that we should be saved was abandoned.

Then, when food was running short, Paul stood before them and said, 'You should have taken my advice, gentlemen, and never put out from Crete, and let yourselves in for this storm and stress. But as things are now, my advice to you is to take heart, for no one will be lost, only the ship. For last night there stood by me an angel of the God whose I am and whom I serve, saying, "Never fear, Paul, you must stand before Caesar. And see, God has given you all those who sail with you." So courage, gentlemen, for I have faith in God that it will turn out exactly as I have been told. But we are to be cast on an island.'

The fourteenth night of our drift across the Adriatic, around midnight, the sailors had the impression they were approaching land. When they took soundings they found twenty fathoms, and

---

* The Day of Atonement, 10th of the 7th month Tishri of the Jewish year, falling in October.
** Lit. 'a typhonic wind' (typhoon).

sounding again after a short interval they found fifteen fathoms. Fearing we should be cast on a rocky coast, they let go four anchors by the stern, and longed for daylight. But some of the sailors tried to abandon the ship, and they were lowering a boat into the sea, on the pretext that they were going to lay anchors from the bow, when Paul said to the centurion and his men, 'If they don't stay on board there is no chance of your being saved.' Then the soldiers hacked away the boat's hawsers, and let her fall away.

While they waited for daybreak Paul encouraged them to take some food, saying, 'This will be the fourteenth day you have been constantly on the alert, and gone without your meals, never taking a bite. I beg you, therefore, to take some nourishment, for this will contribute to your preservation. In no case will a hair of your heads be lost.' Having said this, he took bread and gave thanks to God before them all, broke it and began to eat. At this they all cheered up and followed his example. All told we were about seventy-six souls on board. Then when they had eaten sufficient food they lightened the ship by throwing out the grain into the sea.

When day came they did not recognize the coast, but they perceived a creek with a sandy shore on which they determined if they could to beach the vessel. Casting off the anchors fore and aft, they left them in the sea, and at the same time loosing the lashings of the rudders and hoisting the foresail to the breeze they held for the shore. Chancing on a place where two seas met, they ran the ship aground. Here the forepart stuck fast and held firm, while the stern went to pieces under the shock.

The soldiers were for killing the prisoners in case any of them should swim off and escape. But the centurion, determined to save Paul, vetoed their suggestion, and ordered those who could swim to jump for it first and get to land, while the rest followed, some on planks and others on any other pieces of the ship that were handy. In this way all came safely to shore.

It was not until we had recovered that we found out that this island was called Melita*. The natives treated us with uncommon civility, for they kindled a fire and made us comfortable because of the drenching and the cold. Paul had been collecting an armful

---

* Now called Malta.

of sticks, and was engaged in laying them on the fire, when a viper drawn out by the heat fastened itself on his hand. Seeing the creature hanging from his hand, the natives said to one another, 'He must be a murderer, whom Justice will not allow to live, even though he has safely escaped the sea.' However, he shook off the creature into the fire and suffered no ill effects, though they fully expected him to swell up or suddenly drop dead. After waiting for some time and seeing nothing out of the ordinary happen to him, they changed their minds and said he must be a god.

Hereabouts was the estate of the chief commissioner of the island, called Publius, who received us and very kindly provided lodging for three days. The father of Publius was laid up with an attack of fever and dysentery. Paul went to his room, and after praying laid his hands on him and cured him. The consequence was that others on the island who had ailments came and were cured. They not only loaded us with handsome presents, but furnished the requisite stores.

Three months later we embarked on an Alexandrian ship displaying the emblem of the Dioscuri that had wintered at the island. Putting in at Syracuse we stayed there three days, and from there by tacking we reached Rhegium. A day later we had the advantage of a south wind which wafted us in two more days to Puteoli, where we found brothers who invited us to spend a week with them.

And so we came to Rome. From there the brothers, who had heard all about us, had come to meet us as far as Market Appii and Three Taverns, and Paul when he saw them thanked God and took courage. When we had entered Rome Paul was allowed to occupy a private lodging with the soldier who acted as guard.

It would appear that the quotation from the Diary Document ends at this point; but it is possible that the remaining passage in the *Acts* may rest on its information.

According to the *Acts*, Paul sent for the heads of the local Jewish community, and later spoke to them about the Messiahship of Jesus. But the language put into Paul's mouth was clearly the work of a Gentile, for he makes Paul speak of 'the Jews' instead of specifying the particular Jewish authorities, and to say, 'Rightly did the holy Spirit say to *your* fathers by the Prophet Isaiah,' etc.

The *Acts* concludes: 'Paul resided two full years in his own rented apartment, and welcomed all who visited him there, proclaiming the Kingdom of God, and teaching all about the Lord Jesus Christ with unrestricted freedom of speech.' Nothing is reported of the hearing of his case by the Emperor Nero, if it ever took place, or of the outcome.

20

The End

Judging by the time indications in the *Acts*, Paul would have reached Rome early in AD62, and if he remained under house arrest there for two years this would bring us to the year 64. In the interval he had not been inactive, receiving visitors and communicating by letter with some of the communities he had founded. It is from some of the letters that we gain an insight into his circumstances and anticipations, and also his concern for the spiritual and moral welfare of these communities. Paul's letters are given in full in the second part of this work; but we must quote here passages from those which were written from Rome.

Writing to the Christian communities in Asia Minor, Paul was anxious to stress that for which he had so long contended, that Gentiles who had accepted Jesus as the Messiah of Israel had ceased to be Gentiles, and had become part of Israel. I quote from the Ephesian copy:

> So bear in mind that you were once Gentiles in the physical sense, who are termed the Uncircumcision by those termed in respect of an operation in the flesh the Circumcision, because at that time you were without benefit of Christ [i.e. the Messiah], aliens to the body politic of Israel, and strangers to the covenants of promise. But now in Christ Jesus you who were once far off have been brought near by the blood of Christ... So now you are no longer strangers and foreigners, but fellow-citizens of the saints, parts of God's house... To this end I, Paul, am the prisoner of Jesus for you Gentiles... You are no longer to behave as the Gentiles behave in the levity of their minds.*

---

* See p.208f., *Eph*.ii.11-13, and 19; also *Eph*.iii.1 and iv.17.

There is a special letter to the community at Philippi, who had sent gifts to Paul by the hand of Epaphroditus. Whether he really believed it or not, he was anxious to assure the community that he expected to be set at liberty and return to them:

Now I want to tell you, brothers, that my circumstances have rather tended to the advancement of the News; for my fetters have publicised Christ to the whole praetorium and everywhere else. The majority of the brothers, having been fired with confidence in the Master by my fetters, have become much more venturesome, giving out God's Message fearlessly. Some of course do it out of envy and rivalry, but others proclaim Christ from good-will. These do it out of regard ... while the former, who are not well-intentioned, announce Christ in a factious spirit trying deliberately to make trouble for me in my fettered state.

What does it matter? The main thing is that, whether in pretence or sincerity, Christ is proclaimed. For this I rejoice. But there is greater joy in store; for I know that this will be the salvation of me thanks to your prayers ... with the earnest hope and expectation I have that I shall in no way be put to shame ... It is useful to me to live, and an advantage to die. But if I am to live physically it means an effort on my part. I am in a quandary between the two, having the longing to depart and be with Christ, for that would be so much better, yet on the other hand to remain in the flesh is more essential for you. Finally convinced of this, I know I am to remain and be at the side of all of you for your advancement and joyfulness in faith, that your exultation in Christ Jesus may abound by me through my reappearance among you.*

The letter was taken back to Philippi by Epaphroditus, who had been seriously ill in Rome, who had fretted 'because you had heard that he was ailing. Indeed he was ailing, almost at death's door. But God took pity on him, and not only on him but on me too that I should not have one distress upon another. So I have sent him more expeditiously, that in seeing him again you may have joy, and I less sorrow. Give him, therefore, a joyful welcome in the Master, and hold such as he in high regard, for in doing the Master's work he came so near death, jeopardizing his life to make good your lack of opportunity to serve me.'

---

* See pp.201-202, *Phil*.i.12-26.

To the community at Colossae Paul wrote:

I rejoice in my sufferings for your sake, and make good in my flesh the deficiencies of the Messianic Woes, for the sake of Christ's Body, namely the Community, of which I was made a minister... As to my affairs, Tychicus, that dear brother and loyal minister and fellow-servant in the Master, will fully inform you. I have dispatched him to you for this express purpose, that you may know how I fare and that he may cheer your hearts, and with him faithful and dear brother Onesimus, who is one of yourselves. They will tell you of all that goes on here.

My fellow-prisoner Aristarchus sends you his regards, as does Barnabas's kinsman Mark (about whom you have been advised: welcome him should he visit you) and so does Jesus, known as Justus. They belong to the Circumcision, and they alone have been my co-workers for the Kingdom of God: they have been a great comfort to me. Epaphras, one of yourselves, a servant of Christ Jesus, sends you his regards. Invariably he contends for you at prayer times that you may stand, sound and fully assured, by the whole will of God. I can testify that he has put up a great fight for you, and for those of Laodicea and Hierapolis. Dear Doctor Luke sends you his regards, and so does Demas.

Give my regards to the brothers at Laodicea, also to Nympha and the community in her house. When this letter has been read by you arrange also for it to be read in the Laodicean community, and get their letter from Laodicea, that you too may read it. And tell Archippus, 'See to it that you carry out the ministry you have received in the Master!'

My regards in my own hand,

PAUL.

Remember my fetters! Wishing you every happiness.

We notice in this letter that Paul had become reconciled to Mark, who had deserted him when at the beginning of his missionary activities he had started to preach to Gentiles. Paul also refers to Onesimus, who had run away from his master Philemon and had come to Paul in Rome. Paul sent Philemon a deeply moving letter about Onesimus:

Out of affection I prefer to appeal to you, being such as I am, that old man Paul, and also at present a prisoner of Jesus Christ. It is for a son of mine I appeal to you, one whom I have begotten in my bonds, Onesimus, who was previously worthless to you, but now is of very real worth both to you and me. I have sent him back to you, which means that I have parted with my own heart. I would much rather have kept him with me, so that he might have served me instead of you in the bonds of the News; but I did not wish to do anything without your assent, in case your kindness might seem an obligation instead of being voluntary. Perhaps the reason he was parted from you for a while may be that you might have him wholly ever after, no longer as just a slave, but over and above a slave, as a dear brother, particularly to me, but how much more so to you with a physical tie as well as in the Master.

In the second part of this work we give a translation of the letter in full, in which again Paul anticipates his own release. But it was not to be.

Of special note are the two letters Paul sent to Timotheus, whom he regarded as his adopted son. These are full of wise counsel. But of special interest, because of subsequent Christian doctrine, is the repetition of Paul's monotheism. Invariably he distinguished Christ from God.

In Paul's first letter to Timotheus he states: 'There is One God, and one intermediary between God and mankind, the Man Jesus Christ' (ii.5). And later: 'I charge you before God and Christ Jesus and the elect Angels to maintain these principles without prejudice' (v.22). In the second letter Paul says: 'Always remember, Jesus Christ of the lineage of David was raised from the dead in my presentation of the News' (ii.8). And further: 'I charge you before God, and before Christ Jesus, who will judge the living and the dead; and in view of his visible appearing and reign, proclaim the Message' (iv.1-2). There is nothing trinitarian here.

It is from Paul's second letter to Timotheus that we learn all that we can positively of Paul's last months. Evidently he had appeared once before the Emperor Nero; but the result was inconclusive, and he was remanded. He could not from prison state plainly what had taken place, because the letter would have been read by the authorities. He faced now the certainty that finally he would be executed. He is writing in the autumn of AD 63, since he is asking for his winter coat.

We quote:

Do your utmost to come to me quickly, for Demas, loving the

present world, has deserted me and gone off to Thessalonica, Crescens has gone to Gaul, Titus to Dalmatia. Only Luke remains with me. Pick up Mark and bring him with you, for he is valuable to me in administrative work, and I have dispatched Tychicus to Ephesus. When you come bring the heavy jacket I left Carpus at Troas, also the books, particularly the parchments. Alexander the blacksmith has shown himself very ill-disposed towards me. The Lord will requite him in accordance with his actions. Watch out for him yourself, for he is strongly opposed to our views. At the first hearing of my defence no one supported me: everyone deserted me. May it not be counted against them! But my Master supported and strengthened me; so that through me the proclamation might ring out, and all the Gentiles might hear it; and I was 'saved from the jaws of the lion.' The Lord will continue to rescue me from every evil agency and preserve me for his heavenly kingdom. To him be glory for ever, and ever. Amen... Do your utmost to come to me before winter sets in.

Earlier in this letter he had spoken more positively of his approaching end. 'I am now on the eve of peace, and the time for my discharge is approaching. I have fought a gallant contest: I have completed the course; I have kept the Faith. There remains in store for me the crown to which I am entitled, which the Master, that honourable judge, will award me on that Day.'

The crackling flames of the Great Fire of Rome in July AD 64, which the Christians were accused of starting, burned away all certainty of how and when Paul met his death. A late tradition has it that he was beheaded not far from the Ostian Way, about two miles outside the city.

Part Two

THE LETTERS

Oxyrhynchus 2157. Fragment containing part of Galatians i. Fourth century.
Photograph courtesy of the Egypt Exploration Society.

INTRODUCTION

The letters of Paul represent the oldest documentary material in the New Testament, and therefore they have a special importance. All of them were written in the middle period of the first century AD, approximately between 51 and 63.

Since the letters were penned from various places to communities of believers in different parts of the Roman Empire, mainly in Asia Minor, they had to be collected subsequent to Paul's death. There is an indication in one letter* that Paul favoured the exchange of his letters between communities, so some would have more than one of them. It is not known how complete the collection is, but we have reference to a letter to the community at Laodicea which is not extant, and also to forged letters in the name of Paul.

The priority and spiritual value of the Pauline correspondence lent them a special status, so that the author of the document known as the *Second Letter of Peter* could say to Christians in Asia: 'Consequently, dear friends... Let us be anxious to be found by him [Jesus] in peace, spotless and unblemished... Our dear brother Paul, according to the wisdom given him, has also written to you to the same effect, as indeed is true of all his letters where he speaks of these matters, letters in which there are certain things by no means easy to understand, which the unskilled and unstable twist to their own ruination as they do the rest of the Scriptures' (*II.Pet*.iii.14-16).

In this presentation of the letters of Paul, unlike the New Testament arrangement, they are presented in chronological order with the approximate dates, which is what we would expect. To achieve this we are almost entirely dependent on the *Acts*, which, though later in date of composition, provides a connected narrative of Paul's life and movements. Archaeological discoveries and various ancient histories have pin-pointed the time of certain episodes. The *Acts*, of course, because its author is seeking to tone down Paul's conflict with the Nazorean authorities at Jerusalem, modifies internal relationships, while Paul's letters, written in the heat of the moment in some instances, are much cruder, for example the letter *To the Communities of Galatia.*

Further, to aid the reader the letters have been arranged in two series, the first covering Paul's activities when he was free to

---

*See *Col.* iv.16, p.219

113

travel, and the second when he was a prisoner in Rome. There is a certain difference of style in some of the later letters, and even vocabulary, but these may be accounted for partly by Paul's circumstances and the available scribal help. Paul had to dictate because of his bad eyesight.

A special case is represented by the letters to the community at Corinth. In the Bible they are given as two letters, whereas as I explain, they actually relate to four letters. Throughout *Part Two* I have furnished notes and references whenever necessary. The reader will be aware that the biblical arrangement of the text in chapters and verses for convenience of reference and Bible study are relatively modern. They do not appear in the ancient manuscripts.*

---

* There was no numbering at all in the first edition of Schonfield's translation of the New Testament, *The Authentic New Testament* (1955). By way of compromise, and for ease of reference, the publishers have in this edition included chapter numbering as commonly given in the New Testament, printed in bold, and have placed the appropriate verse number at the beginning of each paragraph.

Series One:

LETTERS ON ACTIVE SERVICE

To the Community at Thessalonica (1)

(Probably written from Corinth about AD 51)

1.1   Paul, Silvanus and Timotheus, to the community of Thessalonians
in God the Father and the Lord Jesus Christ. May peace and
prosperity be yours.

We invariably thank God for all of you, making mention of you in our
prayers, continually remembering in the presence of God our Father
the intensity of your faith, the ardour of your love, and the constancy
of your hope in the Lord Jesus Christ.

4   I[1] know, brothers dear to God, how truly chosen you are, because
my News came to you not merely with speech, but with power, with
inspiration, and with strong conviction; even as *you* know the kind of
man I was with you for your sakes. You became imitators of me, and
of the Master, welcoming the Message in circumstances of great
difficulty with fervent joy,[2] so that you became an example to all the
believers in Macedonia and Achaia. For from you the Master's Message resounded not only throughout Macedonia and Achaia, but indeed
far and wide your faith in God has penetrated, so that there is no need
for me to speak of it. The people of those parts themselves tell of the
effect of my visit to you, how you turned from idols to serve the Living and True God, and to await his Son from heaven, whom he raised
from the dead, Jesus our rescuer from the coming Wrath.

2.1   You yourselves know, brothers, that my visit to you was by no means
ineffective. Though I had previously suffered and been ill-treated, as
you are aware, at Philippi,[3] I made bold in God with a great effort to
give you God's News.[4] My appeal to you was without imposture or
impure motives, neither did I use guile. I spoke as one approved by
God as worthy to be entrusted with the News, not as one who seeks to
please men, but God who tries my heart.[5] For I was never in speech a
flatterer, as you know, nor one with covetous designs, God is my
witness, nor one who seeks human commendation, neither from you
nor anyone else, though entitled to be of consequence as an envoy of

Christ. Rather was I very tender with you, as if I were a foster-mother nursing her own children. Thus yearning over you, I was delighted to impart to you, not only God's News but my very life, so dear had you become to me.

9   Only call to mind, brothers, my toil and drudgery. Night and day I laboured so as not to be a burden to you in any way while proclaiming God's News. You are witnesses, and God also, how correctly, honourably and blamelessly I acted towards you believers, just as you know how I exhorted, encouraged and charged every single one of you, as a father his own children, to behave worthy of God who has invited you to share his sovereignty and state.

13   I do indeed thank God constantly for this, that on acceptance of God's Message as you heard it from me, you welcomed it not as a human message, but for what it truly is – God's Message, which is certainly operative in you believers. For, brothers, you became counterparts of the communities of God in Judea which are in Christ Jesus; for you yourselves have suffered similarly from your own countrymen as they from the Judeans, who put to death the Lord Jesus and the Prophets, and hounded me out, who incur God's displeasure, setting themselves against everyone, hindering me from speaking to the Gentiles that they might be saved and so filling up in every way the measure of their sins. Thus, 'Wrath to the full has fallen on them.'[6]

17   But though separated from you for a while, brothers, in presence not in mind, I have been exceedingly anxious and greatly longing to see your faces. Consequently I, Paul, wanted personally to visit you time and again, but Satan put difficulties in my way. For what, if not you, is my hope or joy or proud crown in the presence of our Lord Jesus at his coming? It is you who are my glory and my joy!

3.1   So when I could bear it no longer, I was content to be left at Athens alone, while I sent Timotheus, our brother and God's agent for the News of Christ, to sustain and encourage you in your faith, that none of you should wilt under these trials. You know yourselves that we are put here for this purpose; and further when I was with you I forewarned you, as you know, "we are bound to have trouble", exactly as it turned out. So, as I say, being unable to bear it any longer, I sent to learn the state of your faith, in case the Tempter had tempted you, and my toil had been in vain.

6   But now, when Timotheus returned to me from visiting you, and gave me the good news of your loyalty and love, and that you always have a pleasant recollection of me and long to see me, as I to see you,

this consoled me as far as you are concerned for all my anguish and distress. Now indeed I live again, since you stand fast in the Master. How can I sufficiently thank God on your account for all the happiness I enjoy because of you in the presence of our God! Night and day I supplicate beyond all bounds that I may be permitted to see your faces and make good any deficiencies in your faith. May God himself, our Father, and our Lord Jesus make it practicable for me to come to you!

12 The Lord make you increase and abound in love for one another and for all others, as my love goes out to you, so as to lift up your hearts blameless in holiness in the presence of God our Father at the coming of our Lord Jesus with all his saints.

4.1 Further, brothers, I entreat and appeal to you in the Lord Jesus, that as you have received from me the manner in which you should conduct yourselves and be pleasing to God – as indeed you do conduct yourselves – so should you do better still. You know that I gave you certain instructions on behalf of the Lord Jesus. Doing the will of God implies your consecration, that you keep clear of immorality, that each of you knows how to possess his own mate[7] in purity and with respect; not swayed by lust like the Gentiles who do not know God,[8] that there be no meddling with or coveting what belongs to your brother; for the Lord will avenge anything of that sort as I warned and solemnly told you. God has not called us to impurity but to consecration. Accordingly, whoever disregards this breaks faith not with men but with God, who has given us his Spirit which is holy.

9 As regards brotherly affection there is no need for me to write to you, for you yourselves are taught by God to love one another; and you do indeed practise it towards all the brothers throughout Macedonia. But I appeal to you, brothers, to do better still, and to make a real effort to be quiet and attend to your own business. Labour with your hands, as I have instructed you, and that you may comport yourselves with dignity towards those outside,[9] and require no one's assistance.[10]

13 Now I do not want you to be ignorant, brothers, about those who are laid to rest, that you do not grieve like those who are without hope. For if we believe that Jesus died and rose again, so do we also that God, by means of Jesus, will bring back those who are laid to rest. I tell you this by the word of the Lord, that we who are alive and survive till the coming of the Master will not forestall those who are laid to rest. The Master will himself descend from heaven with a cry of

119

command, with archangelic voice and divine trumpet blast, and the dead in Christ will rise first. Next we who are alive and survive will be caught up with them by clouds to meet the Master in the air; and so shall we be ever with the Master. Cheer one another, therefore, with this information.

5.1   As regards dates and times, brothers, there is no need for me to write to you, for you yourselves know perfectly well that the Day of the Lord will come like a thief in the night.[11] Just when they are saying, "A peaceful night, and all's well", then suddenly destruction will be upon them like pangs on a pregnant woman, and they will have no chance of escape.[12] But you, brothers, are not in darkness, that the Day should catch you like a thief; for all of you are Children of the Light[13] and beings of the day. We do not belong to the night or to darkness.

6   Well then, let us not slumber like others, but be wakeful and sober. For those who slumber slumber at night, and those who are drunkards are drunk at night. But let us who belong to the day be sober, clad in the corselet of faith and love, and helmeted with the hope of deliverance. For God has not destined us to Wrath, but to be preserved for Deliverance by our Lord Jesus Christ, who died for us, that at once – whether awake or sleeping – we should be alive with him. So encourage one another and fortify each other, as indeed you are doing.

12   But I do beg you, brothers, to acknowledge those who work so hard among you and act as your leaders in the Master, and advise you. Hold them in extra-special affection for their work. Be at peace among yourselves.

14   I appeal to you, brothers, give fair warning to the disorderly, encourage the faint-hearted, stand by the weak, be patient with all. See to it that none renders to any injury for injury, but always do the right thing by each other and everyone else. Always be cheerful, pray constantly, give thanks for everything; for this is God's will in Christ for you. Do not still the Spirit, or scorn prophesies. Test everything: retain the good.[14] Refrain from anything that looks at all wrong.

23   Now may the God of peace himself sanctify you completely, and may you in your entirety, spirit, soul and body, be kept blameless till the coming of the Lord Jesus Christ. He who calls you is faithful, who indeed will accomplish this. Brothers, pray for us also.

26   Convey our regards to all the brothers with a chaste kiss. I adjure you by the Lord to have this letter read to all the brothers. The loving-kindness of our Lord Jesus Christ be with you.

NOTES AND REFERENCES

1. Paul uses the first person plural out of courtesy to his associates. But here and in his other letters the singular has been substituted where Paul's personal views and experiences are referred to.
2. Lit. 'joy of holy Spirit'.
3. See above p. 52-53 (*Acts*.xvi.12-40).
4. See above p. 53 (*Acts*.xvii.1-10).
5. Cf. *Prov*.xvii.3.
6. From *Testaments of the XII Patriarchs* (*Test.Levi* vi.11).
7. Or 'his own person'.
8. Cf. *Ps*.lxxix.6.
9. People in general.
10. Some believers, expecting the speedy return of Jesus, were neglecting employment. See also the second letter to the Thessalonians.
11. Cf. *Matthew* xxiv.43.
12. See *Joel* ii.1-11.
13. An expression favoured by the Essenes, contrasting the Children of Light with the Children of Darkness (see *Manual of Discipline*).
14. A saying of Jesus quoted in the Patristic literature was: 'Become skilled money-changers, rejecting some things, but retaining what is good.'

To the Community at Thessalonica (2)

(Probably written from Corinth about AD 52)

1.1   Paul, Silvanus and Timotheus, to the community of Thessalonians in God our Father and the Lord Jesus Christ. May peace and prosperity be yours from God the Father and the Lord Jesus Christ.

3   We are bound invariably to thank God for you, brothers, as it is only right, because your faith is so wonderfully increasing, and the love of each and all of you for one another is ever deepening; so that we ourselves boast of you in the communities of God, of your constancy and loyalty in all the persecutions and trials with which you have had to contend.

5   This is evidence of God's strict justice, in having treated you as worthy of the Kingdom of God, for which indeed you suffer. For that being so, it becomes just on God's part to repay affliction to those who afflict you, and to give you who are afflicted relief with us when the Lord Jesus is revealed from heaven with his mighty angels with flaming fire, inflicting retribution on those who do not acknowledge God and do not respond to the News of our Lord Jesus.[1] They shall pay the penalty of perpetual exclusion from the presence of the Master, and the splendour of his majesty, when he comes at that time to be praised by his saints and admired by all who have believed because our testimony to you was believed. To this end we invariably pray for you, that our God may make you worthy of your vocation, and enable you to accomplish every praiseworthy object and devoted deed which may serve to glorify the name of our Lord Jesus among you, and you in him, by the loving-kindness of our God and the Lord Jesus Christ.

2.1   Now I beg you, brothers, as regards the coming of our Lord Jesus Christ and our being gathered to him, not to take speedy leave of your senses or become agitated, either by a spirit intimation, or by a speech, or by any letter purporting to be from me, under the impression that the Day of the Lord has begun. Let no one deceive you in any way whatever; for it will not begin before the Defection has first taken place and the Lawless Man has been revealed, the Doomed One who opposes, and elevates himself above everything regarded as a god or as an object of worship, so that he himself sits in God's Temple claiming to be God.[2] Do you not recall that this is what I told you while I was still with you?

6   So now you know what is the retarding factor, that the Lawless One may be revealed at his proper time. Indeed, the process[3] of lawlessness is already at work, only there is one who is a retarding factor until his removal. And then the Lawless One will be revealed, whom the Lord Jesus will consume with the breath of his mouth and annihilate with the radiance of his presence,[4] that one whose coming is attended, in the way Satan works, by every kind of mendacious trickery practised on those who are perishing, because they have not welcomed the love of truth so as to be spared. For that reason God will send them a spirit of delusion so as to believe the lie, that all may be condemned who have not credited truth, but have taken pleasure in falsehood.

13   But I am bound invariably to thank God for you, brothers dear to the Master, because God has chosen you from the very beginning for deliverance, for the acquistion of the glory of our Lord Jesus Christ, by that consecration of spirit and attachment to truth to which he called you by my News. So then, brothers, stand fast, and keep a firm hold on the traditions you have been taught whether by my speech or correspondence.

16   May our Master himself, Jesus Christ, and God our Father, who has loved us and graciously granted us solid consolation and good hope, encourage and confirm your minds by every fair word and deed!

3.1   Finally, brothers, pray for me, that the word of the Lord may speed and be honoured as in your case, and that I may be delivered from inhuman and wicked men;[5] for faith is not found in everyone. But the Lord is faithful, and will establish you and shield you from harm. I have confidence in you in the Master, that you are following and will continue to follow my injunctions. The Lord direct your minds to the love of God and the constancy of Christ!

6   But in the name of the Lord Jesus Christ, brothers, I bid you shun every brother who behaves as a shirker, and not in accordance with the tradition you have received from me. You are well aware that you

ought to copy me; for I was no shirker among you, neither did I accept free meals from anyone.[6] Rather with toil and hardship did I labour night and day so as not to be a burden to you in any way. Not that I have not the right; but that I personally should set you an example, so that you should copy me. That is why when I was with you I gave you this order, 'He who will not work, neither shall he eat.' For I hear there are some among you behaving as shirkers, not busy but busybodies. I order and exhort such as these in the Lord Jesus Christ, that going quietly about their work they eat their own bread.

13   As for you, brothers, never hesitate to do the right thing; but if anyone pays no attention to what I say in this letter, mark that man, and have nothing to do with him, that he may be ashamed. Yet do not treat him as an enemy, but warn him as a brother.

16   Now may the Lord of peace himself give you peace always in all circumstances![7] The Lord be with you all.

17   The greeting I subjoin in my own, Paul's, hand. It is the mark of authenticity in every letter.[8] This is how I write. *The loving-kindness of the Lord Jesus Christ be with you all.*[9]

NOTES AND REFERENCES

1. Cf. The Essene *Damascus Rule*, ii.4: 'And power and might and great fury with flames of fire – all the angels of destruction – for those who turned aside from the Way and abhorred the statute.'
2. The Devil incarnate of apocalyptic thought. The Emperor Gaius Caligula (AD 40) tried to set up his statue as a god in the Temple at Jerusalem.
3. Lit. 'mystery'.
4. Cf. *Isa*.xi.4; *Mt*.xxiv.27.
5. A Jewish morning prayer supplicated God for 'deliverance from arrogant and wicked men.'
6. Lit. 'Neither did I eat anyone's bread for nothing.'
7. See the Aaronic Benediction, *Num*.vi.26.
8. As is evident from these words, and an earlier reference in the letter, at least one forged letter in the name of Paul was in existence at this time, and had perhaps reached the Thessalonians. The practice was common in those days, and much early Christian material, including certain parts of the New Testament, are forgeries. In this instance, the Nazarene 'Zealots for the Law' were no doubt responsible. These did all they could to turn Paul's converts against him, with considerable success, and did not scruple to pervert his teaching. See *Rom*.iii.8.
9. The words italicised were added by Paul in his own handwriting with his signature. He suffered from bad eyesight, and therefore had to dictate his letters, since otherwise they would have been largely illegible.

To the Communities of Galatia

(Probably written from Antioch in the early summer of AD 53)[1]

1.1　Paul the envoy – not from any body of men or appointed by any man, but by Jesus Christ and God the Father who raised him from the dead – and all the brothers who are with me, to the communities of Galatia. May peace and prosperity be yours from God our Father and the Lord Jesus Christ, who gave himself for our sins to reclaim us from the present evil world in accordance with the will of our God and Father, to whom be praise for evermore.[2] Amen.

6　I am amazed that you have so quickly turned your backs on the one who called you in Christ's mercy for some other version of the News. It is not really another, but there are certain people who are confusing you and want to alter the terms of the News of Christ. But even should I, or an angel from heaven, proclaim to you anything different to what I did proclaim to you, cursed be he! Having said that, I am going to repeat it. If anyone proclaims to you anything different to what you received, cursed be he!

10　Is it men I have to satisfy, or is it God? Or is it men I am trying to please? If I were still pleasing men I should be no servant of Christ. I must make it clear to you, brothers, that the News as proclaimed by me is no human contrivance, for I neither obtained it from anyone, nor was I taught it: it came through Jesus Christ's own revelation.

13　You have heard, of course, of my behaviour when I practised Judaism,[3] how I ruthlessly hounded down God's Community and ravaged it, and how I advanced in Judaism far beyond many students of my own age; for none was more keenly enthusiastic than I to master the traditions of my ancestors. But when it pleased God, who separated me from my mother's womb and called me by his mercy, to reveal his Son to me that I should proclaim him to the Gentiles, I did not take immediate steps to consult any earthly authority, neither did I go up to Jerusalem to interview those who were envoys before me. Instead I went away to Arabia, and returned again to Damascus.

Not until three years had elapsed did I go up to Jerusalem to report to Cephas,[4] and I remained with him fifteen days. But I met none of the other envoys except James the Master's brother.[5] These are the facts I am giving you. Before God, I am telling no lie!

21   After that I went to the regions of Syria and Cilicia, and remained unknown by sight to the Nazorean communities of Judea. They only heard that 'he who formerly persecuted us now proclaims the conviction he once attacked', and they praised God for me.

2.1   After that, some fourteen years later, I again went up to Jerusalem with Barnabas, and also took Titus with me. I went there by a revelation and reported to them the terms of the News I proclaim to the Gentiles. This was privately to those of repute, in case I should strive or had been striving to no purpose. But there was no forcing of Titus, who accompanied me, to be circumcised, Greek though he was, despite the infiltrated false brothers who had crept in to spy out the liberty we enjoy in Christ Jesus in order to enslave us. Not for an instant did we strike our colours, so that the true character of the News might be preserved for you.

6   As for those of repute – whatever they were makes no difference to me: God takes no one at face value – they imposed on me nothing additional. Quite the contrary. When they saw that I had been entrusted with the News for the Uncircumcised, as Peter for the Circumcised – for he who stimulated Peter to envoyship of the Circumcised stimulated me also in going to the Gentiles – and when they realized the privilege that had been granted me, then James, Cephas and John, the reputed 'Pillars', extended to myself and Barnabas the right hand of fellowship. We were to go to the Gentiles, they to the Circumcised.[6] Oh yes, they did add one more thing, we were to remember the poor,[7] which personally I was only too ready to do.

11   So when Cephas came to Antioch I opposed him publicly, because he deserved censure. Before certain persons came from James he had eaten with Gentiles. But after their arrival he drew back and separated himself out of fear of those of the Circumcision. The other Jews played up to him, so that even Barnabas was carried away by their hypocrisy.

14   So when I saw that they were not acting in conformity with the true character of the News, I said to Peter in front of them all, 'If you, a born Jew, live like a Gentile, why do you force the Gentiles to keep Jewish ways? We who are of Jewish race and not Gentile sinners,[8] knowing that no one is exonerated by following regulations but by faith in Jesus Christ, even we have trusted in Jesus Christ

so as to be exonerated by faith in Christ and not by following regulations; for by following regulations "not a single human being will be exonerated."[9] But if, while seeking to be exonerated in Christ, we ourselves are found to be sinners, does that make Christ sin's agent? God forbid! So if I rebuild what I have demolished it is I who become a transgressor of my own accord. For in law I have died in the legal sense, so as to live in the divine sense. I have shared Christ's crucifixion. I am alive, it is true, but strictly speaking it is not I who live, but Christ who lives in me. My present physical existence is by virtue of the life of God's Son, who loved me and gave himself for me. I am not going to be the one to refuse God's mercy. For if rectitude could be assured by law then Christ died in vain.'

3.1   You senseless Galatians, who has cast a spell over you, you before whose gaze Jesus Christ was publicly displayed[10] as crucified? I only wish to know this from you, did you receive the Spirit by following regulations or by the response of faith? Are you so senseless, that having made a start spiritually you are now going to end up physically? Have you experienced so much to no purpose – if it is to no purpose? Does he who mediates the Spirit to you, and effects miracles among you, do it by following regulations or by the response of faith, just as Abraham 'believed God, and it was accounted to him as rectitude'?[11]

7   Observe, then, that it is those with faith who are the children of Abraham. And the Scriptures, foreseeing that God would exonerate the Gentiles by faith, proclaimed in advance the News to Abraham, 'in you shall all the nations be blessed'.[12] So it is those with faith who are blessed along with believing Abraham. All those who follow regulations are under a curse, for it is stated, 'Cursed is everyone who does not adhere to and observe all the precepts set down in the Code of Law.'[13]

11   Thus it is evident that no one is exonerated before God by law, because 'the just shall live *by faith*.'[14] But the Law is not 'by faith': it stipulates that 'he who keeps the commandments shall live by them.'[15] Christ has released us from the Law's curse by becoming a curse on our behalf, for it is stated, 'Cursed is everyone hanged on a tree',[16] so that Abraham's blessing might come to the Gentiles by Jesus Christ, that we all should receive the promise of the Spirit *by faith*.

15   Brothers, I speak in human terms; even in human practice a covenant once ratified cannot be set aside or amended. The undertakings were clearly given to Abraham 'and to his seed.'[17] It does not say 'and to seeds', implying a number, but distinctly one, 'and to your seed', that is to say 'to Christ.'[18] So I say this, that the Law which came into

force four hundred and thirty years later[19] cannot abrogate the covenant previously ratified by God so as to nullify the promise; and God wanted to show his appreciation to Abraham by making a promise.

19   Why then was the Law given? It was introduced to deal with infringements until such time as the promised Seed should come, drawn up in due form by angels acting through a spokesman.[20] Since, however, a spokesman does not act for *one*, while God is ONE, does that mean that the Law is at variance with God's undertakings? God forbid! Certainly if a law could have been given capable of conferring life, then rectitude would have been by law. As it is, the Scripture classes all together as sinners, that the promise by faith in Jesus Christ might be granted to those who believe.[21]

23   Before faith came we were under law's strict tutelage: we were classmates until the future faith should be revealed. Consequently, the Law was our disciplinarian till Christ came, so that we should be exonerated by faith. Now that faith has come we are no longer under a disciplinarian. You are all Sons of God by faith in Jesus Christ; for those who have been identified with Christ by immersion have assumed Christ's personality. It is impossible for there to be Jew or Greek, slave or freeman, male or female;[22] for in Jesus Christ you are all one and the same person. If you are *in* Christ you *are* 'the Seed of Abraham', heirs in accordance with the promise.

4.1   What I am saying is this, that so long as the heir is under age, though he is actually master of the estate, his position hardly differs from that of a slave: he remains under supervisors and managers until the time fixed by his father. So it is with us. We too were under age, in subjection to the elemental forces of the universe. Then, when the set time had arrived, God sent out his Son, born of a woman, born under law,[23] that those under law might be redeemed, that we might receive adoption as sons. And because you are now sons, God has sent his Son's spirit into our hearts, crying, '*Abba*!'(Father!). Thus no longer is it a slave crying, but a son, and if a son, then by God's providence an heir also.

8   There was a time when not knowing God you were enslaved to those who in reality are no gods. But now acknowledging God, or rather being acknowledged by God, how comes it that you have turned back to the feeble and abject elemental forces? Do you intend to be enslaved to them all over again? You have begun to observe special days and months, seasons and years. I begin to fear for you that I may have been wearing myself out for you to no purpose.

12   Do become as I am, that I in turn may be as you are, I do entreat

you. I assure you that you have not wronged me. You well know how through physical infirmity I proclaimed the News to you originally. But the temptation afforded you by my physical condition did not induce you to mock or express disgust. Instead, you welcomed me as if I were God's messenger,[24] as if I were Christ Jesus in person. What has become of the delight you exhibited? For I can testify that if need be you would have plucked out your eyes and given them to me. Have I become your enemy by being frank with you? They are paying court to you[25] for no good purpose: they really intend to ostracize you so that you should court them. It is good to be courted for a good purpose on all occasions, and not just when I am present with you, my children, for whom I travail once more until Christ is formed in you. I only wish I could be with you at this moment, and change my tone, for I am quite distracted about you.

21   Tell me, you that want to be under law, do you never listen to the reading of the Law? For it is stated that Abraham had two sons, one by the slave-girl and one by the free-woman. But while the child of the slave-girl was of physical origin, the child of the free-woman was born by promise. These are allegorical matters, for these women represent two covenants. The one is of Mount Sinai bearing children for servitude. This is Hagar – for in Arabia *hajar* means Mount Sinai[26] – and corresponds to the present Jerusalem which is in servitude with her children.[27] But the Jerusalem Above[28] is free, which is our mother Sarah,[29] for it is stated,

> Rejoice, you barren one who do not bear!
> Cry out with joy, you who do not travail!
> For more are the children of the desolate
> Than of the woman who has a husband. [30]

28   Now we, brothers, like Isaac, are children of promise. But just as then the child of physical origin persecuted the child of spiritual origin, so it is now. Yet what does the Scripture say? 'Cast out the slave-girl and her son, for the son of the slave-girl shall not share the inheritance with the son of the free-woman.'[31] Consequently, brothers, we are not the children of the slave-girl, but of the free-woman, with the com-
5.1   plete freedom Christ has given us. Stand firm, then, and refuse to be harnessed again to a yoke of bondage.[32]

2   I, Paul, tell you plainly, that if you become circumcised Christ is of no avail to you. And I declare to every circumcised person that he is obligated to observe the whole Law. You have become severed from

Christ, those of you who would be exonerated by law: you have fallen from grace. For it is spiritually, by faith, that we hold the expectation of rectitude; for in Christ Jesus it is neither circumcision nor un-circumcision that is efficacious, but faith stimulated by love.

7   You were running so well. Who brought you to a halt by making you lose confidence in the truth? That idea you have got never came from the one who called you. It takes little leaven to leaven the mass. I personally am convinced of you in the Master that you will change your minds. He who is confusing you must bear the blame, whoever he may be. And what of me, brothers? If I am still preaching circum-cision, why am I still being persecuted? So much for the 'abolition of the obstacle of the cross'![33] It would be a good thing if those who unsettle you over circumcision would cut themselves off as well!

13   Now you have been called to freedom, brothers. That does not mean freedom merely as an excuse for physical indulgence: it means that you are to serve one another through love. For the whole Law is sum-med up in this one precept, 'You are to love your neighbour as yourself.'[34] But if you bite and devour each other, take care that you do not exterminate one another. I say, therefore, conduct yourselves spiritually, and do not allow your physical passions to have their way. For the physical nature has passions contrary to the spiritual nature, and the spiritual nature contrary to the physical, because these are in opposition to one another. So you are not free to do as you please. Yet if you are spiritually guided you are not under law.

19   Now the deeds of the physical nature are obvious: they are adultery, impurity, sensuality, idolatry, sorcery, enmity, quarrelling, envy, passions, intrigues, dissensions, factions, malice, heavy drinking, revelling, and everything of the same description about which I have warned you, just as I am warning you now, that those who act in this way will not inherit the Kingdom of God. But the spiritual product is love, joy, peace, forbearance, kindliness, goodness, loyalty, gentle-ness, self-control. Against these no law is operative. Those who are in Christ Jesus have crucified the physical nature with its passions and desires. If we are to live spiritually, let us also accept spiritual discip-line. Let us not become self-assertive, defying one another, malicious to one another.

6.1   Brothers, if anyone has been detected in some fault, you who are spiritually-minded should correct him in a mild manner, having an eye on yourself in case you should be tested. Bear one another's burdens, and thus carry out Christ's law.[35] But if anyone fancies himself to be somebody, when he is nothing of the kind, he suffers from self-delusion. Each must carefully examine his own work, and then he can have something to be proud of in his own right instead of in another's; for each must shoulder his own load. But let him who has the Message imparted to him share all credit with his instructor.

7 Harbour no illusions. God is not to be hoodwinked. Whatever a man sows he will also reap. He who sows for his physical nature will reap decay as the physical consequences, while he who sows for the spiritual nature will reap eternal life as the spiritual consequences. Let us never grow weary of doing what is right; for by never relaxing we shall reap in due course. So as opportunity is afforded us let us labour for the welfare of all, particularly of our kinsmen in faith.

11 Look how I have written to you in large characters with my own hand![36] Those who want to make a favourable impression in the physical sense press you to be circumcised, but only to evade persecution of Christ's cross.[37] It is not as if these circumcised people were themselves observant. They only want you to be circumcised so that they can boast of your physical condition. For myself, God forbid that I should boast of anything but the cross of our Lord Jesus Christ, by which the world has been crucified to me, and I to the world! It is neither circumcision nor uncircumcision that counts for anything, but a new creation. To all who toe this line, peace and mercy be upon them, and upon the Israel of God.[38]

17 From now on let no one deal me any more blows, for I carry the scars of Jesus on my body.[39]

The loving-kindness of the Lord Jesus Christ be with your spirit, brothers. Amen.

132

Notes and References

1. Some would date the letter as late as AD57, perhaps from Corinth. *To the Communities of Galatia* is one of the more difficult letters of Paul to translate, as largely it is based on the views of Jewish mystics, of whom Paul was one, that the Hebrew Bible is oracular, having an inner as well as an outer significance. The inner significance seems often very far-fetched, related to particular sounds and sentiments.
2. Paul constantly follows the practice of the pious Jew in adding a doxology when speaking of the ways of God.
3. The Jewish way of life. Paul had followed the views and practices of the Pharisees, including their occult teachings. His beliefs remained Jewish.
4. The Hebrew form of the nickname Peter (meaning 'Rock').
5. Paul's account of his movements should be compared with what is related in the *Acts*.ix.1-31. James (Jacob), the next younger brother of Jesus, was at this time head of all believers in Jesus as Messiah (Christ).
6. Actually Paul had wanted Gentile believers to be reckoned as Israelites by faith. But this had been refused, unless they were full proselytes to Judaism. Paul would not accept this ruling.
7. i.e. the poor saints at Jerusalem. Paul is being sarcastic.
8. As idolaters, living in violation of the Commandments.
9. Cf. *Ps*.cxliii.2.
10. The word used signifies public placarding, but Paul probably had in mind the lifting up of the serpent in the wilderness. See *Num*.xxi.9, and cf. *Jn*.iii.14.
11. *Gen*.xv.6.
12. *Gen*.xii.3.
13. *Deut*.xxvii.26.
14. *Hab*.ii.4.
15. *Lev*.xviii.5.
16. *Deut*.xxi.23.
17. *Gen*.xii.3.
18. Pauline casuistry.
19. The time of the sojourn of Israel in Egypt, *Exod*.xii.40.
20. i.e. the angels, by whom in Jewish legend the Law was given to Moses, whose spokesman was the Angel of the Covenant.
21. Paul's argument is challenged by *James' Epistle*.
22. Jewish daily prayer, where a man thanks God for not making him a heathen, a slave, or a woman, in the order given here.
23. Paul knows nothing about a Virgin Birth. Jesus had been born a Jew in the normal manner. See Schonfield, *The Messianic Mystery*, Chapter 10.
24. See *Acts*.xiv.12, where Paul is taken for Hermes (Mercury), messenger of the gods. In early Christian apologetics Jesus was likened to Mercury.

25. The emissaries of James seeking the conversion of believing Gentiles to the faith of Israel, since they accepted the Messiah (Christ) as their king, and identified themselves with Israel.

26. The Sinai peninsular, called by the Arabs *el-Tijahah*.

27. To the Romans.

28. The heavenly Jerusalem (Jerusalem Above). The Jewish mystics believed in the idea of 'as above so below'. See *Rev*.xxi.2.

29. In the text the name has been dropped, and perhaps also the author's explanation of the name which means 'noble'.

30. *Isa*.liv.1.

31. *Gen*.xxi.9-10.

32. Paul was so concerned that Gentile converts should not be required to be bound by the Mosaic Law that he refused sufficiently to appreciate the consequence of telling them they were free from the Law. He was dealing with people who had been pagans, many of them slaves prone to immorality. Having been brought up himself as a strict Jew he was shocked by the behaviour he discovered.

33. Paul seems here to be borrowing a phrase from the propaganda of the Zealots for the Law. The idea of a crucified Messiah was repugnant to Jews, see *I.Cor*.i.23 (p.141 of current edition). The death of Jesus had to be explained as the means by which he had entered into his glory.

34. *Lev*.xix.18 (cf.*Mt*.xxii.39-40; *Rom*.xiii.9-10).

35. Cf. *Isa*.liii.4; *Mt*.viii.27

36. As a mark of esteem. Paul had bad eyesight and dictated his letters.

37. Judaism was a religion licensed by the Roman Empire, while Christianity was illegal, officially regarded as hostile to the Empire and subversive.

38. Cf. the Jewish doxology, 'May he bestow peace on us, and upon all Israel'. The Israel of God, or 'ideal Israel', as distinguished from the physical Israel.

39. Paul had been flogged by the Roman authorities as Jesus had been.

To the Community at Corinth (1)

(Written from Ephesus probably in AD 55)[1]

[Excerpt One][2]

9.1 ...Am I not a freeman? Am I not an envoy? Have I not seen Jesus our Master? Are you not the product of my labour for the Master? If I am not regarded by others as an envoy, surely I am by you, for you are the confirmation of my envoyship for the Master.

3 Here, then, is my reply to those who cross-examine me. Have we not the right to eat and drink? Have we not the right to take around with us a believing wife[3] like the other envoys do, and the Master's brothers,[4] and Cephas? Is it only I and Barnabas who have no right to give up our occupations? Whoever goes on military service at his own expense? Who plants a vineyard and does not partake of its fruit? Who herds a flock and does not eat the curds obtained from the flock? Am I speaking in human fashion, or does not the Law say the same thing?

9 Surely it is stated in the Law of Moses, 'You are not to muzzle the ox that treads out the corn'.[5] Is God concerned here for oxen, or speaking entirely for our benefit? For our benefit, surely, so that the plough-man should have something to expect from his ploughing, and the thresher from his part of the work. If we have sown spiritual seed in you, is it too much to expect if we reap material things from you? If you grant others that right, should you not much more us, even if we have taken no advantage of that right, but have fended for ourselves entirely lest we should afford the slightest hindrance to the News of Christ?[6] Are you ignorant that those who perform priestly duties partake of the Temple dues, and that those who serve the altar share in what is offered at the altar?[7] In the same way the Master has laid down that those who proclaim the News should live off the News.[8]

15 Yet I have availed myself of none of these rights, and I have not mentioned them here with a view to getting anything for myself. I would sooner die first! Let no one take that as an empty boast. Granted that I do proclaim the News, there is nothing in that for me to boast of, for I am constrained to do it. Woe to me if I do not proclaim the

News! Yet if I do it in a voluntary capacity I receive a reward. But if I am engaged to do it, it is my professional employment. What is the nature of my reward? It is that when I proclaim the News I can give it out free of charge by not exercising my rights.

19 But though I am in every sense a freeman, I have made myself everyone's slave so as to win over far more. So I have been a Jew to Jews to win over Jews. I have been subject to law to those under law – not being under law myself – to win over those under law. I have been alien to law to those without law – though not alien to God's Law[9] and legally bound to Christ – to win over those without law. I have been subject to limitations[10] to those with limitations, to win over those with limitations. To everyone I have been as they are, that at all events I should save some. And whatever I do it is for the News, that I may assure my share in it.

24 Are you ignorant that though all the runners race on the course only one receives the prize? So run as if you meant to win. And every contestant exercises complete self-mastery; but they do it for a perishable garland, we for an imperishable. That is how *I* run, in no uncertain fashion, and that is how *I* fight, with no threshing the air. I pummel my body and make it my slave, in case having preached to others I should fail to pass the test myself.

10.1 I would not have you ignorant, brothers, that our ancestors[11] were all under cover of the cloud and all passed through the sea, and all were immersed with the Mosaic immersion in the cloud and in the sea.[12] And they all partook of the same spiritual food[13] and drank the same spiritual drink; for they drank from that accompanying rock,[14] the rock that was Christ.[15] But God was not pleased with the majority of them, and they were laid low in the wilderness.

6 Now these things have become illustrations to us not to covet what is bad, as they did; not to be idolaters, as some of them were, as it is stated, 'the people sat down to eat and drink and rose up to play';[16] not to indulge in immorality, as some of them did, and twenty-three thousand fell in one day; not to test the Lord, as some of them did, and perished by snake bites; not to murmur, as some of them did, and perished by the destroyer.

11 Now these things happened to those people to furnish illustrations, and they were set down as a warning to us with whom the Consummation of the Ages has been reached.[17] So let him who stands have a care lest he fall. No superhuman temptation has come your way. God is faithful: he will never allow you to be tested beyond your

strength, but along with the test he will provide a loop-hole also, to enable you to extricate yourself from it.

14 Consequently, dear friends, make good your escape from idolatry. I am talking to men of sense. Consider carefully what I say. Is not the cup of blessing that we bless fellowship with Christ's blood? Is not the bread we break fellowship with Christ's body?[18] For we many are one loaf of bread, one body, since we all have a part of the one loaf of bread. Look at the physical Israel.[19] Are not those who partake of the sacrifices in fellowship with the altar of sacrifice? Of course I am not suggesting by this that an offering to an idol is anything, or that an idol is anything. Of course not. What the Gentiles sacrifice they sacrifice to demons, and not to God, and I want you to have no fellowship with

21 demons. You cannot drink the Lord's cup and the cup of demons. Neither can you share the Lord's table and the table of demons.[20] Are we to arouse the Lord's jealousy? Are we stronger than he?

[Excerpt Two][21]

II.Cor.

6.14 ...Do not be ill-matched[22] with unbelievers. For what has rectitude in common with lawlessness? Or what fellowship has light with darkness? What harmony has Christ with Beliar?[23] Or what share has the faithful with the faithless? And what agreement has the temple of God with idols? For we are the temple of the Living God, as God has said,

> I will dwell with them and walk with them,
> And I will be their God, and they my people, [24]
> Therefore come out from among them,
> And be separate,' says the Lord.
> Have no contact with the unclean.[25]
> And I will admit you within,
> And I will be a Father to you,
> And you shall be my sons and daughters, [26]
> Says the Lord of hosts.

7.1 Having therefore these promises,[27] dear friends, let us cleanse ourselves from all physical and spiritual defilement, discharging our sacred duties[28] in the fear of the Lord...

NOTES AND REFERENCES

1. The two letters to the Corinthians in the New Testament are a combination of the original four. The *first* letter is referred to in *I.Cor.*v. 9 (p.144); the *second* letter is largely represented by *I.Corinthians*. The *third* letter is mentioned in *II.Cor.*vii.8 (p.171), and the *fourth* corresponds to the greater part of *II.Corinthians*. The *original first letter* dealt in part with the theme of association with immoral persons. As presented here *I.Cor.*ix.1 – x.22 and *II.Cor.*vi.14 – vii.1 would belong to it.
2. The first excerpt here answers to *I.Cor.*ix.1 – x.22.
3. Lit. a sister-wife.
4. Evidently the brothers of Jesus also acted as envoys.
5. *Deut.*xxv.4.
6. Paul uses the plural, but has himself in mind.
7. Cf. *Lev.*ii.3, vi.18.
8. Cf. *Lk.*x.7.
9. See below *To the Believers at Rome*, p.196, Note 23.
10. Conscientious objectors in matters of diet, etc.
11. Paul always insisted that all Gentile converts were now Israelites, as being in and subject to the Messiah as Israel's king.
12. *Exod.*xiv.19-21, 31
13. *Exod.*xvi.15, the manna.
14. *Num.*xvii.6, xx.8. In Jewish legend the rock was shaped like a beehive, which rolled along beside the Israelites. When they camped it gave water as the people sang, 'Spring up, O well' (*Num.*xxi.17).
15. The Messiah was believed to be prefigured by a rock or stone (*Ps.*cxviii.22; *Isa.*viii.14; *Mt.*xxi.42, and also xvi.18).
16. *Exod.*xxxii.6.
17. We must always have in mind that for Jesus and his followers, as for most Jews at this period, the end of the present world was imminent, to be replaced by the new World Order of the Kingdom of God.
18. Referring to the ceremonial blessing of bread and wine (Heb. *Kiddush*) at communal meals, especially on religious occasions.
19. Those who are Israelites by descent.
20. In the Graeco-Roman world the sacrificial meal was regarded as the table of the god (e.g. 'the table of the Lord Serapis'). The Jews regarded their communal meal as the table of the Lord. See *I.Cor.*viii.4 -7 (p.147f.), and cf. the *Mishnah, Aboth.*iii.4.
21. This excerpt may have followed the previous one almost directly.
22. Lit. 'yoked with another kind', relating to the Law of Diverse Kinds (*Deut.*xxii.9-11). A clean beast was not to be yoked with an unclean (*Mishnah, Kilaim* viii.2).
23. Beliar, Beelzebub, the prince of the demons.

24. *Lev.*xxvi.11-12.
25. *Isa.*lii.11.
26. Cf.*Jer.*xxxi.1, 9; *Isa.*xliii.6.
27. As just quoted. But see also *Ezek.*xxxvii.2, 23, 28 (xi.17, 20 in LXX) where, in verse 17 of the Greek version, *eisdechomai* ('admit within') is used.
28. As priests of God's temple.

To the Community at Corinth (2)

(Written from Ephesus possibly in the autumn of AD 55)[1]

1.Cor.

1.1   Paul, by the will of God a chosen envoy of Jesus Christ, with brother Sosthenes, to the community of God at Corinth, consecrated in Jesus Christ as members of the holy assembly[2] in common with all who in every place invoke the name of our Lord Jesus Christ, their Master and ours. May peace and prosperity be yours from God our Father and the Lord Jesus Christ.

4   Invariably I thank God for you, for the way he has favoured you in Christ Jesus, because he has so enriched you in every respect, both in speech and knowledge. Just as the testimony to Christ was so firmly established among you, so have you never lacked for any spiritual gifts while waiting for the revelation of our Lord Jesus Christ. He will keep you steadfast to the end, that you may be without reproach on the Day of our Lord Jesus Christ. God is faithful, who has chosen you for fellowship with his Son Jesus Christ our Master.

10   Now in the name of our Lord Jesus Christ I urge you, brothers, all to hold together and not to have divisions among yourselves, but to accommodate yourselves to the selfsame outlook and viewpoint. For it has been conveyed to me about you, brothers, by Chloe's people, that quarrelling is going on among you. I mean this, that you are variously saying, 'I side with Paul', or, 'I go with Apollos', 'I take Cephas's view', or, 'I take Christ's'. Has Christ been split up? Was Paul crucified on your behalf? Or were you immersed in the name of Paul? I am thankful I immersed none of you but Crispus[3] and Gaius, so that no one can say you were immersed in my name. Oh, yes, I also immersed the household of Stephanas. Otherwise I do not recall that I immersed anyone else. For Christ did not send me out to immerse but to proclaim the News; and not with clever words either, in case Christ's cross should lose all its potency. The message of the cross may be foolish to those who are perishing, but to those who are

being saved – to us – it is the power of God; for it is stated,

> 'I will destroy the wisdom of the sages,
> And nullify the intellect of the intelligent.' [4]

20 What becomes of the sage, the scribe, the scholar of this world? Has not God made nonsense of the world's wisdom?[5] For since in God's wisdom the world failed to know God by wisdom, it pleased God to save those who believe by the folly of preaching. For while the Jews demand a sign, and the Greeks require wisdom, we preach a crucified Christ,[6] an obstacle to Jews and nonsense to Gentiles. But to those who are chosen – Jews and Greeks alike – a Christ who is the power of God and the wisdom of God. For God's 'folly' is wiser than men, and God's 'weakness' is stronger than men.

26 As regards the choice, take yourselves, brothers. There are not many sages among you in the world's sense, not many persons of consequence, not many highborn. Instead, God has selected what is foolish in the world to shame the wise, and what is weak to shame the mighty, and what is of base origin and treated with contempt God has chosen, and even what is non-existent[7] to bring to an end the existing order, that not a single human being should boast in God's presence. But you are his offspring in Christ Jesus, who was begotten to be wisdom to us from God, yes, and vindication, consecration and ransom, so that, as it is stated, 'Let him who boasts do it in the Lord'.[8]

2.1 So when I came to you, brothers, I did not come disclosing to you the Divine Secret with imposing speech or wisdom; for I was determined to be conscious of nothing while among you but of Jesus Christ, and of him as crucified. And so it was in weakness, and in fear, and in great trepidation, that I arrived among you; and my speech and proclamation was with no persuasive words of wisdom, but with spiritual and phenomenal demonstration, so that your conviction should rest not on human wisdom but on divine power.

6 There is a wisdom we employ with the initiated, but it is a wisdom that has nothing to do with this world, or with the transient forces governing this world.[9] It is the hidden Wisdom of God contained in a mystery,[10] which God formulated of old to be our glory before the Ages began, unknown to any of the forces governing this world; for had they known it they would never have crucified the Lord of glory. But as it is stated,

> What eye has never seen, nor ear heard, what never entered
> the mind of man, God has prepared for those who love him. [11]

10   Yet God has revealed it to us by the Spirit; for the Spirit delves into everything, even into the profundities of God. For who among men knows a man's ideas except the human spirit which is in him? So too none can know God's ideas except the Divine Spirit. Now what we have received is not the spirit of the created world, but the Spirit that emanates from God, so that we may know what God graciously grants us to know.[12] Those are the things we speak of, not in the language that human wisdom provides, but in the fashion of spiritual instruction, bringing spiritually-equipped people into touch with spiritual realities. The materialist cannot entertain the ideas of the Divine Spirit: to him they are nonsense, and he cannot grasp them, because they have to be discerned spiritually. But the spiritually-equipped person discerns all these things, though they are to be discerned by no one unaided, 'for who has ever known the mind of the Lord, that he should teach him?'[13] But we have Christ's mind.

3.1   It was impossible however, brothers, for me to speak to you as spiritually-equipped people, only as physically-equipped, as infants in Christ. I had to feed you with milk rather than solid food, for you were not equal to it. Neither are you equal to it yet, for you are still at the physical stage.[14] As long as there is rivalry and wrangling among you, are you not physical and behaving in human fashion? Whenever someone comes out with, "I take Paul's side", and another, "I am with Apollos", are you not human? What then is Apollos, and what is Paul? Simply the agents, each as the Lord endowed him, by whom you believed. I did the planting, and Apollos did the watering, but God caused the growth. Consequently, neither the planter nor the waterer counts, only God the Grower. Both the planter and the waterer have the same standing, yet each will receive his individual reward according to his individual labour; for we are God's co-workers, and you are God's culture, God's construction.

10   By virtue of God's favour bestowed on me, I, like a skilled master-builder have laid the foundation, while another will build on it. Only let each take care in what way he builds on it. There can never be any other foundation laid than what has been laid,[15] the foundation that is Jesus Christ. But upon it it is open to anyone to erect an edifice of gold, silver, precious stones, wood, straw, or rush. The material in each case will be evident, for the Day will reveal it. Since fire will be the means of disclosure, the flame itself will prove what kind of material it is. If the material which anyone has used for building survives, he will receive a reward. If anyone's material is burnt up,

142

he will pay the penalty, though he will be saved himself, but barely, as if he had come through the flame.

16   Do you not realize that you are God's temple, and that the Divine Spirit resides in you? If anyone dishonours God's temple God will dishonour him; for God's temple is holy, as you are meant to be.

18   Let no one delude himself. If any of you considers he is what passes for a wise man in this age, let him become a fool, so that he may become really wise; for this world's wisdom is folly to God, for it is stated, 'He catches the wise at their knavery',[16] and again, 'The Lord knows how trivial are the arguments of the wise'.[17]

21   So let no one boast of individuals. Everything is yours as it is, whether Paul, Apollos, Cephas, the whole created world, life and death, the present and future, all is yours, and you are Christ's, and

4.1 Christ is God's. Consequently, we should be regarded merely as Christ's assistants, stewards of the Divine Mysteries, which implies the requirement in stewards that they should be found reliable. So it is of small concern to me whether I am examined by you or any human standard. I do not even examine myself. I am not aware of anything to my detriment; but that does not exonerate me. It is the Master who will examine me. So do not judge prematurely, before the Master has come, who will bring dark secrets to light and reveal the heart's design; and then the praise that is appropriate will be accorded by God to each.

6   Now these things, brothers, I have applied figuratively to myself and Apollos for your benefit, that you may learn the truth by us 'Not beyond what is ordained',[18] so that you may not get puffed up over one as compared with another. For who has singled you out? Or what do you possess that you have not received? And if you have received it, why do you boast as if you had not received it? Already you are glutted! Already you have grown rich! Already you have occupied the throne! And I only wish that you had taken the throne, so that we could reign with you. As it seems to me, God has kept us envoys for the end of the show, like those doomed to death;[19] for we have become a spectacle for the universe, for angels and men. We for Christ's sake are fools, while you in Christ are sensible people! We are weak, but you are strong! You stand in high esteem, while we are in disgrace! To this very moment we hunger and thirst, we are ragged and knocked about, vagrant and toil-worn, labouring with our hands. When insulted we are polite, when persecuted we submit to it, when cursed we are conciliatory. Right up to now we are treated as the scum of the universe, the offscouring of everything.[20]

143

14   I am not writing this to shame you, but as dear children of mine I am reminding you. Should you have ten thousand guardians in Christ, you do not have that number of fathers. It is I, in Christ, who have begotten you by the News. Copy me, therefore, I entreat you. That is why I have dispatched Timotheus to you, who is not only a dear child of mine but loyal to the Master, to recall to you the course I follow in Christ, which I commend everywhere to all the communities. There are some who are full of bluster under the impression that I shall not be coming to visit you. But if the Lord wills I shall be visiting you quite soon; and when I do I shall take cognizance not of the speech but of the spiritual power of the blusterers. For the Kingdom of God consists not in speech but in spiritual power. Which do you prefer, that I visit you with a stick or in a mild and affectionate spirit?

5.1   I am reliably informed that there is immorality among you, immorality such as has no parallel among the Gentiles, that one should have his father's wife. And you are full of elation, instead of grieving, to the end that the person responsible should be removed from among you. I, however, absent as I am in body but present in spirit, have already – as if I were present – condemned the perpetrator of such a crime in the name of the Lord Jesus. Before the assembled company of yourselves and my spirit, invested with the authority of the Lord Jesus, the sentence is that the person concerned be consigned to Satan for his physical destruction[21] that his spirit may be saved when the Day of the Lord comes.

6   There is no justification for your boasting. Are you not aware that 'a little leaven leavens the whole lump'? Get rid of the old leaven that you may be a new lump, once more in the unleavened state, for our passover – Christ – has been sacrificed.[22] Consequently, let us observe the festival, not with the old leaven, nor with the leaven of vice and immorality, but with the unleavened bread of purity and sincerity.

9   In my letter[23] I wrote to you not to keep company with immoral characters, not specifically the immoral of contemporary society, any more than with usurers, extortioners and idolaters, for in that case you would have to exclude yourselves completely from society. But I am writing to you now not to keep company at all with anyone bearing the name of brother if he is immoral, or a usurer, or idolater, or foulmouthed, or a drunkard, or extortioner. You are not even to take meals with such people. Is it for me to judge those outside when you do not judge those inside? Leave God to judge those outside, while you 'put away the wicked from among you'.[24]

6.1   Has any of you with a grievance against his fellow the temerity to bring his case before the evil-doers instead of before the saints? Or are you ignorant that the saints are to judge the world?[25] So if the world is to be judged by you, are you unqualified to deal with minor issues? Are you ignorant that we are to judge angels, let alone mundane matters? So if you have any mundane issues let those be appointed to try them who are the most looked down on members of the community. I say this deliberately to shame you. Can it be possible that there is not a wise man among you competent to decide between one brother and another? But brother must go to law with brother, and before unbelievers too!

7   It is already an admission of complete failure on your part that you have any causes between yourselves. Why not rather let yourselves be injured? Why not rather let yourself be defrauded? Instead, you injure and defraud, and your own brothers too! Are you ignorant that evil-doers shall not inherit the Kingdom of God? Do not delude yourselves. Neither the immoral, nor idolaters, nor adulterers, nor homosexuals, nor thieves, nor usurers, nor drunkards, nor the foul-mouthed, nor extortioners, shall inherit the Kingdom of God. That is what some of you were; but you have been cleansed, you have been consecrated, you have been exonerated by the name of our Lord Jesus Christ, and by the Spirit of our God.

12   'I am free to do everything.'[26] Yes, but everything is not advantageous. I am free to do everything, provided I do not fall into its power. 'Food is for appetite, and appetite for food', but God will do away with both the one and the other. For the body is not for prostitution, but for the Master, and the Master for the body. And the God who raised up the Master will also by his power raise us up.

15   Are you ignorant that your bodies are the organs of Christ? Am I then to make the organs of Christ the organs of a prostitute? God forbid! Or are you ignorant that he who unites himself with a prostitute forms a single body, for 'the two', it is said, 'shall become one flesh'?[27] But he who unites himself with the Master forms a single spirit. Shun prostitution. Any other kind of sin a man may commit is independent of the body, but the immoral man sins against his own body. Or are you ignorant that your body is the temple of the holy Spirit which is in you, which you have received from God, and that you are not your own, having been acquired at a high price? Then praise God with your body.

7.1   Now to turn to the matters on which you have written me. It is preferable for a man not to have intercourse with a woman.[28] But to avoid prostitution each should take himself a wife, and each woman should have her own husband. The husband should fulfil his obligations to his wife, and similarly the wife to her husband. The wife has not the control of her own body but the husband. Similarly the husband has not the control of his own body but the wife. Do not deprive one another, unless by agreement for a time to devote yourselves to prayer.[29] But then renew your association, so that Satan should not tempt you through your unhealthy behaviour. I say this by way of accommodation, not of instruction. I would prefer everyone to be as I am. But each has his own gift from God, one in this way, another in that. Though I do say to the unmarried and to widows that it is preferable for them to remain like me. Yet if they cannot exercise self-control they should marry; for it is decidedly better to marry than to burn.

10   For those who are married, however, I stipulate – not indeed I but the Master – that the wife is not to separate from her husband, and if she is separated she must remain unwed or be reconciled to her husband; and the husband is not to divorce his wife.[30] Beyond that, I say – not the Master – that if a brother has an unbelieving wife, and she is agreeable to living with him, he is not to divorce her. So with the wife who has an unbelieving husband, if he is agreeable to living with her, she is not to divorce her husband. For the unbelieving husband is consecrated by his wife, and the unbelieving wife is consecrated by the brother in faith. Otherwise your children would be impure instead of holy as they are now. But if the unbelieving partner insists on separation, let them separate. In such case neither a brother nor a sister is under duress; for God has decreed that you should be at peace. And you, wife, how can you tell whether you will not save your husband? Or you, husband, how can you tell whether you will not save your wife?

17   Otherwise, 'to each as the Lord has assigned, for each as God has decreed'.[31] So let him conduct himself, and so have I prescribed for all the communities.

18   Let anyone who was circumcised when he was called not undo the operation. If he was called in uncircumcision let him not be circumcised. Circumcision is of no consequence, neither is uncircumcision; it is the keeping of God's commandments. Let each remain in the category in which he was called. Were you called as a slave, do not let it fret you; though if you have opportunity to procure your freedom use it to the full. For the slave called by the Master is the Master's freedman. Similarly the freeman who is called is Christ's slave. You have been acquired at a high price. Do not become

slaves of men. Each as he was called, brothers, so let him continue before God.

25 Now as regards the unmarried I have no instructions from the Master, but I offer my opinion as one who has mercifully been permitted by the Lord to be continent. I consider, therefore, in view of the present stress that a man is better off if he is celibate. If you are united with a wife, do not seek to be free. If you are free of a wife, do not seek one; though if you should marry you have done nothing wrong. And if a girl should marry she has done nothing wrong either. But those who take this step face the cares of married life, which I would spare you.

29 Only I would urge this, brothers, time grows short. So from now on let those who have wives be as though they had none, and those who mourn as though they did not mourn, and those who rejoice as though they did not rejoice, and those who acquire as though they did not possess, and those who are on friendly terms with society as though they were unsociable; for the existing order is passing away. I would have you carefree. The unmarried man is concerned with the Master's affairs, how he may please the Master; but the married man is concerned with social affairs, how he may please his wife, and he is torn two ways. So too the unmarried woman and girl is concerned with the Master's affairs, that she may be devoted physically and mentally; but the married woman is concerned with social affairs, how she may please her husband. I am saying this in your own interest, not to hold you on a rein, but rather that not being pulled this way and that you may be more considerate and attentive to the Master.

36 However, if anyone feels he is being inconsiderate to his maiden, should she be passing her bloom, and therefore he owes it to her, let it be as he wishes: he does nothing wrong. Let them be married. But he who maintains a firm resolve, not having necessity, and is in full control of his own will, and has determined in his own mind to keep his maiden inviolate, will do well. So he who marries his maiden does well, but he who does not marry will do better still.

39 A wife is bound for her husband's entire lifetime; but should the husband go to his rest she is free to marry whom she will, so long as he is in the Master. But in my opinion she is happier to stay as she is, and there I think I have the Spirit of God.

8.1 Now as regards offerings to idols, we are aware that we all have knowledge. But knowledge puffs up while affection builds up. If anyone thinks he knows something, he still does not know it as well as he should. But if anyone is devoted to God he is given insight by him. For example, as regards food offered to idols, we are aware that an idol has no actual life, and that there is no God other than the One. For even if there are so-called gods, whether of heaven or earth – since there are many 'gods' and many 'lords', for us there is still only One God, the Father, from whom all things derive, and to whom we belong,[32] and one Lord Jesus Christ, through whom all things come, and by whom we are. But this knowledge is not general. There are some who are so accustomed to the idea of idols that they eat such food as being actually offered to an idol, and their conscience being weak is defiled.

8.8   But the food will not bring us near to God; for neither by not consuming are we retarded, nor by consuming are we advanced. But take care that your 'right' does not prove a hindrance to those whose conscience is weak. For if anyone sees you who have knowledge sitting at table in an idol temple[33] will not he whose conscience is weak conclude from this that there is some benefit to be gained by eating what is offered to idols? So the weak one will be ruined by the very thing you know, that brother of yours for whom Christ died. Consequently, by sinning against your brothers and wounding their weak conscience you are sinning against Christ. For that reason, if food makes my brother stumble, then rather than be the cause of that I will never eat meat again.[34]

10.23   I am free to do everything, but everything is not advantageous. I am free to do everything, but not everything is beneficial. Let no one study his own interests, but those of his fellow. Eat whatever is sold in the meat-market without making inquiries, for 'the earth is the Lord's with all it contains'.[35] And if any unbeliever gives you an invitation, and you feel like accepting, eat whatever is placed before you without making inquiries. But if someone says to you, 'This is sacrificial food', then do not eat it, both for the sake of your informant and for conscience's sake. I say conscience, not yours but the other man's. But why should my freedom be governed by another man's conscience? If I partake with pleasure, why should I be abused over what I am thankful for? The answer is, that whether you eat or drink, or whatever you do, do everything for the glory of God. Be free from offence both to Jews and Gentiles, and to God's Community, just as I accommodate myself to everyone in every way, not studying my own convenience but that of the multitude, that they may be saved. Copy me, as I copy Christ.

11.2   I do thank you for reminding yourselves of me in every way, and for maintaining the traditions as I transmitted them to you. But I want you to know that the head of every man is Christ, while the head of woman is man, and the head of Christ is God. Every man who prays or prophesies with covered head dishonours his head, while every woman who prays or prophesies with unconcealed head dishonours her head; for it is just as if she were shaven. If the woman is not covered, let her also be shorn. If it is a shame for a woman to be shaven or shorn, let her be covered.[36] But it is not proper for a man to have his head concealed, being the image and glory of God;[37] but the woman is the glory of man. For man is not derived from woman, but woman from man;[38] and man was not created for the sake of woman, but woman for the sake of man.[39] For this reason the woman ought to wear some head-covering[40] because of the angels. Beyond this, as relates to the Master, woman is not distinguished from man, nor man from woman. For just as the woman derives from man, so does the man owe his being to woman; and equally they derive from God.

13   Judge for yourselves whether it is seemly for a woman to be uncovered when praying to God. Does not nature itself teach you that when a man has long tresses it is a disgrace to him? But if a woman has long tresses it is her glory, for her tresses are given her as a natural drapery. If someone is inclined to be contentious on this issue, I can entertain no such practice, nor the communities of God.

17   But here is news I do not appreciate, that when you assemble it is not for the better but for the worse. I learn first of all that when you hold your meetings there are divisions among you, and to a certain extent I believe it. Obviously there must be some variations among you, that those who are particularly worthy among you may be distinguished. But is not your coming together for the common purpose of eating the supper that is specifically the Master's? In partaking of this it is for each of you to have had his own supper beforehand. Yet one is famished and another is consumed with thirst. Have you no homes in which to eat and drink? Or do you mean to treat God's Community with contempt, and humiliate those who have no homes? What am I to say to you? Shall I commend you? This is something I cannot commend.

23   I indeed received from the Master what I have transmitted to you, that the Lord Jesus on the night he was betrayed took bread, and when he had given thanks broke it and said, 'This signifies my body broken on your behalf. Do this in commemoration of me.'[41] In the same way he took the cup after the meal, saying, 'This cup signifies the new covenant in my blood. Do this, as often as you drink it, in

commemoration of me.' So as often as you eat this bread and drink this cup you are making mention of the Master's death until he returns. Consequently, whoever eats the bread or drinks the cup unworthily will be held responsible for the Master's body and blood. So let a man examine himself, and after that eat the bread and drink from the cup; for he who eats and drinks is eating and drinking a judgment on himself, not discerning the body. That is why many of you are infirm and ailing, and a number have gone to their rest. If we have passed judgment on ourselves we shall not be judged; but if we are judged by the Master we shall be punished, so as not to be condemned with the world. Consequently, my brothers, when you assemble to eat this meal await your turn. But if anyone is famished let him eat at home, so that you do not come together for condemnation. As for other matters, I will settle these when I come.

12.1   Now about spiritual manifestations, brothers, I would not have you ignorant. You know the kind of Gentiles you were as regards dumb idols, misguided just as you were led. So I must inform you that no one speaking by the divine Spirit says, 'Cursed be Jesus!' And no one is able to say, 'Lord Jesus!' except by the holy Spirit. But there are different kinds of gifts, though the same Spirit, and different kinds of function, though the same Master, and different kinds of motivation, though the same God, who motivates everything universally. And to each has been given that particular spiritual manifestation which was appropriate. For one has been given through the Spirit the faculty of wisdom, another according to the same Spirit the faculty of insight, and yet another the faculty of faith by the same Spirit. To another, still by the one Spirit, has been given gifts of healing, to another the effecting of miracles, to another prophecy, to another the discerning of the nature of spirits, to yet another variety of tongues, to another interpretation of tongues. For all these manifestations one and the same Spirit is responsible, allocating specifically to each at will.

12   For just as the body is a unity while possessing many organs, and all the organs of the body, though many, form a single body, so is Christ a unity. For by one Spirit we have all been immersed into one body, whether Jews or Gentiles, slaves or freemen,[42] and we have all been given a draught of the one Spirit. For the body is no single organ, but many. If the foot should say, 'I am not part of the body because I am not the hand', is it therefore any less a part of the body? Or if the ear should say, 'I am not part of the body because I am not the eye', is it therefore any less a part of the body? If the entire body was eye

150

where would be hearing? If the entire body was hearing where would be smelling? But we find that God has placed the organs in the body, every single one of them, exactly as he wanted. If it were entirely one organ, where would be the body? As it is, there are many organs but one body. The eye cannot say to the hand, 'I do not require you'. Nor can the head say to the feet, 'I do not require you'.

22   Much more are those organs of the body found to be requisite which are more delicate, and those which seem of less consequence are those to which we devote far more attention. It is our unattractive features that come in for beautifying treatment, for which our attractive features have no need. But God interrelates the body to give added dignity to what is inferior, so that there may be no discrimination in the body, but that all the organs shall have the same concern for one another. So if one organ suffers, all the organs suffer with it, and if one organ is esteemed, all the organs rejoice with it.

27   Now you are Christ's body, and its respective organs, and God has placed these in the Community as follows: first envoys, second prophets, third teachers, next mediums, next those with gifts of healing, those with intuition, those who give guidance, and those with varied tongues. Are all envoys? Are all prophets? Are all teachers? Are all mediums? Have all gifts of healing? Do all speak in tongues? Are all interpreters? Make the higher gifts your aim. Yet let me point out to you a still better course to pursue.

13.1   Though I speak the tongues of men and angels, and have not love, I have become a clanging gong or clashing cymbal. Even if I possess the power of prophecy and know all mysteries and secret lore, and have such faith that I can remove mountains,[43] if I have not love I am of no account. Even if I share out my possessions[44] and give my body to be burnt, if I have not love it avails me nothing.

4   Love is long-suffering and kind. Love is never jealous, self-assertive, blustering or inconsiderate. It never seeks its own ends, is never irritable, keeps no score of wrongs, never rejoices in injustice, but delights in truth.

7   Love is ever protective, ever trustful, ever hopeful, ever constant. Love never fails, but whether it is prophesyings, they will come to an end, or whether it is tongues, they will cease, whether it is know-ledge, it will come to an end. For we only know imperfectly, and prophesy imperfectly. But when perfection is reached what is imperfect will come to an end. When I was a child, I talked like a child, I reasoned like a child, I argued like a child; but when I became

a man I put an end to childish ways. So far we see indistinctly as in a mirror,[45] but then it will be face to face. So far I know imperfectly, but then I shall know as fully as I am known. At present faith, hope and love, all three, continue; but the most enduring of them is love.

14.1   So pursue love, and make spiritual manifestations your aim, particularly the capacity to prophesy.[46] For he who speaks in a tongue addresses God, not his fellows, since no one can follow him. He is speaking mysterious things in spirit language.[47] But he who prophesies addresses his fellows for their benefit, encouragement and cheer. He who speaks in a tongue benefits himself, while he who prophesies benefits the community. I wish you could all speak in tongues, but preferably that you could prophesy; for he who prophesies is greater than one who speaks in tongues, unless he can interpret so that the community is benefited.

6   Supposing, brothers, that I were to come to you speaking in tongues, how should I benefit you if I did not also speak by revelation, by knowledge, by prophecy, or by teaching? It would be like inanimate objects that emit a sound, such as a flute or harp. If no clear distinction of notes is rendered, how is it to be recognised what is being played on them? And if the trumpet sounds an uncertain call, who will prepare for battle? So with your tongues, if you do not utter plain speech how is it to be understood what you are saying? You will be talking to the air. Still more, as there happen to be such a medley of sounds in the world, and nothing is soundless, should I not know the implications of a sound I shall be a barbarian to the speaker, and he will be a barbarian to me.

12   So with you, since you are ambitious for spiritual manifestations, aim at those which benefit the community, that you may excel. Therefore let him who speaks in a tongue pray for the ability to interpret. For if I pray in a tongue, my spirit is engaged in prayer, but my intelligence is not functioning. Is it not desirable, therefore, that I pray not only with the spirit, but also with the intellect? Otherwise, if you only bless God in spirit, how is one who is unlearned to make the 'Amen' response at the end of your thanksgiving, since he does not know what you are saying? You are giving thanks fittingly, but the other is not inspired by it. I thank God I speak in tongues more than all of you, but in the community I would rather speak five words with my intelligence so as to instruct others than ten thousand words in a tongue.

20   Brothers, do not be mentally childish, though in evil be as innocent as you please. But in mentality be adult. It is stated in the Law,

'By those of alien tongues and lips will I address this people,
Yet for all that they will not heed me,' says the Lord.[48]

22 So tongues are a sign not to believers but to unbelievers, while prophecy is not for unbelievers but for believers. If, therefore, you hold a meeting of the whole community, and all speak in tongues, and unlearned people or unbelievers come in, will they not say you are mad? But if all prophesy, and an unbeliever or unlearned person enters, he will be convinced by all he hears, he will be searched by all he hears, and the secrets of his heart will be laid bare. And so, falling upon his face, he will worship God, declaring, 'Truly God is with you!'

26 Is it not desirable then, brothers, that when you come together each should have a psalm, an instruction, a revelation, a tongue, or an interpretation, so that everything contributes to edification?

27 When someone speaks in a tongue, or perhaps two do so, or three at most, and then in turn, there should be one to interpret. If there should be no interpreter let the speaker in a tongue keep silence in the community and speak inwardly to God. And let two or three prophets speak, and the others draw conclusions. But if a revelation comes to anyone seated there let the previous speaker keep silence; for you can all continue prophesying after the one with the revelation has finished, since the spirits of the prophets remain under their control,[49] that all
33 may learn and all be encouraged. God is a God of order, not of chaos.

As is the practice in all the communities of the saints let the married
34 women keep silence in the communities; for they are not entitled to speak, being in a subordinate position, as also says the Law.[50] If there is anything they wish to learn let them consult their husbands at home, for it is indecorous for married women to speak at meetings.

36 Did the Message of God go out from you, or did it in fact come to you? If anyone regards himself as a prophet or medium let him acknowledge that what I am writing to you is a commandment of the Master. If anyone is ignorant, however, let him be ignorant. Consequently, my brothers, be ambitious to prophesy, and do not prevent speaking in tongues. But let everything be done decently and in an orderly manner.

15.1 Now I would draw your attention, brothers, to the News I proclaimed to you (which you accepted, on which you have based yourselves, by means of which you are being saved) in the very form in which I proclaimed it to you, if you have retained it, unless you believed in a heedless manner. For I delivered to you as basic what I had myself received: 'That Christ died for our sins in accordance with the Scriptures; that he was buried and raised up on the third day in accordance with the Scriptures; that he was seen by Cephas, then by the twelve, after that on one occasion by more than five hundred brothers (some of whom are gone to their rest); after that he was seen by James,[51] then by all the envoys.'[52] Last of all, as if by an untimely birth, he was seen even by me; for I am the most insignificant of the envoys, who does not deserve to be called an envoy, because I persecuted God's Community. But by God's mercy I am what I am, and his favour to me was not wasted, for I toiled harder than all of them, though not indeed I but God's favour that was with me. But whether it was myself or the others, this is what we proclaimed, and this is what you believed.

12   If then Christ was proclaimed as having been raised from the dead, how do some of you say that there is no resurrection of the dead? For if there is no resurrection of the dead, Christ cannot have been raised. And if Christ was not raised our proclamation was in vain and our faith in vain and we are exposed as false witnesses of God, since we have testified of God that he raised up Christ. This he cannot have done if the dead are not to be raised. For if the dead are not to be raised, neither can Christ have been raised. And if Christ has not been raised your faith is worthless: you are still in your sins. Then, too, all who have gone to their rest in Christ have perished. If we are merely to have hope in Christ in this life we are to be pitied above all men.

20   But in fact Christ *has* been raised from the dead as the first-fruits of those who had gone to their rest. For since by man came death,[53] so by man also[54] came resurrection from the dead. For as in Adam all die, so in Christ will all be brought to life, though each in his proper order, first Christ, followed at his coming by those who belong to Christ, then the remainder[55] when he has handed over the Kingdom of God to the Father, after abolishing all other government, authority and power. For he himself must rule until 'he has put all enemies under his feet'.[56] The final enemy to be abolished is death,[57] for *everything* is to be brought into subjection beneath his feet. But when it is said, 'everything has been subjected',[58] it is obvious that this excludes the One who has made everything subject to him. When, then, everything is subject to him, even the Son will be subjected to the One who has subjected everything to him, that God may reign supreme.

29   Otherwise, what are they doing who are immersed on behalf of the dead?[59] If the dead are not raised why be immersed on their behalf?

154

And why do we risk our lives all the time? 'I am ready to die any day', you say. Yes, that is your boast, brothers, which I make good in Christ Jesus our Master. If, to borrow a human phrase, I have 'fought with wild beasts at Ephesus',[60] how am I the gainer? If the dead are not raised, 'Let us eat and drink, for tomorrow we die'.[61] Oh no, do not delude yourselves! 'Bad company ruins good character.'[62] Sober up completely, and do not go to the bad; for some of you seem to ignore God's existence. I say this to shame you.

35 But someone may say, "How are the dead raised, and what kind of body do they have?" You dunce! Surely what you sow does not spring to life before it dies! And what you sow you do not sow in the bodily form that will emerge, but as bare grain, perhaps of wheat, or maybe of some other cereal. It is God who furnishes it with the body he wishes, each seed with its particular body. All flesh is not identical. There is the human, and besides that the flesh of animals, the flesh of birds, and the flesh of fish. There are also celestial and terrestrial bodies. But the glory of the celestial is one thing, and that of the terrestrial is another. Apart from the glory of the sun, there is the glory of the moon, and of the stars, and star even differs from star in glory.

42 So is it with the resurrection of the dead. What is sown as perishable is raised imperishable. What is sown in humiliation is raised in honour. What is sown in weakness is raised in vitality. What is sown as a physical body is raised as a spiritual body. If there is such a thing as a physical body, there is also such a thing as a spiritual body. Just as it is stated, 'The first man (Adam) became a living soul',[63] so the last Adam[64] became a vitalizing spirit. It was not the spiritual that came first but the physical, and after that the spiritual. The first man was 'dust from the earth':[65] the second man was from heaven.[66] As is the nature of dust so are the creatures of dust; and as is the heavenly nature, so are the heavenly beings. Just as we have worn the likeness of the dust nature, so shall we wear the likeness of the heavenly nature.

50 I tell you this, brothers, that flesh and blood cannot inherit the Kingdom of God, neither can the perishable inherit the imperishable. See, I will let you into a secret, we shall not all be laid to rest, but all of us will experience a change, in an instant, in the flicker of an eyelid, on the final trumpet note. For the trumpet will sound, and the dead will be raised up imperishable, and we shall experience a change. For this perishable nature must be invested with imperishability, and this mortal nature must be invested with immortality. And when this mortal nature has been invested with immortality, then the

saying that is written will come true, 'Death has been swallowed up in victory'.[67]

Where, O death, is your victory?
Where, O grave, is your sting? [68]

56 The sting of death is sin, and the strength of sin is the Law. But thanks be to God, who has given us victory through our Lord Jesus Christ!

58 Consequently, dear brothers, be firm and immovable, always fully engaged in the Master's work, knowing that your toil for the Master is not in vain.

16.1 Now as regards the fund for the saints, follow the same arrangement as I have made with the communities of Galatia. The day after the sabbath let each of you put by savings as he has prospered, so that collections do not have to be made when I come. Then when I come I will send whoever you designate by letter to convey your bounty to Jerusalem. If it is desirable that I should go too, they can travel with me. I propose to visit you when I pass through Macedonia – for I intend to go through Macedonia – and perhaps I may settle down with you, or at least spend the winter, so that you can forward me on your further journey. I do not want to see you merely in passing; for it is my hope, if the Lord permits, to stay some time with you. I shall remain at Ephesus at any rate until Pentecost, for a wide and much frequented gateway has been opened to me, and there is considerable opposition. Should Timotheus come, be sure you put him at his ease, for he is as much involved in the Master's work as I am. So let no one be disrespectful to him. And forward him on his way in peace that he may come to me, for I am expecting him with the brothers.

12 Regarding Brother Apollos, I urged him strongly to visit you with the brothers, but he was very much against coming just now. However, he will come when convenient.

13 Be alert, stand firm in the faith, be manly and sturdy! I beg you, brothers, conduct all your affairs in a loving spirit. You know how the house of Stephanas was the first-fruits in Achaia, and how much it has devoted itself to ministering to the saints. It is for you to submit yourselves to people like these, and to all who collaborate and work so hard. I rejoice at the arrival of Stephanas, Fortunatus and Achaicus, which compensates for the lack of your presence; for they relieve my mind and yours. You should esteem such people.

19 The communities of Asia send you their regards. Aquila and

Prisca[69] send you their regards in the Master together with the community at their house. All the brothers send you their regards. Convey our regards to one and all with a chaste kiss.

My personal regards in my own hand,

PAUL

If someone[70] does not love the Master, let him be accursed.[71] *Maranatha!*[72]

The loving-kindness of the Lord Jesus be with you. My love to you all in Christ Jesus.

NOTES AND REFERENCES

1. Commonly known as *I.Corinthians*.
2. Answering to Heb. *mikra kodesh* ('holy convocation'), as in *Exod*.xii.16.
3. See *Acts*.xviii.8.
4. *Isa*.xxix.14.
5. Cf.*Isa*.xxxiii.18; xliv.25.
6. Christ ('the Anointed') always means the Jewish Messiah.
7. In the Graeco-Roman world a slave was literally a 'non-entity'.
8. *Jer*.ix.24.
9. The spirit-powers ruling the planet.
10. Paul here uses the language of the Mystery cults. The Jewish (Pharisee) mystics had two branches of Hidden Wisdom, the Lore of Creation (in *Gen*.i.) and the Lore of the Chariot (in *Ezekiel*). Paul had been initiated into the former, as revealed in his letters. This dealt with the Heavenly Man as the image of God, the Messiah Above.
11. *Isa*.lxiv.4.
12. *Deut*.xxix.29. Jewish *Amidah* prayer, *Bened*.4: 'Thou favourest man with knowledge'.
13. *Isa*.xl.13.
14. Paul speaks as a Jewish adept in mysticism.
15. Christ ('Messiah') as Foundation Stone, cf. *I.Pet*.ii.4-6.
16. *Job*.v.13
17. *Ps*.xciv.11.
18. The source is not known, but cf. the saying of Paul's Jewish contemporary Johanan ben Zaccai, 'If you have learnt much Divine Doctrine claim no merit for yourself, for to that end you were created' (*Aboth* ii.8).
19. Like condemned criminals in the arena.
20. The metaphor is taken from the Athenian custom in the event of some dire calamity of throwing some of the human 'scum' of the city into the sea, to 'clean off' the guilt of the people.

21. The form of excommunication may have been akin to that of the Essenes. The expelled person was evidently expected to die.

22. The passover sacrifice immediately preceded the Feast of Unleavened Bread. All the old leaven was destroyed before the festival.

23. Two probable excerpts from this letter are given above, pp.135-137.

24. *Deut*.xxii.24.

25. When the Kingdom of God comes on Earth. *Mt*.xix.28.

26. This quotation and the one that follows may have been in the letter from the Corinthians to which Paul is replying.

27. *Gen*.ii.24

28. In view of the imminence of the Messianic Age.

29. *Test.XII Patriarchs*. 'There is a season for a man to embrace his wife and a season to abstain therefrom for his prayer' (*Test.Napht*.viii.8).

30. *Mk*.x.8-9.

31. Source of quotation unknown to translator.

32. Paul invariably distinguishes the Christ from God. See *I.Cor*.xi.3.(p.148-149).

33. It was a pagan custom to send invitations to dine at the table of the god. (See p.137, verse 21)

34. The argument is interrupted here by *I.Cor*.ix.1 – x. 22 (p.135), which seems to belong to the previous letter mentioned in *I.Cor*.v. 9 (p.144) in conjunction with *II.Cor*.vi – vii.1 (p.137).

35. *Ps*.xxiv.1.

36. Paul may be speaking of married women acting like prostitutes.

37. *Gen*.i.26.

38. *Gen*.ii.23.

39. *Gen*.ii.18.

40. Lit. 'control over her head'. And see *Gen*.vi.1-2.

41. Cf. *Lk*.xxii.19.

42. In a morning prayer a Jew thanks God for not making him a heathen, a woman, or a slave. See *Gal*.iii.48.

43. See *Mt*.xvii.20.

44. See *Mk*.x.21.

45. Mirrors of burnished bronze as then used.

46. To prophesy was to give an inspired address, not specially to predict.

47. Speaking in tongues meant giving vent to sounds articulated as in speech not necessarily belonging to any language used in human intercourse.

48. *Isa*.xxviii.11. Quoted from the Prophets, not the Law.

49. A revelation took precedence over every other form of spirit message as a direct communication by the holy Spirit, with the one who gave it out acting only as a medium not in control of what he said.

50. *Gen*.iii.16.

51. The brother of Jesus, as related in the *Gospel of the Hebrews*.

52. This section has been placed within single quotes as in the nature of a credo.
53. *Gen*.iii.
54. The Messiah as being a human being, the Son of Man.
55. Gr. *telos*, here used not in the sense of 'the End' but the 'tail end' – the vast majority. The order is processional, the general, his staff, and finally the main body. See *Rev*.xx.4-6.
56. *Ps*.cx.1.
57. See *Rev*.xx.14.
58. See *Ps*.viii.6.
59. A Christian custom of substitionary baptism for and on behalf of dear ones already dead.
60. Paul is using a figure of speech.
61. *Isa*.xxii.13.
62. From Menander, Athenian dramatist, 342 – 291BC.
63. *Gen*.ii.7.
64. Jesus.
65. *Gen*.ii.7.
66. According to the Jewish mystics God created the Heavenly Man as his image, the archetypal Son of Man, in whose likeness Adam was formed. The Heavenly Man (Messiah Above) incarnated in Jesus as Messiah Below, thus constituting him as the Second Adam, as Paul elaborated. See his letters to the Asian communities, and those at Philippi and Colossae, and particularly the *Book of Enoch*.
67. *Isa*.xxv.8.
68. *Hos*.xiii.14.
69. The same as Priscilla. See *Acts*.xviii.2.
70. Possibly a particular person is meant who is not named. Alternatively read 'anyone'.
71. 'Accursed' (*anathema*). Possibly a scribe's error, and we should read, 'let him be ardent again' (*anatherma*). Cf. *Mt*.xxiv.12.
72. Aram. 'Our Master, come' (*Marana tha*). Cf. *Rev*.xxii.20.

To the Community at Corinth (3)

(Probably written from Ephesus in the spring of AD 56)[1]

II.Cor.

[Commencement lacking]

10.1 ... Now I, Paul, personally entreat you by the mildness and moderation of Christ, I who am 'humble when in your presence, but overbearing towards you when absent.'[2] I pray that I do not have to be overbearing when I am present with the kind of persuasion I contemplate employing against those who reckon me as one who 'moves on the material plane.' In a material body I do move, but I do not fight with material weapons; for the weapons of my warfare are of no material character, but divine armaments for reducing strongholds, demolishing arguments, and every high and mighty position taken up in opposition to God's assured knowledge, bringing every design into subjection to the authority of Christ, and being ever ready to punish any insubordination once your submission is complete.

7   Face the facts squarely. If a certain individual is convinced he is acting for Christ, let him consider this as well, that as he acts for Christ so do I. For even if I should seem to boast unduly of my authority, which the Master has given me to build you up not to pull you down, I would not be ashamed, so long as it does not appear as if I am bent on intimidating you with my letters. For 'his letters', says that individual, 'are weighty and powerful, but his physical appearance is insignificant and his speech is contemptible.'[3]

11   Let that individual mark this, that what I am in word by letter when absent I am also in deed when present. I would not dream of classing or comparing myself with those who indulge in self-commendation; for these measuring themselves by themselves and comparing themselves with themselves cease to be relative. I will not boast so disproportionately, but in terms of the extent of the line the God of measurement has measured out for me, reaching as

far as to you. Clearly I am not overreaching myself where my line did not extend to you, for right the way to you I was first with the News of Christ.[4] I do not boast 'beyond measure' where others have laboured, but I trust, when your faith has expanded, to have my own line considerably prolonged by you, so as to allow me to proclaim the News to the regions beyond you, instead of boasting along another's line where the ground was already covered. 'Let him who boasts boast in the Lord.'[5] For it is not the man who commends himself who is approved, but he whom the Lord commends.

11.1   O that you would put up with a little of my 'folly', or at least put up with me! For I am jealous for you with a divine jealousy; for I have bespoken you as a chaste virgin for one husband that I may give you to Christ. But I am afraid in case, as the Serpent beguiled Eve with his wiles, your minds should be corrupted from the simplicity and virtuousness to which Christ is entitled. For if someone who comes along can proclaim another Jesus whom I did not proclaim, or you can receive a different Spirit than you did receive, or a different News than you accepted, you can well put up with me. For I reckon myself in no way inferior to such 'super-envoys'. Even if I am uncultured in speech, I am not in knowledge, and managed to make everything clear to you.

7   Did I make a mistake in abasing myself that you might be exalted, by proclaiming the News to you free of charge? I stripped other communities, taking payment to apply to your service. And when I was staying with you and went short, I was a dead weight to no one, for my shortage was fully made up by the brothers who came from Macedonia. In every way I kept myself – and shall go on keeping myself – from being any burden to you. As Christ's truth is in me, I am not going to be denied this boast in the regions of Achaia! Why? Because I have no regard for you? God knows I have! But I make and am going on making this boast, that I may remove the pretext of those who want a pretext, that in what they can boast of they will be found to be my equals. Such people are false envoys, deceitful agents, masquerading as envoys of Christ. And no wonder, when Satan himself masquerades as an angel of light! So it is hardly surprising if his ministers masquerade as ministers of religion, whose fate will correspond to their actions.

16   I say again, let no one take me for a fool. But if they must, then accept me as a fool, so that I may do a little boasting. What I am saying then, I am not saying sensibly, but as in folly, on this basis of boasting. Since many boast in human fashion, I too will boast; for sensible as you are you gladly put up with fools. You even put up with it when

somebody reduces you to cringing impotence, when somebody devours, grabs, makes a mat of you, and grinds your faces under his heel.

21 I am speaking insultingly because I am so sick of it all.

In whatever way anyone may make sweeping claims – I am keeping
22 up this fool talk – so can I. Are they Hebrews? So am I. Are they Israelites? So am I. Are they the seed of Abraham? So am I. Are they agents of Christ? Mad as it sounds, I am even more so. My labours have been harder, my terms of imprisonment longer, my floggings beyond all bounds, my risks of death more frequent. Five times I received from the Jews forty strokes less one,[6] three times I have been beaten with Roman rods, once I was stoned,[7] three times shipwrecked, a night and a day consigned to the deep. Often have I taken the road, in peril of rivers, in peril of brigands, in peril from my own nation, in peril from Gentiles, in peril in town, in peril in the country, in peril at sea, in peril from false brothers, in toil and hardship, often sleepless, in hunger and thirst, often fasting, in cold and in nakedness. On top of all this there has been my daily concern, the care of all the communities. Who is ailing, and I do not share his ailment? Who is offended, and I do not share his indignation?

30 If I must boast, I will boast of my disabilities. He who is blessed for ever, the God and Father of our Lord Jesus, knows I am not lying. At Damascus the ethnarch of King Haretath picketed the city of the Damascenes to hem me in; but through a loophole I was let down the wall in a basket, and so escaped his clutches.[8]

12.1 If I must continue to boast, undesirable as that is, I will come to visions and revelations of the Master. I know a man in Christ, who fourteen years ago – whether in the physical or astral state, I do not know, God knows – was caught up as far as the third heaven.[9] I know that this man – whether in the physical state or otherwise, I do not know, God knows – was caught up into 'the Garden'[10] and heard ineffable words which no human is permitted to utter. Of someone like this I will boast, but about myself I will not boast, only of my disabilities.[11]

6 Even should I want to boast I should be no fool, for I state the truth. But I will refrain, in case anyone should think more of me than what he sees and hears. But with the transcendence of the revelations, in case I should be too elated, there was given me a spike in the flesh, an emissary of Satan, to prod me. On this score three times I entreated the Master to make it leave me. But he told me, 'My favour is enough for you, for power is brought to full strength in weakness'. Most gladly,

therefore, will I rather boast of disabilities, that the power of Christ may take up its quarters in me. So I am content with disabilities, assaults, physical punishments, persecutions and close confinements, for Christ's sake. For when I am weak then I am strong.

11   There, I have played the fool. You have driven me to it. For I ought to have had your championship; for in no way am I inferior to those super-envoys, even if I am of no consequence. Indeed, the marks of an envoy were produced among you persistently in signs, wonders and miracles. For in what were you outdone by the rest of the communities, except that I personally was no dead weight to you? Forgive me this injustice.

14   Observe, this is my third time of readiness to come to you. But I will be no dead weight to you; for I do not seek what is yours but *you*. For it is not the children who should provide for their parents but the parents for their children. Most gladly will I spend and be spent to safeguard you. If I love you so dearly, should I not be loved as much? But there it is, I did not burden you. But 'being naturally unscrupulous I took from you by guile', eh? Was it by anyone I have sent to you that I defrauded you? I begged Titus to visit you, and with him I sent our brother. Was it Titus who defrauded you? Have we not acted in the same spirit, followed in the same steps? Do not think from this that I am defending myself. I am speaking before God in Christ. Everything I say, dear friends, is entirely for your benefit; for I fear much in case when I come I shall not find you in the frame of mind I would wish, nor you find me in the frame of mind you would wish. I fear in case there should be strife, rivalry, high-feeling, faction, recrimination, vilification, protestation and uproar, in case at my coming my God should humiliate me in front of you, and that I should break down over many who have fallen into sin, and have not repented of the impurity, immorality and licentiousness of which they have been guilty.

13.1   This is my third time of coming to you. 'By the mouth of two or three witnesses every word shall be confirmed.'[13] I have said previously, and being absent now I give warning as if present a second time,[14] to those who have fallen into sin and to all the others, that should I come once more I will not spare, since it is proof you require that Christ speaks to me. He at least is not weak, but powerful among you. For though he was crucified from weakness, he lives now by the power of God. And though we are weak in him, we too live with him by the power of God. Test yourselves, examine yourselves, whether *you* are in the faith. Or do you yourselves not know that Jesus Christ is in you, whether by any chance you are frauds? But I trust you will realize that I am no fraud.

7   Now I pray God you may do no wrong in any way. Not that I may be shown to be genuine, but that you may do the right thing even did I appear a fraud. For I have no power against the truth, only on behalf of truth. I am happy whenever I am weak and you are strong. This too I pray for, your perfection. That is why being absent I write as I do, that when present I should not have to employ severity, in accordance with the authority the Master has given me to build up, not to pull down.

11   Finally, brothers, rejoice, put yourselves to rights, take courage, be of the same mind, be at peace, and the God of love and peace be with you. Convey my regards to one and all with a chaste kiss. All the saints send you their regards.

14   The loving-kindness of the Lord Jesus Christ, the love of God, and the fellowship of the holy Spirit, be with you all.

NOTES AND REFERENCES

1. Corresponding to *II.Cor.*x – xiii. We have only the last part of the letter, but perhaps only brief introductory lines are missing.
2. Here and elsewhere Paul appears to be quoting remarks adverse to himself which had been reported to him.
3. In early tradition Paul is depicted as a rather ugly baldheaded man with a hooked nose and bow legs. A complaint affected his speech and he had poor eyesight.
4. The author is playing on the idea of measurement in more than one sense.
5. *Jer.*ix.24.
6. *Deut.*xxv.2-3. See *Jewish Encyclopaedia*, article *Stripes*.
7. *Acts.*xiv.19.
8. *Acts.*ix.25.
9. Seven heavens were imagined, one above another.
10. 'The Garden' (Paradise) was the third heaven, answering to the third degree of blessedness in Jewish occultism. See *Talmud, Chagigah* 12a-b.
11. The reference none the less is to Paul's personal experience, when, as he wrote to the Galatians, he had spent some time in Arabia, possibly with a community of the Essenes. The *Acts* omits this circumstance.
12. The cause of this twinge would appear to have been rheumatic.
13. *Deut.*xix.15.
14. It is clear from the next letter that Paul had paid a short 'distressing visit' to Corinth. The present letter was in lieu of a second visit. He therefore thinks of his readiness to come again as a third visit.

To the Community at Corinth (4)

(Probably written from Philippi in the summer of AD 56)[1]

II.Cor.

1.1   Paul, by the will of God an envoy of Christ Jesus, with brother Timotheus, to the community of God at Corinth and to all the saints resident throughout Achaia. May peace and prosperity be yours from God our Father and the Lord Jesus Christ.

3   Blessed be the God and Father of our Lord Jesus Christ, Father of mercies and God of all comfort, who comforts us in all our afflictions, that we may be enabled to comfort those who are in any affliction with the same comfort we have received. Blessed be he, that just as a full share of Christ's sufferings has come to me, so equally have I had my full share of comfort through Christ. And whether I am afflicted for your comfort and well-being, or comforted for your comfort, which is a stimulus to the endurance of the same sufferings that I suffer, my hope for you is constant, knowing that as we are fellows in suffering so are we in comfort also.

8   I would not have you ignorant, brothers, of the trying experience I have been through in Asia, how I was subjected to a weight so crushing in the extreme as to pass endurance, so that I had the gravest doubt whether I would survive. Rather for myself did I take it to be sentence of death, so that I should place no reliance on myself but on God who raises the dead. It was he who shielded me from imminent death, and shields me now, and whom I trust – with your co-operation in prayer on my behalf – to continue to shield me, so that thanksgiving to God on my account may be made by many persons for the kindness of so many towards me.

12   My pride, the testimony of my conscience, is this, that I have conducted myself in the world, not by means of any materialist philosophy but by divine mercy, in all innocence and utter sincerity, especially in my relations with you. I am consequently writing to you nothing but what you already well know or recognize, as indeed to some extent you have acknowledged, that I shall be your pride when the Day of our Lord Jesus comes, just as you will be mine.

15   It was from this confidence that I purposed visiting you previously, that you might have a second pleasure, both by my passing via yourselves on the way to Macedonia and visiting you again on my return from Macedonia, when you would forward me on my way to Judea. Was I merely proposing this casually? Or when I make proposals do I do so in the ordinary casual way, so that my 'yes, yes' can equally mean 'no, no'? As God is true, my word to you is never 'yes-and-no'! For the Son of God, Jesus Christ, he who was proclaimed to you by us – by myself, Silvanus and Timotheus – did not come as a 'yes-and-no'. In him there came 'Yes', for every promise of God is fulfilled in him who is the 'Yes'. That is why, through him, we make the affirmation 'Amen'[2] to God in praising him. It is God who has secured both us and you for Christ, who has had us duly signed and sealed, and has given us the advance payment of the Spirit in our hearts. I call God to witness for my life, that it is to spare you I have not come again to Corinth! Not that I claim any jurisdiction over your faith: I am but a contributor to your happiness. In faith you have your own stand-

2.1   ing. But I made up my mind not to pay you another distressing visit, for if I distress you, who is going to cheer me except those I distress? So I wrote then and there,[3] in case by coming I should be grieved by those who should give me joy, being convinced of all of you that it is my happiness that is the concern of you all. I wrote to you in great trouble and anguish of mind, shedding many tears, not to grieve you, but because of the very deep affection you know I have for you.

5   If a certain individual has caused distress, he has not caused me distress, at least not to an extent that I have to burden all of you with it. Let his censure by the majority suffice for that person, just as on the other hand it is for you to cheer and comfort him in case he should be completely overcome by the depth of his grief. Consequently, I entreat you to assure him of your affection. This was part of my object in writing, to ascertain your worth, whether you answer to all requirements. Whoever you forgive, so do I. Really, if anyone has to be forgiven, I am the one who has to be forgiven by you before Christ, in case Satan should catch me out; for I am not ignorant of his wiles.

12   Well, when I came to Troas in the interest of the News of Christ, and found a door opened to me by the Lord, I had no liberty of spirit because I did not find Brother Titus there. So taking leave of them I went off to Macedonia. Thanks be to God, who leads me in triumph in Christ, and makes the perfume of the knowledge of him rise up through me in every place! For I am Christ's fragrance to God both among those who

167

are being saved and among those who are perishing.[4] To the latter it is the odour of death leading to Death, while to the former it is the odour of life leading to Life. Who is adequate for such things? For I am not like the majority who water down God's message: I speak purely and plainly as from God, as standing in God's presence in Christ.

3.1   Have I begun to commend myself again? Or ought I like some to have procured letters of commendation to you or from you? Surely you are my letter, recorded on my heart, scrutinized and perused by all men. It is plain for all to see that you are Christ's letter composed on my behalf, recorded not in ink but in the Spirit of the Living God, not on tablets of stone but on tablets of the human heart.

4   Such is the confidence I have towards God through Christ. It is not that I am adequate in myself to deal with anything as of myself. My competence comes from God, who has qualified me to act as an administrator of a New Covenant, not in letter but in spirit; for the letter kills, but the Spirit vitalizes.[5]

7   Yet if the administration of death[6] in letters engraved on stones was glorious, so that the children of Israel could not look at Moses's face because of the transient shining of his face,[7] how much more shall the administration of the Spirit be glorious? For if the administration of condemnation was glorious, much more glorious still shall be the administration of vindication. Even what did shine could hardly be said to shine in comparison with that surpassing glory. For if what was transient had a glory, much more glorious shall be that which is to endure.

12   So having an expectation like this I speak plainly, and not like Moses, who had to veil his face so that the children of Israel could not look at the conclusion of what was transient. Their perceptions were blinded; and down to this very day the same veil over the implication of the Old Covenant remains unremoved, since it is in Christ that it is dispensed with. For till to-day, whenever Moses is read, the veil lies upon their mind. Yet whenever that mind 'shall be turned to the Lord' the veil will be taken off.[8] 'The Lord' means the Spirit, and where the Spirit of the Lord is there is freedom. So all of us, having our face unveiled to the glory of the Lord, reflecting as in a mirror the same image, are being transformed from glory to glory, as from the Lord who is Spirit.[9]

4.1   Having this administration, therefore, as mercy has been shown me, I am no shirker, but have renounced base subterfuges. I do not use cunning devices, nor water down God's Message, but by plain truth make contact with every human conscience in the sight of God. If my News is veiled at all, it is veiled to those who are perishing, where the god of this world has blinded the perception of the infidels, so that they should not see clearly the luminosity of the News of the glory of Christ, who[10] is the image of God. For I do not proclaim myself but Christ Jesus as Master, and myself as your servant for Jesus's sake, because it is the God who said, 'Let light shine out of darkness', who has illumined my mind with the luminosity of the knowledge of God's glory on the face of Christ.

7   I have this treasure in an earthen vessel,[11] however, that the superabundance of the power may be of God, and not emanate from myself. I am harassed on every side, but not hemmed in; in great straits, but not devoid of resources; hard-pressed, but not abandoned; struck down, but not destroyed, always carrying around in my body the death-state of Jesus, that the life of Jesus may also be evident in my body. For always I who live am delivered up to death for Jesus's sake, that the life of Jesus may also be evident in my mortal frame. So then death is at work in me, but life in you.

13   Yet having the selfsame spirit of faith as is stated, 'I have believed, therefore have I spoken',[12] I too believe, and therefore speak, knowing that he who raised up Jesus will also raise me up with Jesus, and set me beside you. For all that has transpired is for your sake, that the mercy having been increased by the greater number participating in it[13] the thanksgiving also may be multiplied to the glory of God.

16   So I am no shirker; but if my exterior self is disabled my inner self is daily renewed. The momentary lightness of my affliction achieves for me correspondingly a lasting weight of glory. I pay no regard to the things that are seen, but to those that are unseen; for the things that are

5.1   seen are temporary, while those that are unseen are permanent. For I know that when my earthly makeshift dwelling is demolished I possess a building from God, a dwelling that is not artificial, permanent in heaven. This is what I sigh for, longing to be under cover of my dwelling from heaven; for so sheltered I shall not be left out in the cold. Yes, that is what I – living in this hutment – sigh for, not wanting to be deprived of cover but to be under cover, so that what is mortal may be swallowed up by Life.

5   God, who has acquired me for this very end, has given me the down payment of the Spirit. So having every confidence, and knowing that while I am at home in the body I am absent from the Master – for I walk by faith and not by sight – I am both confident and content rather

to be absent from the body and at home with the Master. That is why I strive so eagerly, whether present or absent, to satisfy him; for we must all stand revealed before Christ's tribunal that each may be requited for his bodily actions, whatever he has done, either useful or worthless.

11   Sensible of the fear of the Lord, therefore, I persuade men while my character stands fully revealed to God, and I trust also to your consciousness. I am not commending myself to you again, but furnishing you with grounds for boasting about me, that you may have something to set against those who boast on the basis of outward appearance instead of the heart. Whether I have been 'raving', it has been for God, or in my senses, it has been for you; for Christ's love deeply affects me. I have reached this conclusion, that as one died for all, all then were dead, and he died for all that those who live should live no longer for themselves but for him who died for them and rose again. From now on, therefore, we know no one in the physical sense. Even if we have known Christ in the physical sense,[14] we do so now no longer.

17   Consequently, if anyone is in Christ, he is a new creation. The old relationships are gone, replaced by the new. It is all God's doing, who through Christ has reconciled us to himself. And he has given us the administration of this reconciliation, the position being that in Christ God was reconciling the world to himself, not charging men's failings against them, and entrusting us with the Message of reconciliation. Accordingly, we plead on Christ's behalf, as though God were entreating by us, we beg you on Christ's behalf, 'Be reconciled to God'. He made him who knew no sin to be as sin for us, that we might be guiltless with God by him.

6.1   As a fellow-worker, I also beg you not to receive the mercy of God to no purpose, for he says,

I have heard you at a time of receptiveness,
And aided you on a day of deliverance.[15]

Assuredly now is the 'time of receptiveness', now is the 'day of deliverance'.

3   It is for me to create no difficulty of any kind, that no blame may attach to the administration. Rather in every way have I to commend myself as God's representative by much patience, afflictions, suffering and anxiety; by lashes, imprisonment and mob violence; by toil, vigil and fasting; by impartiality, insight and perseverance; by kindness, spiritual fervour and unfeigned love; by honest speech and divine

170

power; by the right and left hand weapons of right conduct; by honour and dishonour, ill-fame and good-fame; as a deceiver yet true; as an unknown yet well known; as a dying man yet very much alive; as disciplined yet not brought to death; as grieved yet ever rejoicing; as poor yet enriching many; as possessing nothing yet owning everything.

11 Well, Corinthians, I have spoken frankly to you. I have bared my
12 bosom. You have put no constraint on me, but you have put constraint
13 on your own feelings. 'Now it's your turn to pay *me* back', as one says to children. Now you too bare *your* bosoms.[16]

7.2 Make room for me. I have wronged no one. I have harmed no one. I have defrauded no one. I am not saying this censoriously; for as I have said before, 'you are in my heart to die with and to live with',[17] I am filled with comfort. I am brim full of happiness despite all my troubles. For when I reached Macedonia I had no physical relief, but troubles on every side, 'conflicts without and terror within'. But God, who comforts the cast down, comforted me by the arrival of Titus, and not only by his arrival but by the cheering report of you he brought, informing me of your longing for me, of your contrition, of your anxiety on my account, so that I was made happier still.

8 Although I grieved you in the letter,[18] I have no regrets. Even if I had regrets, seeing that the letter in question had to cause you even an hour's distress, I am glad now, not that you were distressed, but because you were distressed into penitence, distressed indeed as God likes to see, so that you were in no way harmed by me. For pain of the divine kind produces penitence leading to restoration, not to be regretted; but pain of the world's kind produces death. Take this very instance of grieving of the divine kind, how much concern it effected in you, instead of defensiveness, indignation, fear, complaint, passion and vindictiveness! In every way you have shown yourselves honourable in this affair. Therefore, though I wrote to you as I did, it was not for the sake of the offender, not even for the sake of the victim, but that your concern for me might be plain to you in the sight of God.

13 That is why I have been cheered. And over and above my personal consolation I was made happier than ever by Titus's happiness, because all of you had set his mind at rest. So there has been no cause to retract anything I have boasted of to him about you. Rather, as I have spoken with complete truthfulness to you, so has the boast I made to Titus been equally truthful. And his heart overflows towards you at the remembrance of the submissiveness of you all as you received with fear and trepidation. I am happy to have complete confidence in you.

8.1   Now I would inform you, brothers, of the divine favour granted to the communities of Macedonia, how during a most testing trial the excess of their joy set against the extremity of their destitution enhanced the lavishness of their generosity, so that to the best of their capacity, I declare, and beyond their capacity, of their own accord and with many entreaties, they begged me for the favour and fellowship of joining in the service for the saints.[19] It was not as I expected of them, but as they expected, that they gave first to the Master then to me by the will of God, so that I encouraged Titus that as he had begun so should he complete with you also the same expression of gratitude,[20] that just as you excel in every way, in faith, in speech, in knowledge, and zeal of every kind, and also in the affection you have for me, so should you excel in this expression of gratitude also.

8   I am not saying this as an order, but because of the zeal of others and in proof of the genuineness of your affection. For you know the graciousness of our Lord Jesus Christ, how being rich he impoverished himself for your sake, that you might be enriched by that poverty. But on this matter I do offer an opinion, for it is desirable that you should not only have initiated, but should maintain what you started a year ago. So now go on to complete what you have initiated, that as is the keenness to keep it up so will be the effectiveness of what is done. For if the keenness is there, whatever one may do is acceptable: it is not as if one does nothing. For it is not a question of others having relief while you are in difficulties, but that in fairness at the present time your superfluity should compensate for their shortage, so that in turn their superfluity may make up for your shortage which will be only right and proper, as it is stated, 'He that had much had not too much, and he that had little did not go short'.[21]

16   Thank God for putting the same concern on your behalf into the mind of Titus, so that he welcomed the proposal, and being so very admirable he visited you initially of his own accord. I have now sent with him the brother approved in the service of the News throughout the communities,[22] and not only so but elected by the communities as my travelling companion in this expression of gratitude administered and pressed forward by me for the honour of the Master. In this way provision has been made that no one should find fault with me over this bounty which is administered by me; for I would be well-respected not only in the Lord's sight but also in the sight of men.[23] So I have sent with him my brother, whom I have proved to be admirable on so many occasions, and now more admirable than ever in the implicit

confidence he places in you. So whether it is Titus, my associate and your fellow-worker, or other brothers, envoys of the communities, they are a credit to Christ. Therefore furnish clear evidence in the sight of the communities in demonstration of your affection and of my boast about you to them.

9.1   It is really quite superfluous for me to be writing to you about this service to the saints, for I am aware of your keenness which is what I boasted about you to the Macedonians. 'Achaia,' I said, 'was all ready a year ago,' and your enthusiasm has stimulated many. Yet I have dispatched the brothers in case my boast about you should have been an empty one in this respect, so that, as I have been saying you are ready, should it happen that Macedonians accompany me and find you are not ready, I, not to say you, would be ashamed in face of this reality. I have considered it advisable, therefore, to propose to the brothers that they should visit you in advance and set in motion that previously announced goodwill-offering of yours, that the same being promptly forthcoming it will be like a goodwill-offering and not like an imposition.

6   There is this to add: 'He that sows sparingly will reap sparingly, while he that sows liberally will reap liberally.'[24] Let each follow his heart's dictate, not acting grudgingly or from necessity, for 'the Lord loves a cheerful giver'.[25] God is able to lavish every blessing upon you, so that always having sufficiency in every way you may be more than adequate for every good deed, just as it is stated,

> He has distributed his means;
> He has given to the poor:
> His beneficence endures for ever.[26]

10   He who supplies 'seed to the sower, and bread for food'[27] will supply and multiply your produce and increase the fruits of your beneficence. So then, being enriched in every way for every act of generosity, whatever is done evokes by my agency thanksgiving to God. For the administration of this service not only makes up the shortage of the saints, but is further augmented by the volume of thanksgiving to God; for in appreciation of this ministration the saints praise God for the strictness of your conformity with the Good News of Christ and the generosity of your fellowship with them and with all others. And their future wishes for you are expressed in prayer on your behalf because

15   of God's overwhelming kindness to you.[28] Thanks be to God for his incomparable gift!

[Conclusion lacking] [29]

NOTES AND REFERENCES

1. Corresponding to *II.Corinthians* (but see below notes 16 and 29).
2. 'So be it', in the words 'through our Lord Jesus Christ. Amen.'
3. Namely the previous letter, the third letter.
4. As God's captive in Christ, Paul sees himself as a victim led along in the triumphal procession, and at the same time as the incense burnt in the victor's honour at various points on the route.
5. Cf. *Jer*.xxxi.31-33.
6. Because with Law came sin, and so death.
7. Cf. *Exod*.xxxiv.28-30.
8. *Exod*.xxxiv.34 (LXX).
9. Paul is conveying that the process of change continues, as we reflect more and more of the Spirit, until final glorification at the resurrection of the dead, when we shall bear the full likeness of the heavenly, the pristine image of God, like Adam when first created (*Gen*.i.26).
10. Like Adam.
11. The physical body. Cf. *Jud*.vii.16; *Jer*.xxxii.14.
12. *Ps*.cxvi.10.
13. Paul refers to those who have been praying for his recovery from the serious illness mentioned in the previous letter.
14. As the family and immediate followers of Jesus had done, and could thus claim more exact knowledge.
15. *Isa*.xlix.8.
16. Omitting here *II.Cor*.vi.14 – vii.1, as being part of a previous letter (1).
17. Quoted perhaps from a part of the third letter, now missing.
18. The previous letter (3), pp.160 – 165.
19. The collection of funds for the poor saints of Judea.
20. For the gift of the message about the Messiah.
21. *Exod*.xvi.18.
22. The unnamed brother has been thought by some to be Luke or Silas, but might be Tychicus or Trophimus. See *Acts*.xx.4.
23. Cf. *Prov*.iii.4 (LXX); *Rom*.xii.17.
24. Cf. *Prov*.xi.24 (LXX).
25. *Prov*.xxii.8 (LXX).
26. *Ps*.cxii.9 (LXX).
27. *Isa*.lv.10 (LXX).
28. In extending to Gentiles participation in the Messianic bliss.
29. The rest of *II.Corinthians* is reproduced as the third letter to the community at Corinth, pp.160 – 165. Probably little more than the concluding greeting is missing from this fourth letter.

To the Believers at Rome

(Probably written from Corinth early in AD 57)[1]

1.1   Paul, servant of Jesus Christ, a chosen envoy, assigned to the proclamation of God's News, which he had previously announced by his Prophets in the Sacred Writings, concerning his Son, Jesus Christ our Master, born in the physical sense of the line of David, but potently demonstrated to be God's Son in the sanctified spiritual sense by resurrection from the dead.[2] By him I have obtained favour and envoyship to procure loyal submission to his authority on the part of all nations, among whom you likewise are summoned by Jesus Christ. To all God's dear ones in Rome, members of the Holy Assembly, may peace and prosperity be yours from God our Father and from the Lord Jesus Christ.

8   In the first place I thank my God through Jesus Christ for all of you that your faith is patent to the whole world. God is my witness, whom I serve devotedly in the cause of the News of his Son, that I never fail to make regular reference to you in my prayers, requesting that somehow at long last, God willing, I may succeed in reaching you. For I do so long to see you, that I may impart to you some spiritual gift for your confirmation,[3] that is to say that I may find common encouragement with you through your and my mutual faith.[4]

13   I do not want you to be in ignorance, brothers, that I have often proposed to visit you, though I have been prevented hitherto, in order that I may obtain some fruit of my labours among you as I have among other nations. I am indebted for such fruit both to Greeks and Barbarians, to the cultured and the uncultured; so I am naturally eager to have the opportunity of proclaiming the News among you in Rome also. For I am not ashamed of the News: it is God's means of deliverance for all who believe, whether Jews or Greeks. For by it God's justice is revealed by faith for faith, as it is stated, 'By faith the just shall live'.[5]

18   But God's wrath is revealed from heaven against all impiety and

iniquity of men who wilfully suppress the truth, since they are well aware of the facts about God, for God has made these plain to them. For ever since the creation of the world those unseen qualities of his, his immaterial nature, power and divinity, could be clearly perceived, apprehended through his works. So there is no excuse for them, when being acquainted with God they have neither praised nor thanked him as God, but have indulged in idle speculations and obscured their senseless minds. Professing to be wise they have behaved with utter folly, and have converted the glory of the imperishable God into the portrayal of the likeness of perishable men, birds, four-footed beasts and reptiles. Therefore God has given them over to their hearts' desire for depravity, to the abuse of their bodies among themselves, they who have exchanged God's truth for a lie, and worshipped and served the thing created instead of the Creator, blessed be he for ever. Amen.

26   Consequently God has given them over to their infamous passion; for their females have changed the normal function into the abnormal. The males, too, abandoning the normal function with females, inflamed with lust for one another, males for males, have engaged in indecency, duly receiving the reward appropriate to their irregularity between themselves. And just as they have not admitted God to a place in their consciousness, so God has given them over to a corrupt mind, to behave in unseemly fashion, perpetrating every kind of iniquity,

29   obscenity, cupidity and depravity.[6] They are brim full of malice, murder, quarrelsomeness, knavery and malignity, slanderers, libellers, antitheistic, insolent, arrogant, brazen, contrivers of evils, defiant to parents, of low mentality, perfidious, lacking in affection, pitiless, the sort who well knowing God's ordinance that those who are guilty of such behaviour deserve death, not only act in this way themselves, but applaud others who do so.

2.1   So there is no excuse for you, sir, whoever you may be, who sit in judgment; for in the very thing you judge others you condemn yourself, since you who judge act in the same way.

2   Now we know that God's sentence is a just one on those who have acted in this fashion. Do you reckon, therefore, you who judge those who have acted like this and yet do the same yourself, that you can escape God's sentence? Or do you affect to scorn the wealth of his consideration, forbearance and long-suffering, ignoring that God's consideration is designed to lead you to repentance, preferring on account of your hard and impenitent heart to store up wrath for yourself in the Day of Wrath and disclosure of God's just doom? He it is

who will 'render to every man according to his deeds';[7] for those who by persistence in worthy actions seek glory, honour and immortality, it will be Eternal Life, while for those who are of a contentious nature and will not comply with the truth – but readily comply with falsehood – it will be wrath and anger. There will be affliction and anguish for every human being who engages in evil, first for Jew then for Gentile;[8] but glory, honour and peace for all who do good, first for Jew then for Greek; for there is no partiality on God's part.

12   As many as have sinned without law[9] shall perish without law, and as many as have sinned under law will be sentenced by law, on the day God judges the hidden things in men's lives by Christ Jesus, according to my presentation of the News. For it is not the hearers of law who are right with God, but the keepers of law who are exonerated. When, therefore, such Gentiles as have no law act instinctively as the Law requires, these having no law are their own law. They thus display the operation of that law which is written in their hearts, their conscience endorsing such action, though in the meantime their reasoning faculties may be engaged in a mutual conflict of accusation and defence.[10]

17   Now you on the other hand are one who bears the name of Jew. You rely on law and boast in God.[11] You are acquainted with his will, and can make clear distinctions,[12] being instructed out of the Law. You are convinced that you are a guide to the blind, a light to those in darkness, a tutor of the backward, a teacher of infants, because in the Law you have the whole corpus of knowledge and truth.

21   Well then, you who teach others, do you never teach yourself? You who proclaim 'not to steal', do you steal? You who say 'not to commit adultery', do you commit adultery? You who detest idols, do you rob temples? You who boast in the Law, do you dishonour God by transgressing the Law? Surely, as it is stated, 'God's name is profaned by you among the heathen'.[13]

25   Circumcision is a definite advantage if you observe the Law; but if you are a lawbreaker your circumcision is converted into uncircumcision. So if the uncircumcised person observes the moral principles of the Law, is not his uncircumcision to be reckoned as circumcision? And has not that uncircumcision which is by nature the right, having carried out the Law, to judge you who in spite of both code and circumcision are a lawbreaker? For he is no Jew who is only one in appearance, nor is circumcision simply what appears physically. The real Jew is he who is one internally, and the real

177

circumcision is that of the heart, spiritual not literal, whose praise comes not from men but from God.

3.1 What merit is there then in being a Jew? Or what advantage does circumcision confer? Much in every respect, primarily because the Jews were entrusted with the Oracles of God. What does it matter if some were untrustworthy? Does their untrustworthiness invalidate God's fidelity? God forbid! If only God be true, it matters not if every man be false, as it is stated,

> That you should have your words vindicated,
> And prevail when you are arraigned.[14]

5 But if your iniquity confirms God's rectitude, what are we to say, that God is unjust to vent his wrath? (I am speaking humanly.) God forbid! For in that case how can God judge the world? But if God's truth has more redounded to his praise by my untruth, why am I still adjudged a sinner? And why not, as I am slanderously reported, and as some, whose condemnation is richly merited, allege that I say, "Let us do evil that good may come of it"?

9 What then? Do we Jews come off any better? Not at all. For we have already charged Jews and Gentiles alike with sinful behaviour, as it is stated:

> None is upright, not a single one.
> None gives heed: none seeks after God.
> All are defective, and worthless beside.
> None serves a useful purpose, not one.
> Their throat is a yawning tomb:
> They employ their tongues for deceit.
> The venom of asps is between their lips,
> Filling their mouth with bane and bitterness.
> Their feet are swift to shed blood:
> Rack and ruin strew their path;
> And the way of peace they have not known.
> There is no fear of God before their eyes.[15]

19 Now we know that whatever the Law states it declares to those who are governed by the Law, so that every mouth may be gagged and all the world become accountable to God, since by following regulations 'not a single human being will be exonerated';[16] for through law comes acquaintance with sin.

21 But now, independent of law, the righteousness of God has been made patent, attested both by the Law and the Prophets, that right-

eousness of God which is by faith in Jesus Christ, available to *all* who believe. (There is no distinction; for *all* have sinned and failed to reach God's standard.) These, by God's mercy, are freely exonerated through the discharge of liability by Christ Jesus, by their reliance on his blood, whom God has appointed as an expiatory sacrifice in demonstration of his righteousness. In God's forbearance he overlooked the sins of past generations in view of the demonstration of his rectitude at the present time, so as to be both just himself, and the exonerator of whoever places his faith in Jesus.

27 Where then does boasting come in? It is excluded. By what law? Of regulations? No, by a law of faith; for we have reckoned that a man is exonerated by faith independent of legal regulations. For is he the God of the Jews only, and not of the Gentiles? Surely of the Gentiles also, if God is truly One. He exonerates the circumcised by their faith, and the uncircumcised by means of their acquired faith. Are we using faith to invalidate law? God forbid! Rather are we confirming law.[17]

4.1 What then are we to say of Abraham, our ancestor in the physical sense? If Abraham was exonerated by regulations he may well boast, though not to God. For what does the Scripture say, 'Abraham relied on God, and it was credited to him as rectitude'.[18] To one who carries out stipulations his reward is not reckoned as a favour, but as a due. But to one who does not carry out stipulations, but relies on him who exonerates the ungodly, his faith is reckoned as rectitude, just as David speaks of the happiness of the man to whom rectitude is accounted independent of regulations:

> Happy are those whose illegalities are forgiven,
> And whose sins are covered over.
> Happy is the man against whom the Lord counts not sin.[19]

9 Is that happiness reserved for the circumcised, or is it not also for the uncircumcised? Surely we have said, his faith was credited to Abraham as rectitude. In what circumstances then was it credited, when he was in a state of circumcision or of uncircumcision? Not in a state of circumcision, surely, but in that of uncircumcision; for he received the mark of circumcision as a ratification of the rectitude arising from the faith he had while uncircumcised, so that he might be the father of all who believe coming from uncircumcision. At the same time he became the father of circumcision to those who – not on account of circumcision alone – follow in the steps of the faith of our father Abraham which he had when uncircumcised.

13   For it was not by law that the promise was made to Abraham, or
to his seed, that he should be 'heir of the world', but by rectitude
deriving from faith. For if those based on law are heirs, faith is an
empty thing and the promise is idle. The Law results in wrath, but
where no law exists there can be no transgression either. Necessarily
it is based on faith, so as to be a matter of favour, that the promise
might be secured to *all* the seed, not only to that which is based on
the Law, but also to that which is based on the faith of Abraham, who
is our common ancestor, as it is stated, 'I have made you father of
many nations'.[20] Anticipating this, he relied on God the 'Giver of life
to the dead',[21] and the Namer of things as existing which as yet are
non-existent. Against hope he relied on hope that he would be 'father
of many nations', as expressed in the words 'so shall your seed be'.[22]
His faith never weakened with consciousness of the impotence of his
own body – he was nearly a hundred years old at the time – and of
Sarah's incapacity for motherhood. He did not challenge the promise
of God incredulously, but fortified by faith he gave God credence,
and was fully assured that what he had promised was practicable, and
that he would carry it out. That is why it was 'credited to him as
rectitude'.

23   Now it was not written in respect of Abraham alone that 'it was
credited to him', but also in respect of us to whom it would subsequently be credited, of those who trust in him who raised up Jesus
our Master from the dead, who was delivered up for our trespasses
and raised up for our exoneration.

5.1   So being exonerated on a basis of faith we enjoy peace with God
through our Lord Jesus Christ, by whom we have secured admission
to that state of favour in which we now stand, and boast in the prospect of God's esteem. And not only this, we even boast in afflictions,
knowing that affliction fosters patience, patience fosters experiment,
experiment fosters expectation, and expectation never disappoints,
because God's love has pervaded our minds by the holy Spirit which
has been given us.

6   Moreover, Christ, when we were still helpless, died in due course
for the ungodly. Now hardly for a devout man would anyone die,
though possibly for a good man someone might dare to die. But God
proves his own love for us, because Christ died for us while we were
still sinners. Much more, therefore, being now exonerated by his
blood, shall we be delivered from wrath through him. If then, as
enemies, we were reconciled to God by the death of his Son, much

180

more, having become reconciled, shall we be delivered by his life. And not only this, we boast in God through our Lord Jesus Christ, by whose instrumentality we have obtained reconciliation.

12   Consequently, as by one man's agency sin entered the world, and by means of sin death, so death became the common lot of mankind, for all have sinned. For up to the time there was law sin was in the world, though sin was not charged as such while no law existed.[23] Nevertheless, death reigned from Adam down to Moses, even over those who technically had not sinned in a manner corresponding to the transgression of Adam, who prefigured him who was to come.[24] But the effect of the act of grace was very different to that of the transgression; for if by the transgression of one man the many died, far more has the mercy of God, and the free gift in mercy represented by the one man Jesus Christ, transcended this for the many. Other, indeed, was the effect of the gift to what happened by one person having sinned. The judgment for one transgression[25] brought condemnation, while the act of grace for many transgressions brought acquittal. Where, by the transgression of one, death reigned on account of the one, far more will those who have obtained the benefit of mercy and the free gift of rectitude, reign in life on account of the one, Jesus Christ.

18   So then, as a single transgression led to condemnation for all mankind, so equally a single worthy action led to acquittal spelling life for all mankind. Just as by one man's disobedience the many were constituted sinners, so also by one man's obedience the many are constituted righteous. Law came in additionally to magnify the transgression; but where sin abounded mercy abounded still more, that as sin reigned by death so should mercy reign through rectitude in Eternal Life by Jesus Christ our Master.

6.1   What are we to say then? Are we to continue in sin that mercy may be magnified? God forbid! We who have died so far as sin is concerned, how can we still live in it? Can you be ignorant that those who have become associated with Christ by immersion have become associated by it with his death? Through this association with him by immersion we are thus united with him in burial, so that as Christ was raised from the dead by means of the Father's glory, we too should conduct ourselves in newness of life. For if we have become identified with the manner of his death, surely we should be with his resurrection also, knowing this, that our former self has been associated in crucifixion to dispose completely of the sinful body, that we should no longer be enslaved to sin; for the dead has met all the claims of sin upon him.

8   If we have died with Christ we believe that we shall also be associated with him in life, realising that Christ having risen from the dead cannot be put to death again: death has no further power over him. As he died, he died permanently so far as sin was concerned, but as alive again, he lives to God. And so you no less can count yourselves dead so far as sin is concerned, but alive to God in Christ Jesus.

12   Therefore do not let sin rule your mortal body by obeying its lusts, nor offer your organs as instruments of iniquity where sin is concerned. Rather offer yourselves to God as alive from the dead, and your organs as instruments of rectitude to God. Sin shall not have dominion over you, for you are not under law but under mercy.

15   What then? Shall we sin because we are not under law but under mercy? God forbid! Do you not know that to whom you offer yourselves in obedience as slaves, to him you obey you are slaves, whether slaves of sin for death or of obedience for righteousness? But God be thanked that though you were slaves of sin you have since obeyed from the heart that model of teaching[26] which has been transmitted to you. Thus freed from sin, you have become enslaved to righteousness. (I am employing human terms because of the limitations of your physical nature.) For just as you offered your organs as slaves to uncleanness and lawlessness, for lawlessness, so have you now offered your organs as slaves to righteousness, for consecration.

20   When you were slaves of sin you were freemen as regards righteousness. What fruit had you then of those things of which you are now ashamed? For the end of those things is death. But now having been freed from sin and having become enslaved to God you have your fruit in consecration, the end of which is Eternal Life. For death is the pittance that sin pays, while God's bounty by Christ Jesus our Master is Eternal Life.

7.1   Can you be ignorant, brothers (for I am speaking to those familiar with law), that the Law is in control for as long as a man lives? For the wife subject to a husband is bound by law for the duration of her husband's life. But if the husband dies she ceases to be subject to marital control. It follows that if she becomes another man's during her husband's lifetime she will be pronounced an adulteress; but if her husband is dead she is free as far as the Law is concerned, so that she will be no adulteress if she then becomes another man's.

4   Consequently, my brothers, you too have been freed in law by death

through the body of Christ, so as to be able to become another man's, his who was raised from the dead, that we should be fruitful to God.[27] For when we stood in the physical relationship the sinful sensations induced by the Law actuated our organs to produce fruit for death. But now we are severed from the Law, that by which we were controlled being dead, so as to serve in a new way of the spirit and not in the old way of the letter.

7   What are we to say then? That the Law is sin? God forbid! But I should not have been acquainted with sin except through law; for I should not have known desire if the Law had not said, 'You are not to covet.'

8   It was sin, seizing the opportunity through the commandment, that provoked in me every kind of desire; for apart from law sin was inert. I was alive once apart from law; but when the commandment came sin sprang to life, and I died.[28.] So I found the commandment which was intended for life tended to death; for sin seizing the opportunity through the commandment completely beguiled me, and through it slew me. Consequently the Law is indeed holy, and the commandment is holy, just and good.

13   Did then what is good become death to me? God forbid! But sin, that sin might be apparent through the good, brought about my death, that sin through the commandment might be exceedingly sinful. For we know that the Law is spiritual, but I on the other hand am physical, the cat's-paw of sin. I do not perceive what I am about; for I find myself doing not what I wish to do, but doing instead what I detest.

16   So if I am doing what I do not wish to do, I grant that the Law is right. But there it is, it is not that I am doing whatever it is, but the indwelling sin in me. For I know that good does not reside in me, that is, in my physical nature.[29] The intention is there, but the capacity to carry out what is right is not; for I do not do the good I intend, but the evil I do not intend. So if I do what I do not intend, it is no longer I who am doing it, but sin that dwells in me. I discover, therefore, the law, that whenever it is my intention to do the right the wrong asserts itself in me. In my inner self I delight in the Law of God,[30] but I perceive another law in my organs, warring against the law of my mind and making me prisoner to the law of sin which exists in my organs. So there it is, I myself intellectually am bound to God's Law, but physically to sin's law. Miserable man that I am! Who will rescue me from this body of death?[31] Thanks be to God

through Jesus Christ our Master! So then mentally I do indeed serve the Law of God, but with the flesh the law of sin.

8.1 Thus there is no condemnation whatever for those who are in Christ Jesus; for the law of the Spirit of Life in Christ Jesus has freed me from the law of sin and death. For the Law's powerlessness, due to its weakness because of the physical factor, was remedied by God sending his own Son in the likeness of sinful physical nature. And as regards sin he passed sentence on sin in Christ's physical being, so that the Law's claims should be satisfied so far as we are concerned, we who do not lead the physical but the spiritual life. For those who are physical are concerned with material matters, while those who are spiritual are concerned with spiritual matters. The materialistic mentality spells death; the spiritual mentality spells life and peace. That is because the materialistic mentality is hostile to God; for it is not subordinated to God's control, nor can it be. Those who have the physical outlook cannot please God.

9 Now you do not have the physical but the spiritual outlook, assuming that God's Spirit resides in you. Naturally, if anyone does not possess the spirit of Christ he does not belong to him. But if Christ is present in you it means that the body is dead as a vehicle of sin, but the spirit is alive as a vehicle of righteousness. And if the Spirit that raised up Jesus from the dead resides in you, then he that raised Christ Jesus from the dead will also give life to your mortal bodies by very reason of his Spirit indwelling in you.

12 So then, brothers, we are under no obligation to our physical nature to live on the material plane; for if you live on the material plane you will surely die. Whereas if by the spiritual you put to death the practices of the body you will live; for it is those who are led by the Spirit of God who are the sons of God. You have not received a servile spirit, to put you again in fear. It is a filial spirit you have received, whereby we cry 'Abba!' (Father!).[32]

16 The Spirit joins its witness to our spirit that we are God's children. And if children then heirs, first heirs of God, and then joint-heirs with Christ. In that case we suffer together so as to be ennobled together also. I, personally, count the sufferings of the present time as quite unworthy to be compared with the future glory that is to be revealed in us.

19 The eager longing of the Creation itself waits expectantly for the revelation of the Sons of God. For the Creation is subject to dissolution, not of its own choice, but through him who subjected it, yet in

expectation that the Creation itself would be freed from servitude to decay to share the glorious freedom of the Children of God. We know indeed that the whole Creation groans and strains until now, and not it alone, but those who already enjoy the spiritual first-fruits – we ourselves – even they moan to themselves, waiting expectantly for the adoption, the redemption of their bodies.[33] For we are kept alive on hope. But hope that is in sight is not hope; for where one *sees*, where is there need for hope? But if we hope for what we do not see, then we persist in our expectant waiting.

26   Likewise the Spirit comes to the assistance of our limitations; for we do not know how to express ourselves adequately in prayer. But the Spirit itself makes intercession with speechless moans, and God who searches hearts knows what is the sense of the Spirit's utterances, that in God's way it is interceding for the saints. We know further, that for those who love God, for those called in accordance with his purpose, God makes everything turn out for the best. For, for those he had in view, he also planned in advance that they should come to resemble his Son, that thus he might be the eldest of many brothers. And those he purposed in advance he duly called, and those he called he duly exonerated, and those he exonerated he will duly ennoble.

31   What then are we to say to all this? If God is for us, who is there against us? He who did not withhold his very own Son, but delivered him up for us all,[34] will he not also with him gladly give us everything else? Who dare accuse God's Elect? When God exonerates, who is there that can condemn? When Christ has died, still more has risen from the dead, is at God's right hand, and also intercedes for us, who is to separate us from Christ's love? Can affliction, or confinement, or persecution, or famine, or destitution, or danger, or sword? As it is stated,

> For your sake we are killed the whole day long:
> We are reckoned as sheep for the slaughter.[35]

Yet in all these circumstances we are easy victors through him who has loved us. I am convinced that neither death nor life, neither angels nor ruling spirits, neither present nor future, neither powers above nor powers below, nor any other created being, will be able to sever us from the love of God which is in Christ Jesus our Master.

9.1   I am telling the truth in Christ, I am not lying, my conscience bearing me witness in the holy Spirit, when I say that I am in great grief and continual mental distress. For I could entreat that I personally was outcast from Christ for my brothers' sake, my kinsmen in the physical sense, who are Israelites, to whom belongs the Adoption,[36] and the Glory,[37] and the Covenants, and the Law-giving, and the Service,[38] and the Promises, whose are the Patriarchs, and above all from whom in the physical sense came Christ, blessed be God for ever. Amen.

6   There is no question of God's word having failed; for it is not all who spring from Israel who are Israel, neither because they are the seed of Abraham are all of them his children. For 'in Isaac shall your seed be called'.[39] That is to say, not the children in the ordinary physical sense are the children of God, but the children of promise are reckoned as the seed. For this is how the promise went: 'About this time I will return, and Sarah will have a son.'[40] And not only so, but when Rebecca had also conceived by one, namely our father Isaac, it was told her, 'the elder shall serve the younger'.[41] This was before the children were born, when they had done nothing either good or bad, in order that the purpose of God as regards choice should stand not on a basis of conduct but of calling, just as it is stated, 'Jacob have I loved, but Esau have I hated.'[42]

14   What are we to say then? That there is injustice on God's part? God forbid! For he says to Moses, 'I will show mercy to whom I would be merciful, and have compassion on whom I would be compassionate.'[43] It follows that it is a matter not of what one wants, or what one tries to do, but of God's mercy; for the Scripture says to Pharoah, 'For this very reason I have raised you up, that through you I may display my power, and my name become known throughout the world.'[44] It follows that he is merciful to whom he wishes, and whom he wishes he makes obdurate.

19   You will then say to me, 'Why does he still blame anyone? For who is a match for his will? If it come to that, who are you, sir, to answer God back? Is it for the model to say to the modeller, 'Why did you make me like this?' Has not the potter in clay a perfect right to make out of the same lump one article as a thing of worth, another as a thing of no worth? Supposing that God, wishing to display his genius and demonstrate his ability, produced with immense pains crude articles[45a] prepared for destruction, in order to display the richness of his imagination on delicate articles[45b] which he designed beforehand for distinction – namely ourselves, whom he has called not from the Jews alone but also from the Gentiles? He does indeed say in *Hosea*:

I will call them my people, who were not my people,
And her beloved, who was not beloved.

In the very place where it was said to them, 'You are not my people,' there shall they be called, 'Sons of the Living God'.[46]

27   Isaiah also cries concerning Israel, 'Though the number of the Children of Israel is as the sand of the sea, only a remnant will be saved. For the Lord will make a full and summary settlement on earth.'[47] And as Isaiah said previously, 'If the Lord of hosts had not left us some seed, we should have become as Sodom, we should have been like Gomorrah.'[48]

30   What are we to say then? That the Gentiles who did not pursue righteousness have overtaken it, the righteousness that arises from faith, while Israel pursuing a law of righteousness has failed to attain it? That is so. Why? Because it was not by faith, but as by regulations. They stumbled at the stumbling-stone, as it is stated,

Lo, I place in Zion a stumbling-stone, a boulder to trip over;
But he who believes in him will not come to grief.[49]

10.1   It is indeed my fondest desire, brothers, and the burden of my petition to God for Israel is that they should be saved. I can testify that they have a deep passion for God, though without discernment. For failing to perceive God's righteousness, while busy with trying to establish their own, they did not subordinate themselves to God's righteousness. To all who believe, Christ is the end of law as regards righteousness: for Moses writes concerning the righteousness that is by law that 'the man who acts up to it shall live by it'.[50] But the righteousness that is by faith speaks thus: 'Do not say to yourself, "Who will ascend to heaven?" (that is, to bring Christ down) or "Who will descend into the abyss?" (that is, to bring Christ up from the dead).' What it declares is, 'The word is very near you, in your mouth and in your mind,'[51] (that is, the word of faith which we proclaim). For if you will affirm 'the word in your mouth' that Jesus is Master, and believe 'in your mind' that God raised him from the dead, you will be saved; for belief is by the mind for righteousness, and affirmation is by the mouth for salvation. The
12   Scripture does indeed say, 'Everyone who believes in him will never come to grief.'[52] There is no distinction between Jew and Gentile: the same universal Lord is sufficient for all who invoke him, 'for *all* who invoke the name of the Lord will be saved'.[53] How then are they to invoke him in whom they have not believed? And how are they to believe what they have not heard? And how are they to hear without a preacher? And how are they to preach

unless they are sent? As it is stated, 'How fair are the feet of those who bring good news!' [54]

16   But not all have responded to the news, for Isaiah says, 'Lord, who has credited our report?'[55] So then faith comes by hearing, and hearing through the proclamation of Christ. But I say, have they not heard? Decidedly they have:

> Their voice has resounded throughout the earth,
> Their utterance to the utmost confines of the world.[56]

And I say, has Israel not known? First Moses says,

> I will make you jealous over what is no nation;
> Over a senseless nation I will anger you.[57]

While Isaiah takes the liberty of saying,

> I have been found by those who did not seek me;
> I have become evident to those who never asked me.[58]

And of Israel he says, 'All day long I have stretched out my hands to a refractory and contradictory people.'[59]

11.1   I ask, therefore, has God rejected his people? God forbid! I myself am an Israelite, of the seed of Abraham, the tribe of Benjamin. God has not rejected his people whom he knew of old. Or are you unaware of what the Scripture says in the person of Elijah, where he speaks to God about Israel, saying, 'Lord, they have killed your prophets, thrown down your altars, and I alone am left, and they seek my life'? But what does his Interlocutor say to him? 'I have reserved for myself seven thousand men, who have not bent the knee to Baal.'[60] Just so at the present time by a merciful choice there is a remnant. If it is by mercy it is no longer by deeds, otherwise mercy would no longer be mercy.

7   What then? Israel has not found what it is seeking, but the chosen part has found it, while the rest were immobilised, exactly as it is stated, 'God has given them a spirit of stupor, eyes that do not see, and ears that do not hear, to this very day.'[61] And David says,

> Let their table become a snare and a trap,
> A hindrance and an obstacle to them.
> Let their eyes be dimmed that they see not,
> And their back be for ever bent! [62]

11   I ask, therefore, have they tripped in order that they should fall? God forbid! Rather that by their blunder salvation has come to the Gentiles to stir them to emulation. But if their blunder is the world's

enrichment, and their discomfiture the Gentiles' enrichment, how
13 much more their complete achievement? (I am speaking to you
Gentiles.)

In so far, then, as I am an envoy to the Gentiles I make much of
14 my office, if in that way I can provoke my own kin to emulation,
and save some of them. For if their loss has been the world's profit,
what will their acquisition be but life from the dead? If the first-
dough is holy, so is the whole lump,[63] and if the stem is holy, so are
the branches.

17 Now if some of the branches have been pruned away, and you from
a wild olive have now been grafted among them, sharing with them
the sap-stream of the main olive stem, do not lord it over the branches.
For if you do lord it, remember that it is not you who carry the stem,
but the stem you. You will say then, 'The branches have been pruned
away that I might be grafted in.' Putting it fairly, they have been
pruned away as lacking in confidence,[64] while you by confidence stand
firm. So do not be arrogant, but fear. For if God did not spare the
natural branches, neither will he spare you.

22 Mark, then, the kindness and severity of God, severity towards those
branches which drooped, kindness to you, provided you continue to
merit his kindness. Otherwise you too will be cut off. While they, unless they continue to remain without trust, will be grafted back; for
God can graft them in again. For if you were cut from an olive tree
wild by nature, and grafted contrary to nature into a cultivated olive,
how much more shall these which are the natural branches be grafted
into their own olive tree?

25 I would not have you ignorant of this secret, brothers, in case you
should 'give yourselves airs',[65] that partial immobility has come to
Israel until the full complement of Gentiles has come in; and so all
Israel will be saved,[66] as it is stated,

> The redeemer will come out of Zion:
> He will banish ungodliness from Jacob.
> For this is my covenant with them,
> When I take away their sins.[67]

28 As regards the News they are out of favour for your sakes, but as
regards the Choice they are dear to God for the Patriarchs' sake,[68] for
God never goes back on his acts of grace and his calling. Even as you
once refused God obedience, but now have had mercy shown you in
respect of their disobedience, so they also have now refused obedi-

ence in respect of the mercy shown to you, so that they may obtain mercy. For God has classed all together as disobedient that he may show mercy to all.

33   Oh, the infinite wealth of God's wisdom and knowledge! How inscrutable are his judgments and mysterious his ways! Who has ever known the mind of the Lord, or who has been his counsellor? Or who has first given to him, that he must be repaid?[69] For from him, and through him, and in him, are all things. To him be glory for ever. Amen.

12.1   I exhort you[70] therefore, brothers, by God's tender mercies, to offer your bodies as a holy living sacrifice well-pleasing to God, which is your plain religious duty. Do not accommodate yourselves to the age we live in, but transform yourselves by a mental renovation, so that you are competent to determine what is the good, well-pleasing, and perfect will of God.

3   By virtue of the favour bestowed on me, I ask every individual among you not to have a higher opinion of himself than he should, but to think of himself modestly, as God has allotted to each his share of worth. For just as we have many organs in one body, and all the organs do not perform the same function, so we are many persons in one body in Christ, and that body as a unity has its respective organs. Possessing, then, a variety of gifts according to the favour granted us, let mutual regard be unfeigned. If the gift is for prophecy, let it be exercised with corresponding faithfulness. If it is for administration, let it be exercised in administration; if for teaching, let it be for teaching; if for exhortation, let it be in exhortation. He who has something to share, let him do it generously. He who supervises, let him do it diligently. He who does a kindness, let him do it cheerfully.

9   Let love be unfeigned. Repudiate what is evil. Cleave to what is good. In brotherly love be affectionate to one another. In honour give precedence to one another. In diligence do not be backward. In spiritual matters be ardent. Be willing slaves to the Master, joyful in hope, patient in affliction, persevering in prayer, sharing in provision for the necessities of the saints, ready with hospitality. Bless those who are so ready,[71] bless and do not curse. Rejoice with those who rejoice. Weep with those who weep. Be like-minded with one another. Do not be high and mighty, but consort with the humble. Do not give yourselves airs.[72] Never return evil for evil. Be well-respected in the sight of all men.[73] If possible, where it rests with you, be at peace with everyone. Do not avenge yourselves, dear friends, but give anger a

wide berth, for it is stated, 'Vengeance is mine, I will requite, says the Lord.'[74] Rather, 'If your enemy is hungry, feed him, if he is thirsty refresh him; for by so doing you will fill him with remorse.'[75] Do not be overcome by evil, but overcome evil with good.

13.1   Let every individual be subject to the responsible authorities; for there is no authority except from God, and those who are constituted hold their appointment from God.[76] Whoever, therefore, opposes the authority sets himself against the divine order, for those who resist it will duly receive punishment. Magistrates are not a terror to well-doers, but to evil-doers. If you would be free from fear of authority be of good behaviour, and you will earn its commendation; for the authority is God's administrator for your welfare. But if you do wrong, then be afraid, for he does not bear the sword without reason. In his capacity as God's administrator it is his official duty to inflict punishment on the evil-doer.

5   Of necessity you must be subject to the laws, not merely from considerations of punishment, but also of conscience, which applies equally to your payment of taxes. Those who levy them are God's officials regularly employed for this very purpose.[77] Render to everyone their dues, tribute to whoever is entitled to it, tax to whoever is entitled to it, respect to whoever is entitled to it, honour to whoever is entitled to it. Owe nothing to anyone except regard for one another; for he who shows another love has met all the requirements of law. 'You are not to commit adultery, you are not to murder, you are not to steal, you are not to covet,'[78] and whatever other commandment there may be is summed up in this, 'You are to love your neighbour as yourself.'[79] He who loves his neighbour will never do him an injury: so love is the sum total of law.

11   This further, because I know the time, that it is high time for you to awaken from sleep; for our deliverance is much nearer than when we believed. The night is far advanced. The day is at hand. Let us therefore lay aside what belongs to the darkness, and put on the habits of the light. Let us conduct ourselves with daytime decorum, not in revels and carousals, not in sexual intimacy and licentiousness, not in wrangling and rivalry. Rather, invest yourselves with the Lord Jesus Christ, and make no provision for the fulfilment of physical desires.

14.1   Associate with the man who is weak in faith, but not for controversial arguments. For one believes he may eat anything, while another of weaker calibre keeps to a vegetarian diet.[80] The man who eats must not be contemptuous of the one who does not. Neither must the man who does not eat condemn the one who does; for God has taken him into his service. Who are you to criticise another's retainer? To his own Master he stands or falls. And stand he will, for the Lord will see to it that he stands.

5   One man distinguishes one day above another, while someone else treats all days alike. Each must fully satisfy his own mind. He who observes a day observes it to the Lord, and he who eats every kind of food eats it to the Lord, because he thanks God for it. He who does not eat, his not eating is also to the Lord, for he too gives God thanks. None of us lives to himself, and none of us dies to himself. If we live, we live to the Lord, and if we die, we die to the Lord. Whether we live, or whether we die, we are the Lord's. That is why Christ died and came alive again, that he might have jurisdiction over both dead and living. Why then do you condemn your brother, or why do you treat your brother with contempt? We must all stand at God's tribunal, for it is stated,

'As I live,' says the Lord, 'every knee shall bend to me,
And every tongue shall make full confession to God.' [81]

12   So then each of us must render an account of himself to God. Therefore let us no longer pass judgment on one another. Rather should you determine this, not to place any obstacle or impediment in your brother's way. I know and am convinced in the Lord Jesus that nothing is impure in itself,[82] but if someone considers anything to be impure, for him it is so. And if your brother is distressed by the food you eat you are not behaving considerately. Do not by your food destroy one for whose sake Christ died. Do not let what is for your well-being be made a means of injury. For the Kingdom of God is not food and drink, but righteousness, peace, and joy in the holy Spirit. Whoever in such matters serves Christ is both well-pleasing to God and agreeable to men.

19   So then let us follow the ways of peace[83] and the things that promote our mutual welfare. For a mere matter of food do not disrupt God's work. Everything is indeed clean; but it is a wrong thing for a man to be a means of offence by what he eats. The right course is neither to eat meat nor to drink wine, nor whatever else it may be that upsets your brother. As to the conviction you hold, hold it privately in the sight of God. Happy is the man who does not condemn himself by what he sanctions. But he who does discriminate stands condemned if he should eat, because it is not from conviction. For whatever is not done from conviction is sin.

15.1   It is the duty of those who are strong to bear the foibles of the weak, and not to gratify ourselves. It is for each of us to put his neighbour at ease so as to promote the general welfare. For even Christ did not please himself, as it is stated, 'The reproaches which they cast on you fell on me.'[84] Whatever, indeed, was set down was written entirely for our guidance, that through the sustaining power and encouragement of the Scriptures we should have hope. May God who sustains and cheers grant you to be like-minded with one another in accordance with Jesus Christ, that in complete unanimity, with one voice, you may praise God, the Father of our Lord Jesus Christ!

7   Therefore associate with one another for the glory of God, just as Christ associated himself with you. For I say that Christ became a representative of circumcision, as God's honour required, so as to make good his promise to the Patriarchs, and that the Gentiles should praise God for his mercy, as it is stated, 'Therefore I will confess you among the Gentiles, and sing praises to your name.'[85] And again it says, 'Rejoice, O Gentiles, with his people,'[86] and further,

> Extol the Lord, all you Gentiles,
> And praise him, all you peoples.[87]

And again Isaiah says, 'There shall be a root of Jesse, and one who arises to rule the Gentiles. In him shall the Gentiles hope.'[88]

13   May the God of hope so fill you with joy and peace in believing, that you overflow with hope by virtue of the holy Spirit!

14   Naturally, I personally am completely convinced of you, my brothers, that you are the very soul of kindness, fully provided with all essential knowledge, and most competent to admonish one another. But I have written to you more outspokenly than was warranted, simply to serve as a reminder to you, because of the favour God has granted me that I should be the ministrant of Christ Jesus for the Gentiles, carrying out the rite of God's News, that the offering up of the Gentiles might be acceptable when consecrated by the holy Spirit.[89] I hold, therefore, a privileged position in Christ Jesus in matters relating to God. I am not so audacious as to speak of anything which Christ has not effected by my agency, by virtue of signs and wonders, by virtue of the holy Spirit, to procure the obedience of the Gentiles in word and deed. So that from Jerusalem as far round as Illyricum[90] I have fully publicised the News of Christ. And thus have I most strenuously proclaimed the News, not where Christ's name was familiar, that I should not build on another's foundation, but rather as it is stated,

> They shall see, to whom he was not reported,
> And those who have not heard shall consider.[91]

22   That is why I have so frequently been prevented from visiting you. But now having nothing more that I may do in these regions, and having had a great longing these many years to visit you, whenever I travel to Spain I trust to have a sight of you in passing through, and to be forwarded by you on my way there after first making the most of my stay with you.[92]

25   Just now, however, I am setting out for Jerusalem to render the saints a service; for Macedonia and Achaia have been pleased to make a contribution of funds for the poor among the saints at Jerusalem.[93] It has pleased them to do so quite properly, since they are their debtors. For if the Gentiles have shared in their spiritual things, they are under obligation for their part to minister to them in material things. When, therefore, I have performed this service, and deposited this aid with them, I shall proceed via yourselves to Spain; and I know that when I come to you it will be with the full blessing of Christ.

30   Now I entreat you, brothers, by our Lord Jesus Christ, and by the bonds of spiritual affection, to aid me with your prayers to God on my behalf, that I may be protected from those in Judea who are disobedient, and that my mission to Jerusalem may be well received by the saints; so that coming on to you joyfully, God willing, I may take my rest in your company. The God of peace be with you all. Amen.

16.21   [94] My fellow-worker Timotheus sends you his regards, and so do my fellow-countrymen Lucius, Jason and Sosipater (I, Tertius, who took down the letter, send you my regards in the Master). My host Gaius sends you his regards, and so does the whole community. Erastus, the city treasurer, sends you his regards, as does Brother Quartus.

25   Now to him who can establish you in accordance with my presentation of the News and the proclamation of Jesus Christ in accordance with the revelation of the mystery for long ages kept secret, but now disclosed through the Prophetic Scriptures by order of the Eternal God, and made known to all nations to procure their

27   loyal submission, to the only wise God be praise through Jesus Christ for ever and ever. Amen.

COVERING NOTE

16.1 This is to commend to you Sister Phoebe, who is an administrator of the Cenchreae[95] community. Welcome her in the Master as befits saints, and assist her in whatever way she may require; for she has been of great assistance to many, including myself.

3 Give my regards to Prisca and Aquila, my fellow-workers in Christ Jesus, who have risked their necks on my behalf, and to whom not only I am grateful, but all the communities among the Gentiles. Give my regards also to the community in their house. Then give my regards to my dear friend Epaenetus, Asia's first-fruits for Christ, also to Mary who has worked so hard for you. My regards to my fellow-countrymen and fellow-captives Andronicus and Junias, famed among the envoys, who also were in Christ before me.

8 My regards in the Master to my dear friend Amplias, also Urban our fellow-worker in Christ, and my dear friend Stachys. My regards to Apelles approved in Christ, and also to the family of Aristobulus. Give my regards to my fellow-countryman Herodion, also those of the family of Narcissus who are in the Master, and those hard workers in the Master, Tryphena and Tryphosa.

12 My regards to dear Persis, who has worked so hard in the Master, also Rufus, chosen in the Master, and his mother, and therefore mine. My regards to Asyncritus, Phlegon, Hermes, Patrobas, Hermas, and the brothers associated with them. My regards to Philologus and Julia, Nereus and his sister, Olympas too, and all the saints associated with them.

16 Convey my regards to one another with a chaste kiss. All the communities of Christ send their regards.

17 Now I exhort you, brothers, to note those who create doubts and difficulties in opposition to the teaching you have learnt,[96] and keep away from them. Such as they do not serve the Lord Christ, but their own appetites, and by fair words and fine phrases seduce the minds of the guileless. But your obedience has become common knowledge. So I am quite happy about you, and only want you to be wise where good is concerned, uncontaminated where evil is concerned.

20 The God of peace will swiftly crush Satan under your heel. The loving-kindness of our Lord Jesus be with you all.

NOTES AND REFERENCES

1. In this letter, a kind of treatise, Paul does not address himself to the community (*ecclesia*) at Rome, which he had no part in creating, but to Jewish and non-Jewish believers. He offers a reasoned statement of his own faith as uncertain whether they hold the same doctrines as himself.
2. See *Lk*.xx.36.
3. Paul only reached Rome as a prisoner in AD 61.
4. Paul finds it hard to modify his own sense of authority, in face of the fact that envoys from Jerusalem had brought News of the Messiah to Rome.
5. *Hab*.ii.4. 'shall live' now and in the Messianic Age.
6. Cf. Tacitus *Annals*, XV.44, 'The City of Rome, the common sewer into which everything infamous and abominable flows from all quarters of the world.'
7. *Ps*.lxii.12.
8. Lit. 'Greek'.
9. Paul has in mind the Law of Moses.
10. Without God's Law as guide the Gentiles cannot always be clear as to what is right and what is wrong.
11. In the Jew's daily affirmation, 'Hear, O Israel, the Lord is our God, the Lord is One.'
12. Between good and evil, what is permitted and what is prohibited.
13. *Mal*.i.11-12.
14. *Ps*.li.4.
15. Linking *Ps*.xiv.1-3, *Ps*.v.9, *Ps*.cxl.3, *Ps*.x.7; *Isa*.lix.7-8; *Ps*.xxxvi.l.
16. *Ps*.cxliii.2.
17. By propounding a law of faith.
18. *Gen*.xv.6.
19. *Ps*.xxxii.1-2.
20. *Gen*.xvii.5.
21. Jewish *Amidah* prayer, *Bened*.2 (*AJP*, p.45).
22. *Gen*.xv.5.
23. Here as elsewhere Paul does not regard law as having existed until the revelation of the Divine law to Moses. That is why he speaks of the non-Jewish nations as being without law. The first century Jewish historian Josephus takes much the same position in his treatise *Against Apion*, where he argues that Gentile philosophers and lawgivers borrowed from the Jews.
24. As the Second Adam, the Son of Man.
25. See *Gen*.iii.
26. Perhaps a manual of instruction on the lines of the *Didache* (*Teaching of the XII Apostles*). See also xvi. 17 (p.195).

27. Paul thinks of the physical Christ as one man, and the Christ after resurrection as another. The believer is now, as it were, the wife of the new spiritual husband to bear him spiritual offspring.
28. A Jewish child was not held responsible for his actions until after the age of twelve when be became *Barmitzvah* ('Son of the Commandment').
29. Cf. *Ps*.xxxviii.3.
30. Cf. *Ps*.cxix.47, etc.
31. Or 'dead body'. Perhaps with reference to the crime of the Etruscan king Mezentius, who bound living persons to dead bodies 'hand to hand and face to face' until they died a lingering ghastly death (Virgil, *Aeneid*, Bᴋ.VIII.481-488).
32. In Aramaic.
33. Relating to the experience of an expectant mother.
34. Cf. the offering up of Isaac by Abraham (*Gen*.xxii.12), to which great spiritual significance was attached.
35. *Ps*.xliv.22.
36. As God's children.
37. i.e. of God in the Temple. The passage relates to the Jewish liturgy. Cf. *AJP*, p.149. 'For the Law, for the Service, for the Prophets ...'
38. i.e. the Temple ritual.
39. *Gen*.xxi.12.
40. *Gen*.xviii.10.
41. *Gen*.xxv.23.
42. *Mal*.i.2-3.
43. *Exod*.xxxiii.19.
44. *Exod*.ix.16.
45. Equally 'vessels of wrath' and 'vessels of mercy'.
46. *Hos*.ii.23.
47. *Isa*.x.22 with xxviii.22.
48. *Isa*.i.9.
49. *Isa*.viii.14 with xxviii.16 (LXX). 'in him' or 'in it' is an addition to the quotation, possibly taken from a collection of Christian OT proofs.
50. *Lev*.xviii.5.
51. *Deut*.xxx.12-14.
52. *Isa*.xxviii.16.
53. *Joel* ii.32.
54. *Isa*.lii.7.
55. *Isa*.liii.1.
56. *Ps*.xix.4.
57. *Deut*.xxxii.21.
58. *Isa*.lxv.1.
59. *Isa*.lxv.2.
60. *I.Ki*.xix.10,18.

61. *Isa*.xxix.10, with *Deut*.xxix.4.
62. *Ps*.lxix.22-23.
63. Cf. *Num*.xv.18-21; *Lev*.xix.23-24.
64. 'Confidence' may be read as 'faith'.
65. Cf. *Prov*.iii.7.
66. 'All Israel have a share in the world to come.' (*Sanhed*.x.1)
67. *Isa*.lix.20-21 with xxvii.9.
68. Cf. *Amidah* prayer, *Bened*.8, 'Who rememberest the pious deeds of the Patriarchs, and in love will bring a redeemer to their children's children' (*AJP*, p.44).
69. Cf. *Ps*.cxlv.3; *Isa*.xl.13-14; *Job* xli.11.
70. What follows is on similar lines to the *Didache* and may derive from an early manual of instruction.
71. The alternative rendering 'those who persecute' is unsuitable in the context. The same word 'ready' has just been used in association with hospitality.
72. *Prov*.iii.7 (LXX).
73. *Prov*.iii.4 (LXX).
74. *Deut*.xxxii.35.
75. *Prov*.xxv.21-22.
76. Paul's teaching follows that of the Essenes. Cf. Jos. *Jewish War* II, esp. 140. The initiate swears 'that he will keep faith with all men, especially with the powers that be, since no ruler attains his office save by the will of God.'
77. But see the teaching of Jesus: *Mt*.xvii.25-26; *Lk*.xxiii.2.
78. *Exod*.xx.13-17.
79. *Lev*.xix.18, cf. *Mt*.xxii.40.
80. This would relate to a mixed company of Jewish and non-Jewish believers, where the former would be vegetarians so as not to break the dietary laws. The position with holy days would be similar.
81. *Isa*.xlv.23.
82. Cf. *Mt*.xv.11.
83. Cf. *Ps*.xxxiv.14.
84. *Ps*.lxix.9.
85. *Ps*.xviii.49.
86. *Deut*.xxxii.43.
87. *Ps*.cxvii.1.
88. *Isa*.xi.1,10.
89. Paul is using a metaphor of a priest's functions.
90. District east of the Adriatic roughly the same as modern Albania.
91. *Isa*.lii.15.
92. Paul never got to Spain, and only reached Rome as a prisoner.
93. See *Acts*.xxiv.17.

94. Some regard **16**.1-20, which is placed here in the Greek, as a short personal note sent with sister Phoebe as the bearer of the letter. This passage has therefore been transferred to the end of the letter.
95. Seaport on the east of the Gulf of Corinth. See *Acts*.xviii.18.
96. Cf. *Didache* (*Teaching of the XII Apostles*) iv.

Series Two:

LETTERS FROM ROME

To the Community at Philippi

(Probably written from Rome about AD 61 – 62)[1]

1.1   Paul and Timotheus, servants of Christ Jesus, to all the saints in Christ Jesus living in Philippi, with their supervisors and administrators. May peace and prosperity be yours from God our Father and the Lord Jesus Christ.

3   Invariably I thank my God for every recollection of you whenever I pray for you. I offer my petition with joy for the fellowship you have had with the News from the very beginning until now, being fully assured that he who promoted such well-doing on your part will maintain it to the Day of Jesus Christ.[2] It is indeed right that I should so think of you all, because I have you so much at heart, all of you having shared in the privilege I have of being in fetters and of defending and championing the News.

8   God is my witness how I long for you with all the yearning of Christ Jesus! And so it is my prayer that your love may bring you ever deeper insight and perception in distinguishing points of difference,[3] that you may be unalloyed and untarnished till the Day of Christ, laden with the fruit of rectitude that comes through Jesus Christ, to the glory and praise of God.

12   Now I want to tell you, brothers, that my circumstances have rather tended to the advancement of the News; for my fetters have publicised Christ to the whole praetorium and everywhere else. The majority of the brothers, having been fired with confidence in the Master by my fetters, have become much more venturesome, giving out God's Message fearlessly. Some of course do it out of envy and rivalry,[4] but others proclaim Christ from good-will. These do it out of regard, knowing that I am thus circumstanced for the defence of the News, while the former, who are not well-intentioned, announce Christ in a factious spirit, trying deliberately to make trouble for me in my fettered state.

18   What does it matter? The main thing is that, whether in pretence

or sincerity, Christ is proclaimed. For this I rejoice. But there is greater joy in store; for I know that this will be the salvation of me thanks to your prayers and the supply of the spirit of Jesus Christ, with the earnest hope and expectation I have that I shall in no way be put to shame, but that freely and fully, now as always, Christ will be magnified in my person whether by life or death.

21   It is useful[5] to me to live, and an advantage to die. But if I am to live physically it means an effort on my part, and I hardly know which to choose. I am in a quandary between the two, having the longing to depart and be with Christ, for that would be so much better. Yet on the other hand to remain in the flesh is more essential for you. Finally convinced of this, I know I am to remain and be at the side of all of you for your advancement and joyfulness in faith, that your exultation in Christ Jesus may abound by me through my reappearance among you.

27   Only let your ordering of affairs be worthy of Christ's News, that whether I come and see you or remain absent I shall hear word of you that you are continuing to be of one spirit, single-mindedly contending for the faith of the News, and not the least alarmed by the tactics of your adversaries. This is a sure sign of defeat for them, but of deliverance for you, and this by God himself; for you have the privilege on Christ's account not only of believing in him[6] but of suffering for his sake. Yours is the same kind of contest in which you have seen me engaged, and now learn that I am still engaging.

2.1   So if there is any encouragement in Christ you can give me, any consolation of affection, any fellowship of spirit, any deep concern and compassion, do fill me with the joy of it. So that in thus thinking alike, having the same affection, being kindred souls with a common viewpoint, there will be no trace of rivalry, no trace of self-importance, but only that humility of mind which regards others as superior to one's self, each studying not his own interests but those of his fellows.

5   Let your disposition, indeed, be that of Christ Jesus, who though he had godlike form, did not regard it as a prize to be God's equal,[7] but divested himself, taking the form of a servant. Appearing in human likeness, and disclosed in physical appearance as a man, he abased himself, and became subject to death, death by the cross.

9   That is why God has so exalted him, that at the name of Jesus every knee, heavenly, earthly and infernal, should bend, and every tongue acclaim Jesus Christ as lord, to the glory of God the Father.[8]

12   Therefore, dear friends, as invariably you have been obedient, not

only when I have been present, but much more creditably now in my absence, earn your salvation with fear and trembling; for it is God who is prompting you both to want and to carry out what is well-pleasing. Do everything without murmuring or argument, that you may be irreproachable and faultless, blameless children of God in the midst of 'a perverse and crooked generation',[9] in which shine out like luminaries in a dark universe, radiating a message of Life,[10] my proud proof on the Day of Christ that I have neither striven nor toiled in vain. But even should I be poured out as the libation and act of worship that your faith is called upon to make, I shall rejoice and congratulate you all, and similarly you will rejoice and congratulate me.[11]

19 Now I hope in the Lord Jesus to send Timotheus to you soon, that I myself may be heartened by knowing how you fare. I have no one better qualified, one who is genuinely concerned with how you fare; for most study their own interests, not those of Christ Jesus. But you know the worth of Timotheus, how he has served with me in the News like a son with his father. Him, then, I hope to send as soon as ever I have a clear impression of my prospects, though I am convinced in the Master that I shall be in a position before long to come personally.

25 But I have considered it essential to send Brother Epaphroditus, my co-worker and campaigner and your envoy and minister to my needs,[12] because he misses you so, and frets because you had heard that he was ailing. Indeed he was ailing, almost at death's door. But God took pity on him, and not only on him but on me too, that I should not have one distress upon another. So I have sent him more expeditiously, that in seeing him again you may have joy, and I less sorrow. Give him, therefore, a joyful welcome in the Master, and hold such as he in high regard, for in doing the Master's work he came so near to death, jeopardizing his life to make good your lack of opportunity to serve me.

3.1 Finally, brothers, rejoice in the Master.

Here are the particular things I must mention to you, where indeed I do not falter while you are firm.[13]

2 Beware of the dogs! Beware of the cowardly workers! Beware of Incision![14] It is we who are the Circumcision, we who are in service to God's Spirit and exult in Jesus Christ, and place no reliance on the physical, though I could well do so. If anyone else thinks he can rely on the physical, I even more so, circumcised as I was on the

eighth day, of the race of Israel, the tribe of Benjamin, a Hebrew sprung from Hebrews, in observances a Pharisee, as regards zeal a persecutor of the Community, as regards legal rectitude irreproachable.

7   But the very things that were an asset to me, these I regard as a dead loss where Christ is concerned. Indeed, I definitely regard everything as a dead loss because of the excellence of the knowledge of Christ Jesus my lord, for whom all is well lost and I regard it as so much rubbish, that I may gain Christ, and be found in him, not with my own rectitude, which derives from law, but with that which is through faith in Christ, the rectitude which derives from God on a basis of faith. My concern is to know him, and the power of his resurrection, to have kinship with his sufferings, entering as closely as possible into the manner of his death, if by any means I may attain the resurrection from the dead. There is no question of my having already obtained it, or of having already been perfected. But I pursue, if I may but overtake, even as I was overtaken by Christ Jesus. Brothers, I do not reckon myself to have overtaken as yet. But there is this at least, forgetting what lies behind, and reaching out to what lies ahead, I drive hard at the mark for the prize of God's high calling in Christ Jesus.[15] Let those who would be perfect be thus minded; but if you feel differently God will surely make this plain to you. The main thing is, to whatever extent we have forged ahead, to keep on the same course.

17   Copy me, brothers, and pay close attention to those who behave as I have set the example. For there are many, as I have often told you, and now tell you even with tears, who behave as enemies of Christ's cross, whose end is destruction, whose god is their appetite, and whose glory is in their shame, whose minds are on earthly matters. But our form of government originates in heaven, from which source we expect as deliverer the Lord Jesus Christ, who will transform the body of our humble state so that it corresponds to his glorious body by the power which enables him to bring everything under his control.

4.1   Therefore, dear and desired brothers, my joy and crown, stand fast in the Master, my dear ones. I beg Euodia and Syntyche to be of one mind in the Master. Yes, I also ask you, true Synzyge,[16] to bring these sisters in faith together, who aided me in the News with Clement and the other co-workers of mine, whose names are in the Book of Life.[17]

4   Rejoice in the Master always. I repeat, rejoice! Let your moderation be known to everyone. The Master is at hand. Have no anxiety, but

always make your requests known to God by prayer and supplication with thanksgiving; and God's peace, which towers above[18] all reasoning, will stand guard over your minds and thoughts in Christ Jesus.

8 Finally, brothers, whatever is honest, whatever is reputable, whatever is just, whatever is pure, whatever is likeable, whatever is elevated, if there is something virtuous or laudable, concentrate on such things. Practise all you have learnt and received and heard and seen in me, and the God of peace be with you.

10 I have rejoiced in the Master greatly that now at last your thought for me could find fresh expression, for indeed you had always thought that way but lacked opportunity. It is not out of considerations of want that I am saying this, for I have learnt to manage however I am situated. I have had experience of being in reduced circumstances and of having plenty. I have been through the whole curriculum, to be replete and to be hungry, to have ample and to go short. I can cope with everything by him who strengthens me. You have none the less done a kindness in associating yourselves with my difficulties.

15 Let me tell you Philippians that in the early days of the News, when I left Macedonia, there was not a single community which associated itself with me in the matter of giving and gaining other than yourselves, so that even at Thessalonica you sent once and again a contribution for my needs. It is not that I am looking for gifts. What I am looking for is the yield that swells your credit account. I have indeed enough and to spare. I am fully supplied, having received from Epaphroditus what your means allowed, a sweet-smelling perfume, an acceptable sacrifice, well-pleasing to God. My God, in turn, will supply every need of yours in Christ Jesus out of his wealth in glory. To God our Father be praise for ever and ever. Amen.

21 Give my regards to every saint in Christ Jesus. The brothers who are with me send you their regards. All the saints send you their regards, particularly those of Caesar's household.

May the loving-kindness of the Lord Jesus Christ be with your spirit.

NOTES AND REFERENCES

1. In Rome Paul was under house-arrest awaiting the hearing of his appeal by the Emperor Nero (*Acts*.xxv.12; xxviii.16).
2. The day of Christ's return to earth at the start of the Messianic Age.

3. Relating to what is right and wrong. Cf. *To the Believers at Rome*, **2**.18.
4. The followers of Jesus at Rome at this time were mainly Jews (see p.195, Note 1), who were naturally opposed to Paul's doctrine, notably his granting of Israelite status to non-Jews without obligation to keep the Mosaic laws.
5. By a scribal error 'Christos' was written for 'chrestos', meaning 'useful'. The mistake was easy since *Chrestos* was a well-known proper name. The Roman historian Suetonius once referred to Christus as Chrestus.
6. 'in him', i.e. 'in God', believing in God on Christ's account.
7. Referring to the sin which Adam, who was Son of God (*Lk*.iii.38), was tempted by Satan to commit, and which Lucifer in his former state had committed (*Gen*.iii.5; *Isa*.xiv.12-14). Moses is said to have had a divine form, and as an infant to have received the crown from Pharaoh's head (Josephus, *Antiq*.Bk.II.232-235). The Christ Above of the Jewish mystics had angelic likeness as a Son of God (*Dan*.iii.25-28, *Job* i.6-7). He discarded his heavenly aspect at his incarnation, but once revealed it when he was transfigured (*Mk*.ix.1-7).
8. The Spirit-Messiah, the heavenly Archetype, became incarnate in the human Jesus, according to Paul (*To the Believers at Rome*,**1**.3-4), thus creating the combination Jesus-Christ. The incarnation was at the baptism of Jesus (*Mk*.i.11).
9. *Deut*.xxxii.5.
10. *Dan*.xii.3.
11. Referring to the pagan practice of mutual congratulation at the close of the temple service, when the ritual was ended involving sacrifice and the pouring of a libation.
12. Epaphroditus was a Philippian who had been sent by his community to Rome with gifts and messages for Paul in prison there.
13. The tone of the letter changes *abruptly* at this point, and what follows was due to problems Paul had with the Jewish adherents of Jesus in Rome, on doctrinal grounds.
14. 'Zealots for the Law' had been *incising* themselves into Paul's Gentile communities to cause them to become Jews. 'Dogs' refers to immoral non-Jews. At the entrance to Roman houses the legend *Cave Canem* ('Beware of the Dog') was often to be read. Paul warns against licentious Gentiles and fanatical Jews.
15. The allusion is to Greek foot races and their finishing post.
16. The name Synzyge means 'Yoke-fellow'. Paul asks him to act up to his name in reconciling the two quarrelling ladies.
17. Cf. *Exod*.xxxii.32.
18. Like a dominating and protective fortress.

To the Communities in Asia
(The Ephesian Copy)
(Probably written from Rome in AD 61 or 62)

1.1 Paul, by the will of God an envoy of Christ Jesus, to the saints resident in (*Ephesus*)[1] and to the faithful in Christ Jesus. May peace and prosperity be yours from God our Father and the Lord Jesus Christ.

3 Blessed be the God and Father of our Lord Jesus Christ, who has blessed us with every spiritual blessing in the heavenly spheres in Christ, just as in him God made choice of us in love[2] before the universe was founded, that we should be holy and blameless in his presence. For he designated us in advance for adoption as his own through Jesus Christ, as it pleased his will, to the great renown of his loving-kindness with which he has favoured us in the Beloved. In Christ we have redemption by his blood, absolution from transgression, by virtue of the wealth of loving-kindness which God has lavished upon us, in having made known to us in all wisdom and understanding,[3] as it pleased him, the secret of his intention, which he purposed in Christ, for that ultimate Government when he shall have brought everything under Christ's jurisdiction both in heaven and on earth. Yes, under him in whom we too have our allotted place, assigned to us in advance, according to the plan of God, who makes everything work out in accordance with his design and intention; so that we should be to his great renown who [as Jews] set our hope in advance on Christ.[4] In him also you [Gentiles] after hearing the Message of Truth, the News of your salvation, and after believing in him, were sealed with the holy Spirit of promise which is the advance payment on our inheritance, the promise to redeem what was purchased, to God's great renown.

15 Consequently, I too, having heard of the faith you have in the Lord Jesus, which is common to all the saints, never cease giving thanks on your account, making mention of you in my prayers, that the God of

207

our Lord Jesus Christ,[5] the Father of glory, may give you a spirit of wisdom and revelation to acquire knowledge of him. I pray that with your mental vision illumined you may know the nature of the hope of God's callings, what is the glorious wealth of his inheritance in the saints, and the surpassing extent of his power available to us who have believed. This was indicated by the operation of the mighty force God employed with Christ in raising him from the dead and seating him at his right hand in the heavenly spheres high above every entity that has existence not only in this world but in that which is to come. He has indeed 'put everything under his feet',[6] and over and above has given him the headship of the whole Community, which is his body, the full dimension of him who fills the entire universe.[7]

2.1   You [Gentiles] too were once dead in the trespasses and sins in which you lived in conformity with the Aeons of this world, the Archon[8] of the government of the lower atmosphere, the spirit of him who now animates the Children of Disobedience. We likewise [all we Jews] were once tarred with the same brush in the indulgence of our physical passions, fulfilling our physical desires and inclinations, and by nature Children of Wrath like the rest. But God being full of compassion because of the great love he had for us even when we were dead in trespasses, has brought us all back to life with Christ – it is by mercy that you have been spared – and has raised us up together, and seated us together in the heavenly spheres in Christ Jesus. For it is by mercy that you have been spared through faith, not in any way by your own efforts, nor by your own deeds – it is God's gift so that no one should boast. We are entirely his handiwork, created in Christ Jesus for those good deeds with which God prearranged that we should be occupied.

11   So bear in mind that you were once Gentiles in the physical sense, who are termed the Uncircumcision by those termed in respect of an operation in the flesh the Circumcision, because at that time you were without benefit of Christ, aliens to the body politic of Israel, and strangers to the covenants of promise. But now in Christ Jesus you who were once far off have been brought near by the blood of Christ. For he is our peacemaker, who has united both Jew and Gentile, having abolished the dividing partition-wall,[9] and having in his person neutralised the cause of enmity, the Law of commandments set down in ordinances, so that the two should in him be welded into one new man. Thus he has reconciled both to God by one body through the cross, having in his own person killed the enmity, and

by his coming proclaimed 'peace to you the far off, and peace to the near',[10] because through him by one Spirit we both have access to the Father.

19   So now you are no longer strangers and foreigners, but fellow-citizens of the saints, parts of God's house, having been built upon the foundation of the Envoys and Prophets with Christ Jesus himself as the coping-stone, where each block having been closely fitted together[11] grows course upon course into a sacred fane in the Master, into which you too have been built as a spiritual abode of God.

3.1   To this end I, Paul, am the prisoner of Jesus for you Gentiles. You must surely have heard of the administration of God's mercy granted me for your benefit, how by revelation he acquainted me with the secret, as I have previously stated it above. From this you may gather how well-versed I am in the Messianic Mystery, which in previous generations was never made known to mankind as now revealed under inspiration to God's holy envoys and prophets, the secret that by the News the Gentiles were to be joint-heirs, jointly incorporated [as Israel] and joint participants in the promise in Christ Jesus.[12] Of this News I was made a minister, by the gift of God's mercy granted me in accordance with the operation of his power. To me, the least of all the saints, was this privilege given, that I should proclaim to the Gentiles the inexhaustible wealth of Christ, and publish the details of the secret kept hidden from the Aeons by God who created all things; so that the wisdom of God in all its multitudinous aspects should now be made known through the Community to the rulers and authorities in the heavenly spheres, in accordance with the Plan of the Ages which God formed in Christ Jesus our Master. In him, by faith in him, we enter God's presence boldly and confidently. So I beg you not to take hardly my trials on your behalf, which are an honour to you.

14   To this end I bend my knees to the Father, from whom every order of being both in heaven and on earth derives its existence, that in accordance with the wealth of his glory he may grant you by his Spirit to be powerfully strengthened in the inner self, that the Christ may make his abode in your minds by faith, that being deep-rooted and well-grounded in love you may be able to grasp with all the saints what is the Breadth, the Length, and Depth and the Height, that you may know, what indeed surpasses knowledge, the love of Christ, that you may be filled with the immensity of God.

20   Now to him who is supremely powerful to do infinitely more

than we can ask or think, in accordance with the power that ope-
rates in us, to him be glory in the Community and in Christ Jesus
to all generations for ever and ever. Amen.

4.1   I entreat you therefore, I the Master's prisoner, to behave in a
manner worthy of the calling with which you have been called, with
all humility and gentleness, with long-suffering, being patient with
one another in love, striving to keep unity of spirit by the binding
force of peace. There is one Body and Spirit, just as you were called with one expectation of your calling, one Master, one Faith, one
Immersion, one God and Father of all, and through all, and in all.

7   And to each one of us there has been granted some favour corresponding to the extent of Christ's bounty, as it is stated, 'Having
ascended on high he made captivity captive, and bestowed gifts on
men.'[13] That he ascended implies that he also descended into the
lower regions of the earth.[14] He who descended is the same as he who
ascended to the uppermost part of the heavens,[15] that he might fill
the universe. To some he gave gifts as envoys, some as prophets,
some as preachers, some as pastors and teachers, for the training
of the saints, for the work of administration, and the development of
the Body of Christ, until we all reach unity of faith and knowledge of
the son of God, the Perfect Man, the measure of the stature of the
full-grown Christ.[16] No longer should we be infants, tossed on the
waves and swept this way and that by every wind of doctrine by
the facile knavery of men practised in the contrivance of deceit;
but speaking the truth in love we should grow up collectively to
him, Christ, who is the Head, from whom the whole Body – closely
joined together and knit by every connecting part has its growth
promoted for the Body's harmonious development.

17   This then I say and solemnly declare in the Master, that you are no
longer to behave as the Gentiles behave in the levity of their minds.
They, having their intellect dimmed, being alien to the divine life
through their ignorance and the obtuseness of their minds, being lost
to decent feelings, have given themselves over to licentiousness, to
indulge in every kind of impurity with avidity. But you have not so
learnt what Christ means – that is, if you have attended to him and
been instructed by him, as the truth is in Jesus – namely, that you
should abandon what accords with the former mode of life of the
old degenerate personality with its treacherous lusts, that you should
have the temper of your minds renovated, and put on the new personality fashioned after God in rectitude and the sanctity of truth.

25   So abandoning falsehood, 'Let each speak the truth to his fellow.'[17] 'Be angry, yet sin not.'[18] Let not the sun go down on your anger, nor give the Devil his opportunity. Let him that stole steal no more. Instead let him toil, putting his hand to worthy employment, that he may have something to give to any who are in need. Let no foul language pass your lips, only what is good for some constructive purpose, that it may give pleasure to the listeners. And do not grieve God's holy Spirit by which you have been sealed for the Day of Redemption. Put aside all bitterness and passion, anger, vituperation and abuse, and every kind of malice. Instead be kindly disposed to one another, large-hearted, merciful to each other as God has been

5.1   merciful to you in Christ. Follow God's example, then, as dear children, and behave with affection, just as Christ loved you and offered himself for you as 'an offering and sacrifice of pleasing odour to God'. But let there be no mention among you of vice and any kind of impurity or lechery, as befits saints, nor obscenity, levity, or facetiousness, which are unbecoming. Preferably let there be thanksgiving. You surely know this, that no immoral person, nor impure, nor rapacious (which means an idol-worshipper), shall have any inheritance in the Kingdom of Christ and of God.

6   Let no one beguile you with empty words, for because of this the wrath of God falls upon the Children of Disobedience. Do not be of their company therefore; for though once you belonged to darkness, now in the Master you belong to the light. Behave like the Children of Light[19] – the Light that has its fruits in every kind of goodness, in uprightness and honesty – approving what is acceptable to the Master. And have no fellowship with the unfruitful works of darkness, but rather refute them, though it is shameful to speak of the things such people do in secret. For whatever is refuted has light thrown upon it, since all visibility is due to light. That is why it is stated,

> Rouse yourself, sleeper,
> And arise from the dead,
> And Christ shall shine on you![20]

15   Pay strict attention, therefore, to the way you behave, as wise people, not unwise, using the time profitably, for these are evil days. So do not be stupid, but comprehending, as to what are the Master's wishes. And do not get drunk with wine, in which is sottishness, but be filled spiritually, chanting psalms and hymns and spiritual odes, singing and making melody in your hearts to the Lord, above all

211

invariably giving thanks to God the Father in the name of our Lord
Jesus Christ.

21   Be submissive to one another in the fear of Christ, the wives to
their husbands as to the Master; for man is the head of woman as
Christ is the head of the Community, being as he is the preserver of
the Body. But as the Community is subject to Christ, so should wives
be to their husbands in every way. Husbands, love your wives, even
as Christ loved the Community and gave himself for her sake, that
he might consecrate her, having been cleansed by the ritual bath of
water,[21] so to speak, that he might take the Community to himself as
a bridge to be proud of, not having a spot[22] or wrinkle, or anything of
the kind, as well as being chaste and unblemished. So ought husbands
to cherish their wives as their own bodies. He who cherishes his wife
cherishes himself; for no one ever hated his own flesh, but cares for
and tends it, as indeed Christ does the Community, since we are
members of his body. 'For this cause a man shall leave father and
mother, and unite with his wife, and the two shall be one flesh.'[23] This
is a great mystery: I am speaking here of the relationship between
Christ and the Community. Just so you too, every one of you, should
thus love his wife as himself; and the wife should respect her husband.

6.1   Children, obey your parents, for it is rightly said, 'Honour your
father and your mother,'[24] which is the first commandment with a
promise attached to it, namely, 'that it may be well with you, and that
you may live long on the earth'. And you fathers, do not provoke your
children, but bring them up in the discipline and admonition of the
Lord.[25]

5   Slaves, obey those who in the physical sense are your masters with
fear and trembling in singleness of mind as you obey Christ, not with
service meant to catch the eye, like those who want to ingratiate
themselves, but as slaves of Christ carrying out God's behests. Give
service with real goodwill, as having the Lord in mind rather than men,
knowing that each one, whether slave or freeman, has whatever good
he may do treasured up by the Lord. And you masters, act in the same
way towards your slaves, refraining from threats, knowing that both
their and your Master is in heaven, and that with him there is no
partiality.

10   Finally, make yourselves strong in the Lord and in the power of
his might. Array yourselves in the full armour of God, so that you
may stand up to the artfulness of the Adversary. For we are not
contending with mortals but with angelic Rulers and Authorities, with

the Overlords of the Dark State, the spirit forces of evil in the heavenly spheres.

13 Therefore take to yourselves the full armour of God that you may be able to withstand in the evil day, and having completely over-come, to go on standing. Stand, therefore, with your loins girded with truth,[26] clad in the corselet of rectitude,[27] with your feet shod with the sureness of the News of peace.[28] To complete your equipment, hold before you the shield of faith with which you will be able to ex-tinguish the flaming darts of the Evil One, and take the helmet of preservation, and the sword of the Spirit — which means God's Word.

18 Pray at all times in the Spirit with every kind of petition and supplication for all the saints, being intent on this with all diligence and entreaty, and on my behalf that fluent speech may be given me boldly to make known the Mystery on account of which I am an ambassador in chains,[29] that even so placed I may speak as boldly as it behoves me to speak.

21 But so that you too may know the state of my affairs, how I fare, Tychicus,[30] that dear brother and loyal minister in the Master, will inform you. I have dispatched him to you for this express purpose, that you may know my concerns and that he may cheer your hearts.

23 Peace be with the brothers, and affection with faith, from God the Father and the Lord Jesus Christ. May well-being be the portion of all who love our Lord Jesus Christ unfeignedly.

NOTES AND REFERENCES

1. While in some MSS Ephesus is given as the destination, in others it is omitted. The letter is of a general character primarily intended for communities in Asia not founded by Paul, of which he had information, possibly through Epaphras (see the letter to Colossae). These may particularly have been Laodicea and Hierapolis.
2. Jewish *Ahabah* prayer, 'Blessed art thou, O Lord, who hast chosen thy people Israel in love.' (*AJP* p.46)
3. Jewish *Amidah* prayer (*Bened*.IV). 'Thou favourest man with knowledge.' (*AJP* pp.39-40)
4. i.e. the Messiah, with reference to the ultimate Messianic Government of the Cosmos under the Son of Man.
5. Early Christian faith carefully distinguished Christ from God (*Acts*.ii.22; vii.55).
6. *Ps*.viii.6.

7. The Jewish mystics held that the Heavenly Man (Son of Man), in whose likeness Adam was created, had reached from earth to heaven. Christ with the Community are here the head and body of this cosmic figure (see further n.16). *Ma'aseh Bereshith* (Mystery of Creation in *Gen*.i-iii) was an aspect of Jewish occultism in which Paul had been trained.

8. 'Aeon', 'Archon'. Spirit powers subordinate to Beliar, the Evil Force controlling the existing world order. To understand Paul it is essential to have a knowledge of Pharisee and Essene occult teaching.

9. The allusion is to the balustrade in the Temple at Jerusalem which separated the Court of the Gentiles from the Court of Israel. Gentiles who trespassed into the Court of Israel did so, as warning notices proclaimed, on pain of death. Paul himself had been accused of taking Greeks through the barrier (*Acts*.xxi.28). In Paul's teaching the Gentile who believed in Christ acquired Israelite status.

10. *Isa*.lvii.19.

11. In the Temple stones were fitted without mortar.

12. It had not before been disclosed that Gentiles, by faith, would become part of the People of God, the new redeemed Israel. Paul claimed to have received this by revelation.

13. *Ps*.lxviii.18.

14. In the early Christian *Odes of Solomon* the descent of Christ to the underworld is described as the Head going down to the Feet (*Ode* xxiii.14).

15. Seven heavens, in layers, were postulated by the Jewish mystics.

16. Here the body is to grow up to the Head, to the stature of the universe-filling Man. See *Jew. Ency*. Artic. *Adam Kadmon* (the Archetypal Man).

17. *Zech*.viii.16.

18. *Ps*.xxxvii.8.

19. An Essene term denoting the Elect.

20. Like the Essenes the early Christians sang hymns at dawn in praise of the 'Sun of righteousness' (Cf. *Mal*.iv.2). These lines may be from one such hymn. See also *Jn*.i.1-17, and *Letter of Pliny to the Emperor Trajan,* 'that they (the Christians) met on a certain fixed day before it was light and sang an antiphonal chant to Christ, as to a god'.

21. Baptism, related to the ritual bath of purification taken by Jewish women, here prior to the marriage ceremony, kiddushin (consecration).

22. Cf. *Cant*.iv.7.

23. *Gen*.ii.24.

24. *Exod*.xx.12.

25. Cf. *Gen*.xviii.19.

26. Cf. *Isa*.xi.5.

27. Cf. *Isa*.lix.17.

28. Cf. *Isa*.lii.7.

29. At this time Paul was in Rome awaiting trial.

30. See *II. Tim*.iv.12.

To the Community at Colossae

(Probably written from Rome in AD 61 or 62)

1.1   Paul, by the will of God an envoy of Christ Jesus, with brother Timotheus, to the saints and faithful brothers in Christ at Colossae. May peace and prosperity be yours from God our Father.

3   I thank God, the Father of our Lord Jesus Christ, and invariably pray for you, having heard of your faith in Christ Jesus and the affection you have for all the saints on account of the hope held in heavenly reserve for you. This hope you first heard expressed in the True Message of the News, which reached you, as it has reached everywhere else in the world, producing fruit and increasing – again as it has done among you – from the very day you heard it. You then became fully conscious of God's mercy as you learnt it from our dear fellow-servant Epaphras. He is a faithful minister of Christ on your behalf, who has also informed me of your spiritual affection.

9   Accordingly, I too, from the day I heard, have never ceased to pray for you, and to request that you may be filled with the knowledge of God's will in all wisdom and spiritual comprehension, so as to behave in a manner worthy of the Master to his entire satisfaction by every good deed you do. You are thus producing fruit and increasing in the knowledge of God, endued by his glorious power with every capacity for much patience and long-suffering with joy.

12   I give thanks to the Father, who has qualified you to share the lot of the saints in Light, who has rescued us from the dominion of Darkness and transferred us to the Kingdom of his dear Son, by whom we obtain redemption, absolution from our sins. He[1] is the image of the Unseen God, the first-born of all creation, that everything in heaven and earth might be founded on him, seen and unseen alike, whether angelic Thrones or Lordships or Rulers or Authorities. Everything was created through him and for him. He is the antecedent of everything, and on him everything was framed.[2] So also is he Head of the

Body, the Community, that is to say, the fount and origin of it, the first-born from the dead, that in every connection he might take precedence. For it pleased God that by him the Whole should be governed, and through him – his making peace through the blood of his cross – to bring everything once more into harmony with the Divine self, whether on earth or in heaven.

21   You yourselves were formerly alienated and hostile in attitude when you were engaged in evil deeds; but now Christ has reconciled you to God by the death of his physical body, so as to present you before God chaste, blameless and irreproachable, assuming that you remain firm and unmoved in the Faith, and do not deviate from the Hope of the News which you have heard, which has been proclaimed to every creature under heaven, and of which I, Paul, was made a minister.

24   So I rejoice in my sufferings for your sake, and make good in my flesh the deficiencies of the Messianic Woes,[3] for the sake of Christ's Body, namely the Community, of which I was made a minister, in accordance with God's mandate granted me for you, to give effect to God's message, the secret kept hidden from all the ages and generations, but now published to his saints. To them God would make known what wealth of glory this secret holds for the Gentiles namely Christ in you, the expectation of glory. He it is whom we proclaim, advising everyone and teaching everyone with all wisdom, that we may present everyone perfect in Christ.

29   This is what I toil for, striving with his energy who so powerfully
2.1 motivates me. Indeed, I wish you to know what a severe trial I am undergoing on your account, and on account of those of Laodicea, and of as many others as have never seen me personally, that their minds may be encouraged, being confirmed in their love and in the solid wealth of absolute certainty in knowledge of God's secret, yes, of Christ himself, in whom are hidden all the treasures of wisdom and knowledge. I say this in case anyone should mislead you with specious argument. For even if I am absent physically I am nevertheless with you in spirit, observing with pleasure your good order and the solidarity of your faith in Christ.

6   As, therefore, you have accepted Christ Jesus as Master, behave in his way, base yourselves and build yourselves on him, and maintain yourselves in the Faith as you have been taught it, excelling in it with thanksgiving.

8   Take care that no one gets hold of you with philosophy and worthless craft belonging to human tradition, to the elemental forces

of the world instead of to Christ; for it is in him that the immensity of the Divine Wisdom corporately dwells, and it is in him – Head of all Rulers and Authorities – that you are made complete. It is in him too that you have been pared by a circumcision not man-made, by the stripping away of the physical body, by Christ's kind of circumcision, being buried with him by immersion. In him equally you have been raised up by faith in the might of God who raised him from the dead.

13 So you who were dead in transgressions, and in your physical uncircumcision, God has brought to life with him, having forgiven us all our transgressions. He not only cancelled the writ against us with its stipulations, which were adverse to us, but also took it away entirely, nailing it to the cross. After having despoiled the angelic Rulers and Authorities, he paraded them in public by the cross.[4]

16 Let no one judge you, therefore, in matters of food and drink, or in such a matter as a Jewish festival, New Moon, or Sabbath, which represent only a shadow of things to come, and of which Christ is the substance. Let no one arbitrarily influence you to fast and engage in the worship of angels,[5] inducing you to share his visions, being vainly puffed up by his physical mind and not holding to the Head, from whom the whole Body, connected and integrated by the joints and ligaments, grows in God's way.

20 If you have died with Christ to the Elemental Forces of the Cosmos, why, as though still living in the world, are you controlled by stipulations – 'Do not handle! Do not taste! Do not touch!' – which imply that everything contaminates[6] by its use, in accordance with human commandments and doctrines? Such prescriptions, indeed, seem to have some sense in them in subordination of the will, fasting and asceticism, but they are not really efficacious against human indulgence.

3.1 If, therefore, you have been raised up with Christ, seek the things that are on high, where Christ is, seated at God's right hand. Set your minds on the things that are above, not on what is on earth; for you have died, and your life has been secreted with Christ in God. When Christ, who enshrines our life, is revealed, then you too will be revealed with him in glory.

5 So treat your organs on earth as dead for fornication, impurity, lust, unlawful desire, and rapacity (which means idol-worship), things that bring down the wrath of God. In such things you once indulged when you led that kind of life. But now you must discard all alike, anger,

rage, malice, abuse, foul language. Do not lie to one another, having divested yourselves of the former man and his deeds, and having put on the new man, renovated in knowledge, in conformity with the likeness of God who created him, where there can be no question of Gentile[7] and Jew, circumcision and uncircumcision, Barbarian, Scythian, slave or freeman, but of Christ wholly and completely.

12 Put on, therefore, as God's Elect, saints and beloved ones, feelings of compassion, benevolence, humility, gentleness, long-suffering, bearing with one another and forgiving one another should any have a complaint against another. As the Lord has forgiven you, do you also forgive. And over and above these qualities put on love, which represents the band[8] that gives the finishing touch. And let Christ's peace direct your minds, the peace to which you were called as one Body. And be thankful. Let the Message of Christ dwell in you richly in all its wisdom, teaching and admonishing one another graciously by psalms, hymns and spiritual odes, singing to God in your hearts. And whatever you do, by word or deed, do it all in the name of the Lord Jesus, giving thanks to God the Father by him.

18 Wives, be submissive to your husbands as is befitting in the Master. Husbands, love your wives and do not treat them harshly. Children, obey your parents in everything, for this is well-pleasing to the Lord.[9] Fathers, do not fret your children, in case they should be discouraged. Slaves, in everything obey those who in the physical sense are your masters, not with service which catches the eye like those who wish to ingratiate themselves, but in singleness of mind, fearing the Lord. Whatever you do, do it with real goodwill, as having the Lord in mind rather than men, knowing that you will receive from the Lord the recompense that is due. Serve the Lord Christ; for he who does wrong will be paid back for his wrong-doing, and there is no partiality shown.

4.1 Masters, treat your slaves equitably and fairly, knowing that you too have a Master in heaven.

2 Apply yourselves constantly to prayer, being incited to it by thankfulness. At the same time pray for me, that God may give me an opportunity to speak, to declare the secret of Christ on account of which I am fettered, that I should disclose it as it behoves me to speak. Behave with circumspection towards those who are 'outside', using the time profitably. Invariably let your speech be gracious, flavoured with salt, that you may know how to answer all and sundry.

7 As for my affairs, Tychicus, that dear brother and loyal minister and fellow-servant in the Master, will fully inform you. I have dis-

patched him to you for this express purpose, that you may know how I fare and that he may cheer your hearts, and with him faithful and dear brother Onesimus,[10] who is one of yourselves. They will tell you all that goes on here.[11]

10   My fellow-prisoner Aristarchus sends you his regards, as does Barnabas's kinsman Mark (about whom you have been advised: welcome him should he visit you), and so does Jesus known as Justus. They belong to the Circumcision, and they alone have been my co-workers for the Kingdom of God; they have been a great comfort to me. Epaphras, one of yourselves, a servant of Christ Jesus, sends you his regards. Invariably he contends for you at prayer times that you may stand, sound and fully assured, by the whole will of God. I can testify that he has put up a great fight for you, and for those of Laodicea and Hierapolis. Dear Doctor Luke sends you his regards, and so does Demas.[12]

15   Give my regards to the brothers at Laodicea, also to Nympha and the community in her house. When this letter has been read by you arrange also for it to be read in the Laodicean community, and get their letter from Laodicea,[13] that you too may read it. And tell Archippus, 'See to it that you carry out the ministry you have received in the Master!'

My regards in my own hand,

PAUL

Remember my fetters![14] Wishing you every happiness.

NOTES AND REFERENCES

1. As the Archetypal Man (Cf. *Gen*.i.26).
2. It was held that the Archetypal Man (Son of Man), the Messiah (Christ) Above, had incarnated in Jesus as the Messiah Below, having in the Beginning served as the Expression (Word) of God on which the Universe was framed. The concept derived from mystical Jewish teaching unfamiliar to the Catholic Creed creators.
3. Known in Jewish teaching as the 'Pangs of Messiah' which would precede the birth of the Messianic Era (the Kingdom of God on earth).
4. Like captives in a victor's procession. In Paul's view the Law had been drawn up by angelic powers. And see *Gal*.iii.13, 19.
5. The heavenly hierarchy of the Jewish mystics.

6. Or 'sends to perdition'.
7. Paul commonly uses the word 'Greek', as here, to represent non-Jews.
8. i.e. the belt or girdle which completes the attire.
9. See *Exod*.xx.12.
10. See the letter *To Philemon*.
11. i.e. in Rome, where Paul was a prisoner.
12. Demas later deserted Paul (*II.Tim*.iv.10).
13. Either the letter *To the Asian Communities* known as the letter to the *Ephesians*, or another which has not been preserved.
14. i.e. in prayer.

To Philemon etc.

(Written from Rome about AD 62)

1.₁ Paul, prisoner of Christ Jesus, with brother Timotheus, to our dear friend and co-worker Philemon, to our sister Apphia, to our fellow-campaigner Archippus,[1] and to the community in your house. May peace and prosperity be yours from God our Father and the Lord Jesus Christ.

4 Invariably I thank God, making mention of you in my prayers, learning of the affection and loyalty you have for the Lord Jesus and for all the saints, whereby the fellowship of your faith may prove effective in securing knowledge of every good thing that is ours in Christ. I have indeed been given much happiness and encouragement by your affection, brother, because through you the hearts of the saints have been refreshed.

8 Consequently, while regarding myself in Christ as quite at liberty to insist on the point, yet out of affection I prefer to appeal to you, being such as I am, that old man Paul, and also at present a prisoner of Christ Jesus.

10 It is for a son of mine I appeal to you, one whom I have begotten in my bonds, Onesimus, who was previously worthless to you, but now is of very real worth both to you and me. I have sent him back to you, which means that I have parted with my own heart. I would much rather have kept him with me, so that he might have served me instead of you in the bonds of the News; but I did not wish to do anything without your assent, in case your kindness might seem an obligation instead of being voluntary. Perhaps the reason he was parted from you for a while may be that you might have him wholly ever after, no longer as just a slave, but over and above a slave, as a dear brother, particularly to me, but how much more so to you with a physical tie as well as in the Master.

17 So if you regard me as a kinsman, receive him as you would myself. If he has wronged you, or owes you anything, put that down

to my account. I, Paul, put this in my own handwriting, 'I will make restitution in full.' Need I say to you that actually you owe me your own self? Well, brother, let me have some 'benefit'[2] out of you in the Master. Refresh my heart in Christ.

21   I am writing to you in full confidence of your compliance, knowing that you will do even more than I ask. At the same time prepare to have me also as your guest, for I anticipate that through your prayers I shall be granted to you.

23   My fellow-prisoner Epaphras[3] sends you his regards in Christ Jesus. So do my fellow-workers[4] Mark, Aristarchus, Demas and Luke.

    The loving-kindness of our Lord Jesus Christ be with your spirit.

Notes and References

1. Mentioned at the close of the letter to Colossae.
2. Playing on the name Onesimus, meaning 'beneficial'. Paul pleads most movingly on behalf of this runaway slave, who has become a Christian. Instead of being beneficial Onesimus had proved worthless to Philemon.
3. See *Col*.iv.12.
4. All these persons are referred to in the letter to *Colossae*.

To Titus

(Probably written from Rome in AD 62)

1.1   Paul, servant of God and envoy of Jesus Christ for purposes of
faith in God, and for the knowledge of the Truth, as it concerns
devoutness in prospect of Eternal Life, which the never false God
promised in the remote past and in due course revealed by his
Message, with the proclamation of which I have been entrusted
by order of God our Saviour, to Titus my true son in our common
faith. May peace and prosperity be yours from God our Father
and Christ Jesus our deliverer.

5   I left you in Crete with good reason, to tie up what loose ends were
left, and to ordain elders for each town as I directed you, assuming
6   there is someone of blameless character, husband of one wife, having
believing children, someone who is not open to the charge of profli-
10   gacy or disorderliness.¹ For there are many disorderly vaporisers and
bamboozlers, particularly those from the Circumcision, people who
must be muzzled, the kind who subvert whole households, teaching
things they have no business to do from mercenary motives. One of
themselves, an exponent of their own,² has said, 'The Cretans, ever
cheats, brute beasts and idle windbags.'³ That is a true description.
For that very reason rebuke them sharply, that they may be sound
in the Faith, paying no heed to Judaic myths and injunctions of men
who have turned away from the truth. To the pure everything is pure,
but to the polluted and unbelieving nothing is pure, because both their
minds and consciences are warped. They profess to know God, but
by their actions they disown him, being disgusting and mutinous,
hopeless for any useful service.

2.1   It is for you to state what is consistent with sound teaching, to tell
the older men to be sober, dignified, discreet, sound in faith, in love,
in constancy. Tell the older women similarly to maintain a condition
suited to a reverent nature, not to be spiteful, not addicted to drink,
but givers of good advice, so that they may influence the young

223

women to be devoted to husband and children, to be sensible, chaste, domesticated, decent, submissive to their husbands, that God's Message may not come into disrepute. In the same way exhort the young men to be temperate. In every connection you yourself should set an example of good behaviour, by purity of teaching, plain sense, and sound principles that cannot be impugned, so that he who is against us may respect our position, finding nothing detrimental to say about us.[4]

9   Slaves should be in subjection to their masters, giving entire satisfaction, not answering back, not pilfering, but giving proof of complete trustworthiness, that in every way they may be a credit to the teaching of God our Saviour. For God's mercy has manifested itself for the salvation of all men, instructing us that, abandoning impiety and worldly passions, we should live temperately, justly and devoutly in the present time, waiting for the blessed Hope and visible manifestation of the glory of the Great God, and of our Deliverer Jesus Christ, who gave himself for us to free us from all our iniquities and to purify for himself a special people eager for good deeds.[5]

15   Declare these things, exhort and reprove, with every possible
3.1 authority. Let no one treat you casually. Remind them to be subject to rulers and authorities, to be law-abiding, ready for every useful service, in no way abusive, to be free from pugnacity, equable, always exhibiting a mild demeanour towards everyone. I myself was once lacking in sense, ungovernable, erratic, a slave to various passions and pleasures, spending my time in resentment and jealousy, gloomy, hating others. But when the goodness and benevolence of God our Saviour became clear, not because of any righteous actions I had performed, but in accordance with his mercy, he saved me by the washing and the renovating power of the holy Spirit which he lavished on me richly through Jesus Christ our Deliverer; so that being exonerated by that act of grace I became an heir in accordance with the expectation of Eternal Life.

8   This is a true saying, and I want you to be very positive about it, that 'those who have believed in God should be concerned to offer themselves for honest employment.' This is a proper and helpful thing for men to do. But avoid foolish issues and genealogies, wrangles and legal quibbles;[6] for these are unhelpful and senseless. Have no more to do with the dissentient man after giving him a first and second warning, seeing that anyone like this has turned away and erred deliberately, and stands self-condemned.

12   When I despatch Artemas to you, or Tychicus,[7] do your utmost to come to me at Nicopolis, for I have decided to pass the winter there.[8] Afford the lawyer Zenas and also Apollos every facility for their journey, so that they are short of nothing. Our people must really learn to offer themselves for honest employment to meet essential needs, so that they are not unproductive.

15   All here send you their regards. My regards to those who truly esteem me.

Wishing you all every happiness.

NOTES AND REFERENCES

1. The following passage, verses 7-9, appears to be a later MS addition: 'For the supervisor (i.e.bishop) should be irreproachable, as God's appointed steward, not domineering, not irritable, not a tippler, not a brawler, not mercenary, but open-handed, one who cares for goodness, is discreet, just, consecrated, disciplined, a close adherent of the trustworthy Message in terms of the Teaching, so that he may be able to exhort by sound instruction and confute opponents.'
2. Cretan poet Epimenides.
3. Poem *On Oracles*, quoted by Callimachus, *Hymn 1. – To Zeus*, 8.
4. Cf. *Acts* xxviii.22. The Christians were already in bad odour.
5. Cf. *Ezek*.xxxvii.23; *Deut*.xiv.2.
6. When Paul was a prisoner in Rome there was conflict between his views and those especially of the Jewish members of the Christian Community there who had formed the majority. See *II.Tim*.iv.14-17. Paul seems to be referring to such points of disagreement (cf. *I.Tim*.i.6-11).
7. Tychicus was bearer of the letters to Asia (Ephesians) and Colossae. It is suggested that the Nicopolis where Paul proposed to spend the winter, assuming he was released, was the one in Epirus on the western coast of Greece.
8. At the time of writing Paul anticipated that he would be released by the Roman government (see *Phil*.i.24-26, and especially *Philemon*, verse 22). But in this he was thwarted by fate.

To Timotheus (1)

(Probably written from Rome in AD 63)

1.1   Paul, envoy of Christ Jesus by appointment of God our Saviour and of Christ Jesus our Hope, to Timotheus my true son in faith. May prosperity, mercy and peace be yours from God the Father and Christ Jesus our Master.

3   As I begged you when you were leaving Macedonia,[1] do stay on at Ephesus to impress on some there not to teach different doctrine, not to concern themselves with myths and interminable genealogies, matters which raise issues rather than promote the divine government which rests on faith. The essence of the precept still is love,[2] love out of a pure heart, a clear conscience, and unfeigned faith. From these some, having missed the mark, have gone off at a tangent into senseless talk, wanting to be teachers of the Law, but neither understanding what they are talking about, nor what they are really driving at.[3]

8   We all know how valuable the Law is if it is consulted legitimately. But we recognise none the less that the Law is not put there for the upright, but for the lawless and refractory, the impious and the sinners, the ungodly and profane, patricides and matricides, those guilty of manslaughter, vicious persons, homosexuals, man-traffickers, liars, perjurers, and whatever else there may be that is opposed to sound teaching in conformity with the News of the Blessed God with which I have been entrusted.

12   I feel deeply grateful to the one who has empowered me, to Christ Jesus our Master, that he considered me sufficiently trustworthy to take into service, I who previously had been a slanderer, a persecutor, and a man of violence. But I obtained mercy because I acted unwittingly in unbelief. But our Master's loving-kindness, together with the faith and love which is in Christ Jesus, was more than adequate.

15   This is a true saying, and deserving of unqualified acceptance, that 'Christ Jesus came into the world to save sinners.' Of these I am foremost. But I obtained mercy for the very reason that by me Christ Jesus might exhibit his full forbearance as a general indication to

those who would come to believe in him for Eternal Life. To the imperishable, invisible King of the Universe,[4] the Only God, be honour and glory for ever and ever. Amen.

18   This signal[5] I transmit to you, son Timotheus, in conformity with the prognostications about you, that in their terms you may set out to wage a gallant campaign, in possession of faith and a clear conscience, a campaign which some having declined have come to grief over the Faith. Among these are Hymenaeus and Alexander,[6] whom I have consigned to Satan that they may be disciplined not to speak profanely.

2.1   In the first place, therefore, I require that petitions, prayers, intercessions and thanksgivings be offered for everyone, for kings and all holding positions of authority, so that we may pass a quiet and tranquil life in all godliness and gravity. This is proper and well-pleasing in the sight of God our Saviour, who desires everyone to be saved and come to acknowledge the Truth. There is One God, and one intermediary between God and mankind, the Man Christ Jesus, who gave himself as a ransom for all, as will be demonstrated in due course. To announce this I was made a herald and envoy – I am telling the truth, I am not lying – a faithful and true teacher of the Gentiles.

8   I therefore desire the men everywhere to offer prayer, raising holy hands free from passion and controversy. Similarly, their wives should dress themselves unobtrusively, with modesty and moderation, not adorning themselves with lace and gold or pearl embroidery or expensive material, but with what is becoming for women professing to be religious, with kind actions. Let a wife learn passively with complete submissiveness. I do not permit a woman to teach, nor to exercise a husband's prerogative, but to be passive. For Adam was formed first, and then Eve. And it was not Adam who was beguiled; but the woman being completely beguiled fell into transgression. Yet she shall be saved by child-bearing,[7] provided the couple remain faithful, affectionate and devoted, and also practise moderation.

3.1   This is a true saying, 'If anyone aspires to be a supervisor he desires honourable employment.' The supervisor ought therefore to be irreproachable, husband of one wife, sober, temperate, mannerly, hospitable, a good teacher, not truculent, nor pugnacious, but equable, pacific, free from avarice, managing his own household wisely, keeping his children in order with all gravity. For if anyone does not know how to manage his own household, how is he to take charge of God's community? He should not be a recent convert, in case by becoming conceited he meets with the Devil's fate. He ought also to be well-spoken of by those 'outside', in case he falls into disrepute and the Devil's snare.

8 Administrators likewise should be grave, not gossipers, not addicted to liberal potations, not money-grubbers, holding the mystery of the Faith with a clear conscience. They should also first be on probation: then let them act as administrators when proved satisfactory. Their wives too should be grave, never malicious, sober and entirely reliable. Let administrators remain married to one wife, managing their children and their own households well. For those who act well as administrators acquire an influential status and great liberty of speech for the Faith that is in Jesus Christ.

14 I am writing to you in this way, hoping to visit you shortly, but in case I am delayed, that you may know how life ought to be lived in the house of God, which is the Community of the Living God, the prop and stay of the Truth. Admittedly it is a great thing, this Mystery of devoutness which [in Christ][8] 'was made visible physically, vindicated spiritually, seen by angels, proclaimed to the Gentiles, believed in in the world, taken up again in glory.'[9]

4.1 Now the Spirit categorically declares, 'In the latter times some will desert the Faith, paying attention to misleading spirits and pronouncements of demons, speaking falsely with intent to deceive,'[10] having their own conscience seared, forbidding marriage, and requiring abstention from foods which God has created to be partaken of with thanksgiving by those who believe and fully understand the truth. For every provision of God is good, and by no means to be refused if it is accepted with thanksgiving; for it is consecrated by the recitation of the grace to God.

6 If you put these things to the brothers you will be a worthy minister of Christ Jesus, primed in the principles of the Faith and in the right teaching you have consistently followed. But deprecate irreverent matters and old wives' tales. Train yourself for devoutness. 'Physical training is of limited usefulness, but devoutness is of unlimited usefulness, providing assurance both for the present life and for that which is to come.' This is a true saying and deserving of unqualified acceptance. That is why we toil and strive, because we have fixed our hope on the Living God, who is the Saviour of all men, particularly of believers. Impress and teach these things.

12 Let no one despise your youth; but set an example to believers by speech, by behaviour, by love, by faith, by purity. Devote yourself until I come to exposition, exhortation and instruction. Do not neglect

the gift you have, which was bestowed on you by a prophetic intimation which accompanied your ordination[11] by the elders. Exercise and develop these faculties, that your progress may be marked by all. Keep a firm hold on yourself and on the doctrine. Be true to them; for by so doing you will save both yourself and those who listen to you.

5.1   Do not reprimand an elder, but appeal to him as if he were your father, and to the younger men as brothers, to the older women as your mother, and to the younger women chastely as sisters. Care for widows who are lone widows. But where a widow has children or grandchildren let these first learn to discharge their filial duty and to make suitable return to the authors of their being, for this is well-pleasing in God's sight. But the lone and solitary widow has her hope in God, and gives herself to prayers and petitions night and day. The fast-living woman, however, is dead in life. Impress these things on them, that they may be irreproachable. So if any man does not provide for his own relations, and especially his own family, he has disavowed the Faith and is worse than an unbeliever.

9   Do not let a widow be put on the register[12] at a lower age than sixty, a woman who has been the wife of one husband, with testimonials to her kind actions, such as that she has brought up children, given hospitality to strāngers, washed the feet of saints, relieved those in distress, or has been responsible for some other good deed.

11   But decline to register the younger widows; for when they become capricious towards Christ they want to marry, earning condemnation for disregarding the first claim on their allegiance. At the same time they learn to be idle, going the round of houses; and not only to be idle, but also gossipers and meddlers, talking about what is none of their business. I therefore prefer the younger women to marry, to have children, keep house, and give no kind of pretext to the ill-disposed to indulge in abuse, for already some have gone off the road after Satan. Should any believers have widows to take care of, let them give them assistance and not burden the community, so that lone widows may be provided for.

17   Let the elders who govern well be treated as deserving of twice as much consideration, particularly those who are occupied with speaking and instruction. The Scripture truly says, 'You are not to muzzle the ox that treads out the corn,'[13] and 'the workman deserves his wages'.[14]

19   Do not admit an accusation against an elder unless it is supported by two or three witnesses. But publicly reprove those that do sin, that it may deter the others. I charge you before God and Christ

Jesus and the elect angels[15] to maintain these principles without prejudice, doing nothing with bias. Do not ordain anyone hastily, nor become involved in the sins of others. Keep yourself unpolluted.

23 Do not be a water drinker any longer, but take a little wine for the sake of your stomach and your chronic ailments. Some men's sins are patent, standing out for condemnation, but with others they are kept in the background. In the same way also their good deeds are patent; but even when they are not they cannot be concealed.

6.1 Let as many as are under the yoke as slaves regard their owners as deserving of every consideration, that the Name of God and the doctrine may not be brought into disrepute. But let not those who have owners who are believers be presumptuous towards them because they are brothers. Rather should they be meticulous in serving because those who are deriving the benefit of the useful service are believers and friends. Teach and advocate these things.

3 If anyone teaches anything different, and does not propound sound principles, those of our Lord Jesus Christ, and instruction that is consistent with godliness, he is befogged, knowing nothing clearly, crazy about issues and fights over words, which give rise to antagonism, rivalry, slanders, evil suspicions, and violent altercations of men whose minds are warped and bereft of truth, imagining good business to be the same thing as godliness. But godliness plus contentment is the best possible business; for we have brought nothing into the world, neither is there anything we can take out of it. Having food and shelter let us be content with these.

9 Those who want to be rich expose themselves to temptations and pitfalls, and to many foolish and harmful cravings, which drag men down to ruin and perdition. The root of all the evils is avarice, and some having clutched at it have strayed from the Faith and racked themselves with many torments.

11 Do you, man of God, fly from these things. But pursue rectitude, devoutness, faith, love, constancy and gentleness. Fight the gallant contest of the Faith to the finish. Put up a real struggle for Eternal Life, to which you were called. Having made the noble confession before many witnesses, I charge you before God the Source of all life,[16] and before Christ Jesus who made the noble confession before Pontius Pilate,[17] to keep the injunction unsullied, unimpeachable, until the visible appearance of our Lord Jesus Christ, which the blessed and sole Sovereign[18] will display in due course, the King of kings and Lord of lords, who alone is deathless, dwelling in unapproachable light,

whom no man has seen, nor can see. To him be honour and ever-lasting might. Amen.

17 Impress on those who are rich in this present world not to be arrogant, nor to build their hopes on such uncertain things as riches, but on God who provides everything in profusion for our enjoyment. Impress on them to be beneficent, rich in kind actions, to be generous and public-spirited, storing up for themselves a useful fund for the future, so as to secure the Life worth living.

20 Guard what is committed to your care, Timotheus, avoiding the ir-reverent jargon and contradictions of the falsely termed 'Knowledge',[19] which some professing have fallen into error regarding the Faith.

Wishing you every happiness.

Notes and References

1. Timotheus appears to have gone from Rome to Ephesus, and at Paul's request to have remained there.
2. *Deut.*vi.5.
3. The New Testament was the product of the Christian communities out-side Israel, so that the views of the Judaeo-Christian envoys and mem-bers are very little represented.
4. Paul is using the language of congregational Jewish prayer and praise.
5. i.e. the doxology just quoted. Here and in the words that follow Paul is using the metaphor of a military expedition by sea.
6. Probably the same as Alexander the blacksmith (*II.Tim.*iv.14).
7. *Gen.*iii.16.
8. 'in Christ' is not in the text but is needed by the sense.
9. From an early hymn or creed.
10. Cf. *Dan.*viii.23-26; *Mt.*xxiv.10-12.
11. Lit. 'laying on of hands'.
12. So as to receive communal maintenance.
13. *Deut.*xxv.4.
14. See *Deut.*xxiv.15 and cf. *Lk.*x.7.
15. Cf. Jos.*Jewish War*, II.401: 'I call your Sanctuary and God's holy angels ... to witness.'
16. Cf. *I.Sam.*ii.6 (LXX).
17. Perhaps from an uncanonical source.
18. i.e. God Almighty.
19. Gr. *Gnosis* (Gnostic systems). This paragraph may be a scribal addition.

To Timotheus (2)

(Probably written from Rome in AD 63)

1.1   Paul, by the will of God an envoy of Christ Jesus in conformity with the promise of Life that is in Christ Jesus, to his dear son Timotheus. May prosperity, mercy and peace be yours from God the Father and Christ Jesus our Master.

3   I am grateful to God, whom I serve with a pure conscience as did my forebears, as I am unremitting in mentioning you to him in my petitions, longing night and day to see you, very mindful of your tears, that I may be filled with joy.

5   I cherish the recollection of your guileless faith, which first resided in your grandma Lois and your mother Eunice, and I am sure does still in you. It is on this ground that I would urge you to fan the flame of the divine gift imparted to you when I ordained you; for God has not given us a spirit of timidity, but of resolution, devotion and correction. So do not be ashamed of the testimony of our Master, nor of me his prisoner, but bear your share of hardship for the News as God enables you. He has saved us and called us with a holy calling, not in accordance with our actions, but in accordance with his own purpose and mercy bestowed on us in Christ Jesus before the Ages began, but now tangibly expressed through the visible appearance of Christ Jesus our Deliverer, who has put death out of action and brought life and imperishability into operation by the News, of which I am appointed herald, envoy and teacher. It is on this ground that I suffer as I do. But I am not ashamed of it, for I know in whom I have put my trust, and am confident that he is able to keep secure what I have entrusted to him until that Day comes.

13   Hold fast the outline of sound principles you have heard from me by the faith and love that is in Christ Jesus. Keep safe that noble deposit which by the holy Spirit resides in us. You are well aware that all the Asiatic believers[1] have turned from me, among them Phygelus and Hermogenes. The Lord have compassion on the house-

232

hold of Onesiphorus,[2] because he often heartened me and was never ashamed of my chain; but on arrival at Rome he made diligent inquiry for me and found out where I was. The Lord grant him to find mercy[3] when the Day comes. And the many ways in which he looked after me in Ephesus you know better than anyone.

2.1 Be resolute therefore, my son, in the loving-kindness that is in Christ Jesus, and what you have heard as from me through many witnesses, commit to reliable persons, who will be competent in turn to teach others. Bear your share of hardship like a good soldier of Christ Jesus. No one going off to war saddles himself with the responsibilities of life, since he aims to satisfy his enlisting officer. Also if anyone contends in the Games, he will not be crowned if he does not adhere to the rules. The farmer who has put in the labour ought to have first claim on the produce. Note what I say. The Lord will grant you complete understanding.

8 Always remember, Jesus Christ of the lineage of David was raised from the dead in my presentation of the News. For this I suffer hardship to the extent of imprisonment, like a malefactor. But God's Message is not fettered. Because of that I submit to everything for the sake of the Elect, that they too may obtain the salvation that is in Christ Jesus with eternal glory. It is a true saying,

> If we have died with him, we shall also live with him.
> If we are constant, we shall also reign with him.
> If we disown him, so will he disown us.
> If we are disloyal, he will still be faithful.

14 Faithful, because he cannot deny himself. Remind them of this, begging them most solemnly before God not to battle over words, which gains nothing, and only disconcerts the listeners. Be at pains to prove yourself competent to God, a workman who has no need to be ashamed, having kept to the straight line with the Message of Truth. But evade irreverent jargon. Those who employ it only further the progress of impiety, and their speech mortifies like a gangrene. Among them are Hymenaeus and Philetus, who have fallen into error regarding the Truth, saying that the resurrection has already taken place,[4] and have overturned the faith of some.

19 At least God's solid foundation stays firm bearing this stamp on it, 'The Lord knows those who are truly his,'[5] and 'Let all who pronounce the name of the Lord stand aside from iniquity.'[6] But in a large establishment there are not only vessels of gold and silver, but also of wood and earthenware, the ones for best and the other for common

use. Should anyone make himself pure from the latter, he will become a vessel for best use, cleansed, fit for the Owner's employment, in complete readiness for every useful service.

22 Fly from youthful passions, but pursue rectitude, faith, love and peace, with those who invoke the name of the Lord with a pure mind. Deprecate foolish and idle issues, knowing that they breed strife. The Master's servant ought not to wrangle, but to be pacific towards all, instructive, forbearing, quietly correcting opponents, so that perhaps God may grant them a change of mind to realise the truth and be brought to their senses, being recovered by him from the Devil's clutches, who had taken possession of them for his own purposes.

3.1 You must know this, however, that in the Last Days hard times are in store; for men will be selfish, money-grubbing, brazen, arrogant, slanderous, defiant to parents, ungrateful, irreligious, lacking in affection, implacable, spiteful, uncontrolled, savage, disliking good, treacherous, headstrong, conceited, preferring pleasure to piety, maintaining a semblance of devoutness but denying its efficacy. Turn away from all such people; for from them come those who gain an entrance into households and captivate immature females, piled high with peccadilloes, swayed by whims and fancies, always learning, but never really able to grasp the Truth. In the same kind of way as Jannes and Jambres[7] opposed Moses, so do these men, warped in mind, unsound in the Faith, oppose the Truth. But they will make no further headway, for their folly will be patent to all, as indeed was that of those magicians.

10 But you have closely followed my teaching, my method, presentation, forbearance, devotion and constancy, the persecutions and sufferings I met with at Antioch, Iconium and Lystra, the various kinds of persecution I underwent, from all of which the Lord rescued me. And indeed all who desire to live dutifully in Christ Jesus must expect persecution. But wicked men and impostors will flourish as time goes by, deceiving and being deceived. You, however, adhere to the things you have learnt and been convinced of, seeing from whom you learnt them, and that from infancy you have known the holy Scriptures, which have power to make you wise for salvation by faith that is in Christ Jesus. Each document is divinely inspired, and consequently advantageous for instruction, reproof, reclamation and moral discipline, so that the Man of God may be expert, fully equipped for every useful undertaking.

4.1 I charge you before God, and before Christ Jesus, who will judge the living and the dead, and in view of his visible appearing and reign, proclaim the Message, apply yourself to this in season and out of season. Reprove, censure, exhort, with all forbearance and diligence. For the time will come when they will not tolerate sound teaching, but following their own desires will load themselves with teachers who tickle the ear, and will turn a deaf ear to the Truth, turning instead to myths.

5   You, however, keep perfectly cool, endure hardships, do your duty as a standard-bearer of the News, fulfil the conditions of your service. For I am now on the eve of peace, and the time of my discharge is approaching. I have fought a gallant contest; I have completed the course; I have kept the Faith. There remains in store for me the crown to which I am entitled, which the Master, that honourable judge, will award me on that Day; and not me alone, but all who delightedly welcomed his personal presence.

9   Do your utmost to come to me quickly, for Demas, loving the présent world, has deserted me and gone off to Thessalonica, Crescens has gone to Gaul, Titus to Dalmatia. Only Luke remains with me. Pick up Mark and bring him with you, for he is valuable to me in administrative work, and I have dispatched Tychicus to Ephesus. When you come bring the heavy jacket I left with Carpus at Troas, also the books, particularly the parchments. Alexander the blacksmith has shown himself very ill-disposed towards me. The Lord will requite him according to his actions.[8] Watch out for him yourself, for he is strongly opposed to our views. At the first hearing of my defence no one supported me: everyone deserted me. May it not be counted against them! But my Master supported and strengthened me; so that through me the proclamation might ring out, and all the Gentiles might hear it; and I was 'saved from the jaws of the lion'.[9] The Lord will continue to rescue me from every evil agency and preserve me for his heavenly Kingdom. To him be glory for ever. Amen.

19   Give my regards to Prisca and Aquila, and to the household of Onesiphorus. Erastus is still at Corinth, while Trophimus I left ill at Miletus. Do your utmost to come to me before winter sets in.

   Eubulus sends you his regards, so do Prudens, Linus, Claudia, and all the brothers.

   The Lord Jesus Christ be with your spirit. Wishing you every happiness.

NOTES AND REFERENCES

1. i.e. those in the Province of Asia, such as at Ephesus.
2. The passage seems to convey that Onesiphorus had died.
3. Lit. 'The Lord grant him to find mercy from the Lord', a Hebraism. Cf. *Gen*.xix.24.
4. i.e. that of the Saints.
5. *Num*.xvi.5 (LXX).
6. Cf. *Num*.xvi.26-27 (LXX).
7. The legendary court magicians of Pharaoh in the time of Moses.
8. Cf. *Ps*.xxviii.4; *II.Sam*.iii.39.
9. Cf. *Ps*.xxii.1. Paul is using a Jewish stock phrase for the power of tyrannical rulers, in this case the Emperor Nero. See Jos. *Antiq*.Bk.XVIII. 228-229. Evidently Paul had had his case deferred.

Select Bibliography

Buttrick, Charles (ed.): *The Interpreter's Dictionary of the Bible*, 4 vols. (Abingdon Press, 1962).

Charles, R H (ed.): *The Apocrypha and Pseudepigrapha of the OT*, 2 vols. (Oxford, 1913, reissued 1963).

Cross, F L: *The Early Christian Fathers* (Duckworth, 1960).

Eusebius: *The History of the Church* (Penguin).

Galling, Kurt (ed.): *Die Religion in Geschichte und Gegenwart*, 7 vols. (Mohr, Tübingen, third edition, 1957).

The Greek New Testament (Η ΚΑΙΝΗ ΔΙΑΘΗΚΗ) Wide Margin Edition (The British and Foreign Bible Society, second edition with revised critical apparatus, 1966).

James, M R: *The Apocryphal New Testament* (Clarendon Press, Oxford, 1969, first edition, 1924).

Josephus, Flavius: *Works* (Loeb Classical Library).

Lawrence, D H: *The Man Who Died* (*Collected Stories*, Heinemann, 1934).

Maccoby, Hyam: *The Mythmaker: Paul and the Invention of Christianity*, (Heinemann, London, 1986).

Marshall, Alfred: *The RSV Interlinear Greek - English New Testament* (Samuel Bagster & Sons Ltd., 1968).

Philo of Alexandria, *Works* (Loeb Classical Library).

Philostratus, *The Life of Apollonius of Tyana*, 2 vols., includes Letters (Loeb Classical Library).

Price, Richard: *Augustine* (Fount Paperbacks, HarperCollins*Publishers*, 1996).

Sanders, E P: *Paul and Palestinian Judaism* (London, 1977).

Schonfield, Hugh J: *The Original New Testament* (Firethorn Press, an imprint of Waterstone & Co Ltd., London, 1985; distributed by Sidgwick & Jackson Ltd.). Published in USA by Harper Row.

The Passover Plot, (Element Books, mass market edition, 1996; first published by Hutchinson, 1965).

Schonfield, Hugh J:

    The Pentecost Revolution (Element Books, 1985; first published by Hutchinson, 1974). Published in USA as *The Jesus Party*.

    Those Incredible Christians (Element Books, 1985; first published by Hutchinson, 1968).

    After the Cross (A S Barnes & Co., USA., 1981).

    The Essene Odyssey (Element Books, third impression 1993).

    The Messianic Mystery (Open Gate Press, 1998).

Singer, S: *Authorised Jewish Prayer Book*.
The Septuagint with Apocrypha - Greek and English (Samuel Bagster).
Vermes, Geza: *The Dead Sea Scrolls in English* (Penguin, 1962).
Wand, J W C: *A History of the Early Church to AD500* (Methuen, 1965).

Principal Sources and Abbreviations

For a full list, see Schonfield *The Original New Testament*, p. 591f.

The Old Testament and Apocrypha. Where the references are to the Greek Version this is indicated by LXX (the Septuagint).

The Letters of Paul of Tarsus, The Acts of the Apostles, etc. The Greek MS Sinaiticus and Codex Alexandrinus; for *Luke – Acts* also Codex D (Bezae).

Rabbinical Literature:
  The Mishnah
  The Talmud
  Midrashim

Jewish, Classical and Patristic Literature as cited in the text.

AJP *Authorised Jewish Prayer Book* (Singer).
LXX The Septuagint
RGG See *Bibliography*, Galling, Kurt.
RSV The Revised Standard Version of the Bible.

Index

Elijah 188
Enoch, Book of 27, 33, 68ff.,
159 (66)
Epaenetus 195
Epaphras (see next entry)
Epaphroditus 107ff., 203, 206 (12),
205, 215, 219, 222
Ephesus 74-78, 84, 155, 156, 160,
226, 232, 233, 235
Epicureans 61
Epimenides 62
Erastus, an associate of Paul 235
Esau 186
Essenes 15, 26, 28, 30-31, 33, 35,
47, 74, 81, 121(13), 125(1),
158(21), 165(11), 214(19 & 20)
Eternal Life 44, 132, 177, 181, 182,
223, 224, 227, 230
Eubulus 235
Eunice, mother of Timotheus 232
Euodia 204
Eusebius 81-82
Eutychus 84
Eve 161, 227
Ezekiel (see also Lore of the Chariot)
9, 26

Fair Havens 101
Faith 73, 128ff., 131, 167, 175,
179f., 187, 228
Felix, Antonius, governor of Judea
81, 92, 93ff., 94, 95ff., 96, 97
Festus, Porcius, governor of Judea
94, 95, 96, 97ff., 99, 100
Fortunatus 156

Gaius, travelling companion of Paul
77, 84
Galatia 9, 24, 29, 34, 49, 113, 156
Gallio, L. Junius, brother of Seneca,
proconsul of Achaia, 66ff
Gamaliel 9, 90
Gaster, Theodor H 35

Gaul 235
Gentiles 3, 4, 5, 14ff., 19ff., 25ff.,
27, 28, 29, 33, 36ff., 37ff., 39, 40,
43, 44ff., 45ff., 47, 48, 58, 63, 64,
65, 68, 71, 73ff., 75, 79, 88, 99ff.,
106, 108, 118, 119, 126, 144, 148,
162, 179ff., 188ff., 193ff., 195,
215ff., 216, 218, 227, 228
God 119, 122ff., 123, 127, 141,
168ff., 176; faith in God 117ff
Gomorrah 187
Gratus, Lucius Valerius 12

Habakkuk 175, 196 (5)
Hadrian, Emperor 59
Hagar 130
Haretath, king of Arabia 32, 33, 162
Hellenists 23, 24
Hermas 195
Hermes 44
Hermogenes 232
Herod the Great 21, 23ff., 56, 95
Herodion 195
Hierapolis 105, 219
Hippolytus 80
Homosexuality 176
Hosea 186
Hymenaeus 227, 233

Iconium 8, 44, 234
Idols 117, 147f
Illyricum 193
Incarnation 206 (8)
Isaac 130, 197(34), 186ff
Isaiah 28, 29; Second Isaiah 29;
Israel 5, 6, 15ff., 17, 35, 42, 49,
134(38)
Italy 58, 101

Jacob, the Patriarch 35, 186
Jambres 234
James, son of Zebedee, one of the
XII envoys 56

Publisher's Note

This book was finished by the author shortly before his death in 1988. Any additional material introduced by the publishers – almost exclusively in the form of supplementary notes based entirely on the author's works – has been clearly marked with an asterisk, thus *.